Sustainable Resource Management

Volume II

Sustainable Resource Management

Volume II

Editors :

K.K.SINGH
ALKA TOMAR
V.PHOGAT
SUMAN PHOGAT

MD Publications Pvt Ltd
New Delhi

Published by

MD Publications Pvt Ltd

"MD House"
11, Darya Ganj
New Delhi-110002
Tel. : +91-11-41562846, 41563325
Fax : +91-11-29235450
E-mail : contact@mdppl.com
Website : www.mdppl.com

ISBN : 978-81-904551-2-1 (Volume 2)
978-81-904551-0-7 (Set of 2 Volumes)

Printed and Published by **MD Publications Pvt Ltd** at Times Press, New Delhi

CONTENTS

FOREWORD

With the technological revolution there was rapid industrialization without restriction and only economic development was supposed to be the parameters of human prosperity, peace and happiness. Unfortunately, some of the very development activities have caused colossal destruction to the global human ecosystem. Air and water pollution, soil degradation, extinction of wildlife species, global warming, depletion of forest wealth, exhaustion of mineral oil/ores and many other forms of environmental degradation have raised doubts about the wisdom of the pattern of development which is being pursued now-a-days. In addition to these, newer problems like encroachment of anthropogenic activities on the limited land available, appearance of non-degradable synthetics, accumulation of toxic wastes, leaching from landfills and mines pose challenges for rational managements of natural resources. Thus, escalating rate of erosion of natural resources is of great concern because the idea of sustainable development and conservation has been bypassed in major developmental planning and implementation.

Of all natural resources, water is most severely threatened by pollution. According to several estimates, 60% of the discharged pollutants (sewage, industrial wastes, fertilizers, pesticides and landfills and mines leachates) reenter the water supplies. Contaminated water kills around 2.2 million people every year. Approximately 40% of world population now faces chronic shortage of fresh water for daily needs. Hence, water pollution control measures are on high priority in many countries and among numerous pollution control agencies. Land degradation is also a principal constraint in meeting the food demands of rising population. Since 1990, two-thirds of the world's farmlands suffer from soil degradation. Over-exploitation of natural resources has further aggravated the situation. At the threshold of the 21st century, a grim scenario is looming large with burgeoning population starved of natural resources and chocked by pollution. To combat the deleterious effects of intensive farming and rapid industrialization, particularly with regards to adverse environmental effects, requires the development and implementation of technologies and policies that will result in sustainable management of natural resources.

The Paris NGO Conference advocated a different way of development, one where ecological and social concerns for all humanity and future generations have given priority. Besides, the question of consumption patterns is becoming a subject of research and public interest in environment and the widespread belief that current rates of resource exploitation are unsustainable. Thus, the challenge of environment versus development is very clear. The choice is upon man, either to turn the direction of development into more sensible and traditional channels or to continue reckless exploitation of the earth's resources and leave a legacy of dissolution and death for our children and the generations to come.

The problems of pollution and reckless degradation of natural resources cannot be solved without proper understanding of their causes and effects. Simultaneously, it is necessary to build up professional capabilities to develop and frame policies, measures and programmes for environmental management. Unless concerted efforts are made to save the biosphere from catastrophic collapse, tomorrow will be too late. Thus, abatement of pollution and conservation of ecosystem is therefore imperative for attaining the goal of sustainable development. In the light of the above facts, the title of the book **'Sustainable Resource**

Management' is very pertinent. The book provides holistic overview of the topical environmental issues the human being has been facing today.

The present book in two volumes addresses various facets of environmental pollution and presents a broad overview of environmental problems and their likely solution. With emphasis on environmental protection and ecological conservation of natural resources it is an excellent reference document. It is hoped that this publication will prove useful to students, teachers, researchers of various disciplines and conservationist.

I appreciate the efforts made by Dr. K.K.Singh, Mrs. Alka Tomar, Dr. V.Phogat and Dr. Suman Phogat for compiling and editing the chapters of this book meticulously. Lastly, I would like to congratulate the authors, editors and publisher for bringing out this book.

Dr. Komal Singh, IAS
Divisional Commissioner
Gwalior (MP)

PREFACE

Air, water, soil and forests constitute the natural resources of a country. For centuries man has exploited these resources of the planet Earth recklessly and destroyed them what nature took millions of years to achieve. It is a grim and dark harvest of poisoned air, polluted water and soil, suffering children and vanishing beauties of lakes, forests and rivers, along with all the varied species of flora and fauna. Stupendous increases in population, industrialization, rapid urbanization and intensive farming have caused tremendous damage resulting in environmental imbalances and degradation on a global scale. The changes in the environment have endangered the very survival of humankind on this planet Earth.

Preservation of the environment is therefore, essential for the very existence of the human beings. Thus, sustainable management of natural resources has emerged as an issue of major international concern. In India too, environmental protection and the conservation of natural resources has been a national priority in the wake of 1972 Stockholm Conference on Human and Environment. The world commission on Environment and Development in its report published in 1987 have stressed the importance of ensuring that today's economic progress is not at the cost of tomorrow's development prospects. The growing interest in the concept of sustainability was given added stimulus at the United Nations Conference on Environment and Development (UNCED), held in Rio de Janeiro in June, 1992. Agenda 21, a major action plan developed at UNCED, focused attention on the need to make development more economically and environmentally sustainable and socially acceptable. It is, therefore, essential to make the masses aware of the changes in the quality of our environment and strategies to prevent the situation from worsening further. Proper monitoring would also help in focusing on the seriousness of the problem of environmental pollution and generate real concern among policy makers.

The contents of this reference book aims to provide a general framework to ensure sustainable management of natural resources for the well being of society through proper strategies of environmental protection, conservation and management. This comprehensive book emphasizes a research perspective for integrated resource management through two volumes covering 19 chapters. Each chapter is well written by the leading experts and scholars having long standing in research in their respective fields.

Chapter 1 describes role of clays in scavenging toxic metals ions. Chapter 2 focuses light on management of flyash through agricultural use. Chapter 3 deals with remediation of cadmium and lead contaminated soils by employing biosurfactant technology. Chapter 4 is devoted to utilization of biologically treated distillery waste water. Chapter 5 describes an eco-friendly approach for treatment and disposal of pulp and paper mill waste water. Chapter 6 describes management of urban wastes for restoration of soil fertility. A critical appraisal of municipal solid wastes management is attempted in Chapter 7. In Chapter 8 radioactive wastes and their storage and disposal are described in detail. Chapter 9 is related to environment and tourism.

The present book in two volumes is the outcome of contribution of various renowned scientists/academicians. We are indebted to a number of institutes and universities of India and abroad who helped us immensely by their respective contributions. It is hoped that this book will be of immense value to students, teachers, researchers of various disciplines, policy makers and planners having concern for the conservation and sustainable management of natural resources. Last but not the least, Shri Vijay Gupta, Publisher, M.D. Publications Pvt. Ltd., New Delhi deserves our all appreciation and thanks for publishing this book in a nice get up.

Editors

LIST OF CONTRIBUTORS

A. Kumar, Scientist, Air Pollution Control Division, NEERI, Nehru Marg, Nagpur-440020.

A.G. Devi Prasad, Post Graduate Dept. of Environmental Sciences, University of Mysore, Manasagangothri, Mysore-570006, Karnataka

A.S. Juwarkar, Environmental Biotechnology Division, NEERI, Nehru Marg, Nagpur-440020

A. Venkateswara Rao, Manager, Technical Services, Aquaculture Products Division, Neospark Drugs and Chemicals Pvt. Ltd., 241 B.L.Bagh, Panjagutta, Hyderabad-500082 (AP)

Aleya Lotfi, Laboratoire de Biologie Environnementale, Universite de Franche-Comte, 1 Place Leclere, 25030 Besancon Cedex (France)

Alka Tomar, Dy.Director & Head, Centre for Media Studies, Saket, New Delhi.

Anjana Chowdhary, Research Scholar, Dept. of Botany, Govt. Dungar College, Bikaner (Raj.)

Asha A. Juwarkar, Environmental Biotechnology Division, National Environmental Engineering Research Institute (NEERI), Nehru Marg, Nagpur-440020

Ashok K. Choudhary, Research Scholar, Dept. of Soil Science, S.K.N. College, Jobner (Raj.)

Bijender Singh, Dept. of Microbiology, University of Delhi, South Campus, New Delhi-110021

G. Kalaichelvan, Fermentation Lab, Tamil Nadu Agricultural University, Coimbatore-641003, (TN)

Gayatri Verma, Principal, S.M. Degree College, Palidogra, Sonkh, Mathura, (U.P.)

K.K. Singh, Research Officer, Project Directorate (Res.), Agriculture and Soil Survey, Krishi Bhawan, Bikaner (Raj.).

K.R. Arun Kumar, Fermentation Lab, Tamil Nadu Agricultural University, Coimbatore-641003, (TN)

K. Ramaswamy, Fermentation Lab, Tamil Nadu Agricultural University, Coimbatore-641003, (TN)

Khattabi Hichan, Laboratoire de Biologie Environnementale, Universite de Franche-Comte, 1 Place Leclere, 25030 Besancon Cedex (France)

Kirti V. Dubey, Environmental Biotechnology Division, NEERI, Nehru Marg, Nagpur-440020

Krishna G. Bhattacharya, Dept. of Chemistry, Gauhati University, Guwahati-781014, Assam.

Mahadevi Singh, Teacher, Sophia Sr. Secondary School, Bikaner (Raj.)-334002.

Mudry Jacques, Laboratoire de Geosciences, Universite de Franche-Comte, 16, route de Gray, 25030, Besancon Cedex (France)

N.R. Rajendra Prasad, Post Graduate Dept. of Environmental Sciences, University of Mysore, Manasagangothri, Mysore-570006, Karnataka

N. Ramalingam, Fermentation Lab, Tamil Nadu Agricultural University, Coimbatore-641003, (TN)

P.R. Thawale, Environmental Biotechnology Division, National Environmental Engineering Research Institute (NEERI), Nehru Marg, Nagpur-440020

Padma S. Rao, Environmental Biotechnology Division, National Environmental Engineering Research Institute (NEERI), Nehru Marg, Nagpur-440020

Parvinder Kaur, Dept. of Microbiology, University of Delhi, South Campus, New Delhi-110021

Ramesh Chandra Parida, Prof., Dept. of Chemistry, College of Basic Science and Humanities, Orissa University of Agriculture and Technology, Bhubaneswar-751003 (Orissa)

S.K. Singh, Environmental Biotechnology Division, National Environmental Engineering Research Institute (NEERI), Nehru Marg, Nagpur-440020

S. Karthikeyan, Fermentation Lab, Tamil Nadu Agricultural University, Coimbatore-641003, (TN)

Suman Phogat, Lecturer, C.R. College of Education, Hisar (Har.)

Sushmita Sen Gupta, Dept. of Chemistry, Gauhati University, Guwahati-781014, Assam.

T. Satyanarayana, Dept. of Microbiology, University of Delhi, South Campus, New Delhi-110021

U. Sivakumar, Fermentation Lab, Tamil Nadu Agricultural University, Coimbatore-641003, (TN)

V. Phogat, Department of Soil Science, CCS Haryana Agricultural University, Hisar (Haryana)

V.S. Saxena, Ex-Additional Secretary, Environment, Rajasthan, A-2, Van Vihar, Tonk Road, Jaipur-302018 (Raj.)

Vinod Singh, Lecturer, Department of Geography, Govt. Dungar College, Bikaner (Raj.)

CHAPTER 1

ROLE OF CLAYS IN KEEPING A CLEAN ENVIRONMENT : SCAVENGING TOXIC METAL IONS FROM AQUEOUS MEDIUM

Krishna G Bhattacharyya[1] and Susmita Sen Gupta[2]

[1] Department of Chemistry, Gauhati University, Guwahati —781014, Assam, India.

[2] Department of Chemistry, B.N. College, Dhubri —783324, Assam, India.

ABSTRACT

Adsorption of metals by clay minerals is a complex process controlled by the different environmental variables. The present work investigates the adsorptive interactions of metal ions with kaolinite and montmorillonite in aqueous medium. Batch adsorption studies were carried out with various metal ions concentrations, amount of clay adsorbents, pH, interaction time and temperature. The higher alkalinity of the adsorption medium favours the removal of metal on clay adsorbents. The uptake was very fast initially and maximum adsorption was observed within 180 min, 240 min and 180 min of agitation for Pb(II), Cd(II) and Ni(II), respectively. The kinetics of the interactions was tested with pseudo first order Lagergren equation, second order kinetics, Elovich equation, liquid film diffusion and intra-particle diffusion mechanism. The adsorption data gave good fits with Langmuir and Freundlich isotherms and yielded Langmuir monolayer capacity of 6.78 to 31.06 mg g^{-1} and Freundlich adsorption capacity of 0.37 to 7.32 $mg^{(1-1/n)}$ $L^{1/n}$ g^{-1} for the clay adsorbents. The adsorption of Pb(II) and Ni(II) on clay adsorbents was exothermic in nature with ΔH in the range of -31.5 to 58.9 KJ mol^{-1} accompanied by decreased in entropy and decrease in Gibbs energy. The adsorption of Cd(II) was endothermic in nature with an increase in entropy and an appreciable decrease in Gibbs energy (ΔG: – 19.8 to – 35.1 KJ mol^{-1}). The results have established good potentiality for kaolinite and montmorillonite to be used as adsorbent for heavy metals like Pb(II) and Cd(II) and Ni(II) ion from aqueous medium.

Key Words : Kaolinite; montmorillonite adsorption; adsorption kinetics; adsorption isotherm, temperature; enthalpy; metal ions.

Introduction

Metallic elements are indispensable and essential for cellular growth and for maintenance of metabolic function in trace amounts. Excessive presence, however, exerts an inhibitory influence on all living forms. Heavy metals in water have severe toxicity towards aquatic life and human beings (Chiron *et al.*, 2003). They are also harmful to the environment as a whole because of their non-biodegradable and persistent nature. They can accumulate in living tissues being biomagnified through the food chain (An *et al.*, 2001). According to the World Health Organization, the metals of most immediate concern are aluminium, chromium, manganese, iron, cobalt, nickel, copper, zinc, cadmium, mercury and lead (Ulmanu *et al.*, 2003).

Toxic effects of Pb(II), Ni(II) and Cd(II)

Lead is a naturally occurring bluish-gray metal found in small amounts in the earth's crust. It has no characteristic taste or smell. Metallic lead does not dissolve in water and does not burn and can combine with other chemicals to form lead compounds or lead salts (ATSDR, 1999a). The main sources of lead pollution are lead smelters, battery manufacturers, paper and pulp industries, boat and ship fuels and ammunition industries. In addition, the production of television picture tubes, pigments, petroleum fuels, printing, glass industries, photographic materials, etc., also adds lead to the environment (Kiff, 1987).

Lead toxicity affects the nervous system, both in adults and in children. Long-term exposure of adults to lead disturbs the nervous system. Lead exposure may cause weakness in fingers, wrists, or ankles. Some studies in humans have suggested that lead exposure may increase blood pressure causing hypertension (Marino *et al.* 1989). Pb(II) ions have affinity for ligands containing thiol and phosphatic groups and they inhibit the biosynthesis of heme (Balasubramanian and Jafar Ahmed, 1998). At high levels of exposure, lead can severely damage the brain and kidneys in adults or children and can cause miscarriage in pregnant women. Cardiovascular effects other than blood pressure changes have also been reported in individuals occupationally exposed to lead.

Children are more sensitive to the effects of lead than adults. A child who swallows large amounts of lead may develop blood anemia, kidney damage, severe stomachache, muscle weakness, and brain damage. Moreover, the consistent pattern of lower IQ values and other neuropsychological deficits among the children exposed to higher lead levels have also been reported (Rummo *et al.*, 1979).

Cadmium is an element that occurs naturally in the earth's crust. Pure cadmium is a soft, silver white metal. Cadmium is released into aqueous system from metal plating, smelting, mining, cadmium-nickel batteries, phosphate fertilizers, paint industries, pigments and alloy industries as well as from sewage (Kadirvelu and Namasivayam, 2003).

Breathing air with very high levels of cadmium can severely damage the lungs and may cause death. Breathing air with lower levels of cadmium over long periods of time (for years) results in a build-up of cadmium in the kidney, which is the main target organ for cadmium toxicity (ATSDR, 1999b). Lung damage and fragile bones are also common problems that occurred by long time exposure of cadmium.

The acute inhalation exposure to cadmium can cause death in humans and animals. Lowered hemoglobin concentrations and decreased packed cell volumes have been observed in some studies of workers occupationally exposed to cadmium. The toxicity of Cd(II) is accredited due to its ability to attach the sulphydryl groups of essential amino acids and enzymes (Kannan and Umamathi, 2003). Case studies indicate that calcium deficiency, osteoporosis, or osteomalcia can develop in some workers after long-term occupational exposure to high levels of cadmium. Adverse health effects due to cadmium such as lung insufficiency, bone lesions, cancer and hypertension in humans are well documented (Yin and Blanch, 1989). Chronic cadmium toxicity has also been the cause of Japanese Itai–Itai disease (Mathialagan and Viraraghavan, 2002).

Pure nickel is a hard, silvery-white metal. Nickel combined with other elements occurs naturally in the earth's crust. It is found in all soil, and is also emitted from volcanoes. Nickel is the 24th most abundant element. Nickel is released into the atmosphere during nickel mining and by industries that make or use nickel, nickel alloys, or nickel compounds. Nickel is also released into the atmosphere by oil-burning power plants, coal-burning power plants, and trash incinerators. The deposition of ash residues from coal combustion and disposal of municipal sewage sludge also act as supplier of Ni(II) to the environment (Poulsen and Hansen, 2000). The most serious harmful health effects from exposure to nickel, such as chronic bronchitis, reduced lung function, and cancer of the lung and nasal sinus, have occurred in people who have breathed dust containing nickel compounds.

The higher nickel load on soils may increase the uptake by plants and lead to adverse effects on ecosystem and human health. Changes in faunal composition and soil fertility due to nickel pollution are observed in many places. The respiratory tract is the most sensitive target of inhaled nickel toxicity. Chronic bronchitis, emphysema, and impaired lung function have been observed in nickel welders and foundry workers. The carcinogenic effect of nickel has been well documented in occupationally exposed individuals (ATSDR, 2003). Humans suffer from allergy due to nickel-containing diets and also due to exposure to nickel-containing materials.

Removal of toxic metals from the environment

Technologies are available to minimize the problem of the non-biodegradable and persistent heavy metals in the environment. Chemical precipitation, ion exchange, solvent extraction, reverse osmosis, adsorption are some of the techniques used for this purpose (Ajmal *et al.*, 1998; Gupta *et al.*, 2003). The removal of heavy metals by reverse osmosis is not cost-effective as the membrane is easily spoiled and needs frequent replacement. Reverse osmosis requires a high operating pressure and some pre-treatment is often required. Solvent extraction and electrolytic processes are also available but they are considered to be economical only for more concentrated solutions. Chemical precipitation and ion exchange techniques are also not very suitable when the heavy metals are present in trace amounts. A large amount of research has been devoted to finding cost-effective alternative methods as well as materials for removal of heavy metals in very small concentration from aqueous medium (Wang *et al.*, 2003).

As a technique for heavy metal removal, adsorption has been found to be very effective and economical, and it has become one of the preferred methods for removal of toxic contaminants from water (Tran *et al.*, 1999). The adsorption of metals by solid surfaces is an important mechanism that controls trace metal concentrations in the aqueous system (Chantawong *et al.*, 2003). Different conventional and non-conventional type of adsorbents have been cited in the literature for removal of metal ions, viz., blast furnace slag (Dimitrova, 1996), red mud (Gupta *et al.*, 2001), silica gel (Tran *et al.*, 1999), canola meal (Al-Asem and Duvnjak, 1999), coconut coirpith (Kadirvelu and Namasivayam, 2003), tree fern (Ho, 2003), chitosan (Jeon and Holl, 2003), activated carbon (Galiatsatou *et al.*, 2002), sewage sludge (Pan *et al.*, 2003), sawdust (Yu *et al.*, 2003), peat (Ho and McKay, 1999a), bituminous coal (Rawat *et al.*, 1991), bone char (Ko *et al.*, 2004), waste wheat bran (Singh *et al.*, 2004), etc.

Role of Clays and Clay minerals in the environment

The clay minerals in soil play an important role in the environment by acting as a natural scavenger of pollutants. As water flows over soil or penetrates underground, clays in soil take up various pollutants from water through ion exchange and adsorption mechanisms. Clays are hydrous aluminosilicates broadly defined as those minerals that make up the colloid fraction ($< 2\mu$) of soils, sediments, rocks and water (Pinnavaia, 1983). The particles of clay minerals may be crystalline or amorphous, platy or fibrous and may vary from colloid dimensions to those above the limit of resolution of an ordinary microscope (Deer *et al.*, 1985). The high specific surface area, chemical and mechanical stability, layered structure, high cation exchange capacity (CEC), etc.,. have made the clays excellent adsorbent materials. The CEC is different for different clay minerals. Montmorillonite has a very high CEC of 80 – 150 meq/100g and kaolinite 3 – 15 meq $100g^{-1}$ (Grim, 1968). Both Bronsted and Lewis type of acidity in clays has been shown by Tanabe (Tanabe, 1981) using various techniques including IR and NMR spectroscopic methods. The Bronsted acidity arises from H^+ ions on the surface, formed by dissociation of water molecules of hydrated exchangeable metal cations on the surface:

$$[M\,(H_2O)_x]^{n+} \rightarrow [M\,(OH)\,(H_2O)_{x-1}]^{(n-1)+} + H^+$$

The Bronsted acidity may also arise if there is a net negative charge on the surface due to the substitution of Si^{4+} by Al^{3+} in some of the tetrahedral positions and if the resultant charge is balanced by H_3O^+ cations. The Lewis acidity arises from exposed trivalent cations, mostly Al^{3+} at the edges, or Al^{3+} arising from rupture of Si-O-Al bonds, or through dehydroxylation of some Bronsted acid sites. Both the types of acid site enhance the adsorption capacity of clay minerals to a great extent.

Structure of kaolinite and montmorillonite

The structure of kaolinite was first suggested by Pauling (1930). Kaolinite is a 1:1 layer silicate where the basic structure consists of a tetrahedral sheet of SiO_4 and an octahedral sheet with Al^{+3} as the octahedral cation. Both the sheets combine to form a common layer such that the tips of the silica tetrahedra point towards the octahedral layer. The tetrahedral layer is inverted over the octahedral layer with the apical 'O' atoms being shared by the two.

In the layer common to the octahedral and tetrahedral sheets, two-thirds of the O-atoms are shared between Si and Al atoms. The remaining one-third of the sites in this layer consists of hydroxyl group coordinated to the octahedral Al atoms alone. Only two-thirds of the possible positions in the octahedral sheet are filled with Al, and there are three possible places of regular population of the octahedral layer with Al. The remaining one-third of the octahedral sites is vacant. The Al-atoms are placed in such a manner that any two Al-atoms are separated by two hydroxyl groups – one above and one below; making a hexagonal distribution in a single plane in the center of the octahedral sheet. The hydroxyl groups are placed directly against the centers of oxygen-hexagons of the basal plane of the tetrahedral layer (Theng, 1979).

The structure of montmorillonite was given by Marshall (1935). Montmorillonite is composed of units made up of two silica tetrahedral sheets with a central alumina octahedral sheet. The tetrahedral and octahedral sheets combine such that the tips of the tetrahedra of each silica sheet and one of the hydroxyl layers of the octahedral sheet form a common layer. The atoms in this layer, which are common to both sheets, become oxygen instead of hydroxyl. It is thus, referred to as a three-layered clay mineral with T-O-T layers making up the structural unit.

The silica-alumina-silica units are continuous in the 'a' and 'b' crystallographic directions and are stacked one above the other in the 'c' direction. In the stacking of these units, oxygen layers of each unit are adjacent to oxygen of the neighboring units. This causes a very weak bond and an excellent cleavage between the units. The outstanding feature of this clay structure is that water and other polar molecules can enter between the layers causing the lattice to expand in the 'c' direction. Thus, the 'c'axis dimension in montmorillonite varies from a minimum value of 9.6 A° when there is no polar molecules between the unit layers and above.

The 'c'axis spacing also varies with the nature of the interlayer cations present between the silicate layers.

Adsorption of heavy metals on clay minerals

A good number of studies have been reported for metal ion removal by using clay minerals from aqueous solution. China clay (Sarma *et al.*, 1991) as well as illite (Echeverria *et al.*, 2002) removed cadmium from hazardous waste. Natural bentonite was used for uptake of zinc from aqueous solution (Mellah and Chegrouche, 1997). Yavuz *et al.* (2003) reported the use of raw kaolin for adsorption of Mn(II), Co(II), Ni(II) and Cu(II) from aqueous solution. Kara *et al.* (2003) used sepiolite for the removal of cobalt. Some authors have been investigating the adsorption capacity of modified clays. The removal of Cr(III), Ni(II), Zn(II), Cu(II) and Cd(II) was studied by using natural and Na-exchanged bentonites (Alvarez-Ayuso and Garcia-Sanchez, 2003). Strawn *et al.* (2004) reported the adsorption of Cu by smectites (montmorillonite and bedellite) whereas Lin and Juang (2002) used surfactant modified montmorillonite for the removal of Cu(II) and Zn(II). Adsorption of Cu ions onto a 1:10 phenanthroline-grafted Brazilian bentonite has been reported by De Leon *et al.* (2003).

The present work was undertaken to investigate the feasibility of using kaolinite and montmorillonite for removal of Pb(II), Cd(II) and Ni(II) in single batch system from aqueous solution by adsorption under various environmental conditions.

Materials and Methods

Synthetic effluents

The adsorption experiments were conducted by using synthetic effluents containing Pb(II), Cd(II) and Ni (II) separately. The stock solution containing 1000 mg of Pb(II), Cd(II) and Ni(II) per liter was prepared by dissolving $Pb(NO_3)_2$ (Glaxo, Mumbai, India), $Cd(NO_3)_2 \cdot 4\,H_2O$ (Qualigens, Mumbai, India) and $Ni(NO_3)_2.6H_2O$ (Qualigens, Mumbai, India) respectively in 1 L of double distilled water and were used to prepare the adsorbate solutions by appropriate dilution.

Clay adsorbents

Kaolinite, Kga-1b (K) and Montmorillonite, Swy-2 (M) were obtained from the University of Missouri-Columbia, Source Clay Minerals Repository, USA. Both the clays were calcined before using them as adsorbents at 773 K for 10 h.

Surface area

The surface areas for the clay adsorbents were estimated according to Sears' method (Sears, 1956; Shawabkeh and Tutunji, 2003). A sample containing 0.5 g of clay was acidified with 0.1 N HCl to pH 3 to 3.5. The volume was made up to 50 ml with distilled water after addition of 10.0 g of NaCl. The titration was carried out with standard 0.1 M NaOH in a thermostatic bath at 298 $\pm$ 0.5 K to pH 4.0, and then to pH 9.0. The volume, V, required to raise the pH from 4.0 to 9.0 was noted and the surface area was computed from the following equation

$$S\ (m^2/g) = 32\ V - 25 \tag{1}$$

Cation Exchange Capacity

The CEC of the clays was estimated by using the copper bisethylenediamine complex method (Bergaya and Vayer, 1997). $CuCl_2$ solution, 1 M was prepared by dissolving 26.89 g $CuCl_2$ (0.2 mole) in 200ml of double distilled water. Ethylenediamine solution 1 M was prepared by dissolving 33.39 ml of ethylenediamine in 500 ml double distilled water.

50 ml of the $CuCl_2$ solution was mixed with 102 ml of the ethylenediamine solution to allow for the formation of the $[Cu(en)_2]^{2+}$ complex. A slight excess of the amine ensures complete formation of the complex. The solution is diluted with water to 1 L to give a 0.05 M solution of the complex. 0.5 g of dry clay sample was mixed with 5 ml of the complex solution in a 100 ml flask, diluted with distilled water to 25 ml and the mixture was agitated for 30 min in a thermostatic water bath shaker and centrifuged. The concentration of the complex remaining in the supernatant is determined by mixing 5 ml of it with 5 ml of 0.1 M HCl to destroy the $[Cu(en)_2]^{2+}$ complex, followed by addition of 0.5 g KI per ml and then titrating iodometrically with 0.02 M NaS_2O_3 in presence of starch as indicator (Bassett *et al.*, 1978). The CEC was calculated from the following formula:

$$\text{CEC (meq/100 g)} = \text{MSV}\,(x\text{-}y)\,/\,1000m \qquad (2)$$

where M is the molar mass of the complex, S the strength of the thio solution, V the volume (ml) of the complex taken for iodometric titration, m the mass of adsorbent taken (g), x the volume (ml) of thio required for blank titration (without the adsorbent) and y the volume (ml) of thio required for the titration (with the adsorbent).

Adsorption experiments

A pre-weighted sample of the adsorbent material and a measured volume of aqueous metal ion solution were taken in 100 ml borosil conical flasks and the mixture was agitated in a thermostatic water bath (NSW, Mumbai, India) for a fixed time interval. The mixture was centrifuged (Remi R 24) and metal ions remaining unadsorbed was determined in the supernatant liquid with Atomic Absorption Spectroscopy (Varian SpectrAA 220 with air-acetylene oxidizing flame, for Pb(II): Lamp current 5 mA, wavelength 217.0 nm, slit width 1.0 nm, optimum working range 0.1–30.0 μg ml^{-1}; for Cd(II):

Lamp current 4 mA, wavelength 228.8 nm, slit width 0.5 nm, optimum working range 0.02–3.0 μg ml^{-1} and for Ni(II): Lamp current 4 mA, wavelength 232 nm, slit width 0.5 nm, optimum working range 0.02–3.0 μg ml^{-1}). The experiments were carried out under different conditions of clay amount, initial metal ion concentration, pH of the medium, interaction time and temperature.

The amount, q, of metal ions adsorbed per unit mass of the adsorbent is computed from the expression (Shawabkeh and Tutunji, 2003):

$$q = (C_o - C_t) / m \tag{3}$$

where C_o (mg L^{-1}) and C_t (mg L^{-1}) are metal ion concentrations before and after adsorption for time t, and m (g) is the amount of clay adsorbent taken for 1 L of solution. The extent of adsorption is given by (Espantaleon *et al.*, 2003):

$$\text{adsorption } (\%) = (C_o - C_t) \times 100 / C_o \tag{4}$$

Theoretical foundation of adsorption

Adsorption process involves an array of phenomena that can alter the distribution of solutes among the constituent phases and interfaces of subsurface system (Weber *et al.*, 1991). Adsorption at a surface or interface is mainly the result of binding forces between the individual atoms, molecules or ions of adsorbate and the surface, all of these forces having origin in electromagnetic interaction. A number of parameters specific for a given adsorption process influence the system. Some of these factors are concentration, molecular weight, molecular size, molecular structure and polarity, steric form of adsorbate, surface area, the physico-chemical nature of the surface, the availability of adsorbate ions, the physical size of adsorbent particles, etc. Sometimes, the extent of adsorption also influences system parameters like pH and temperature (Weber, 1985).

The adsorption equilibrium is usually described by an isotherm equation (Ho and McKay, 1999a) whose parameters express the surface properties and affinity of the adsorbent, at a fixed temperature and pH. Thus, an accurate mathematical description of the equilibrium isotherm, preferably based on a correct sorption mechanism, is essential to the effective design of adsorption systems (Ho *et al.*, 2002a). An adsorption process is usually described by the following two widely used isotherms (Gharaibeh *et al.*, 1998):

(*a*) Freundlich isotherm: $q_e = K_f C_e^n$ (5)

where C_e is the concentration of the adsorbate at equilibrium in the liquid phase and q_e is the corresponding concentration of the adsorbate in the solid phase, K_f and n being Freundlich coefficients.

(*b*) Langmuir isotherm: $C_e/q_e = 1/(bq_m) + (1/q_m)\, C_e$ (6)

where b and q_m are Langmuir coefficients representing the equilibrium constant for the adsorbate-adsorbent equilibrium and the monolayer capacity.

The linear Freundlich and Langmuir plots are obtained by plotting (i) log q_e vs. log C_e and (ii) C_e/q_e vs. C_e respectively, from which the adsorption coefficients could be evaluated. The Langmuir equation is also used to obtain R_L, the dimensionless equilibrium parameter or the separation factor (Ghosh, 2000) from the expression:

$R_L = 1/(1+bC_o)$ (7)

where C_o is the initial concentration of the adsorptive. The shapes of the isotherms are indicated by R_L values as follows (Ho *et al.*, 2002b; Ho, 2003):

R_L value	Type of isotherm
$0 < R_L < 1$	Favourable
$R_L > 1$	Unfavourable
$R_L = 1$	Linear
$R_L = 0$	Irreversible

Kinetics of adsorption

The adsorption kinetics normally includes two phases: a rapid removal stage followed by a much slower stage before the equilibrium is established (Ho and McKay, 1999b; Chen and Wang, 2004). According to Ho and McKay (1999c), the rate law has three primary requirements :

(*i*) Knowledge of all the molecular details of the reaction including the energetics and stereochemistry,

(*ii*) Interatomic distances and angles throughout the course of the reaction and,

(*iii*) The individual molecular steps involved in the mechanism.

Lagergren pseudo first order kinetics

Assuming pseudo first order kinetics, the rate of the adsorptive interactions can be evaluated by using the simple Lagergren equation (Ho and McKay, 1998a; Keskinkan *et al.*, 2004):

$$dq_t / dt = k_1 (q_e - q_t) \quad (8)$$

where k_1 is the pseudo first order adsorption rate constant. Integrating equation (8) for the boundary condition t = 0 to t = t and q_t = 0 to $q_t = q_t$, gives,

$$\ln (q_e - q_t) = \ln q_e - k_1 t \quad (9)$$

where q_e and q_t are the values of amount adsorbed per unit mass at equilibrium and at any time t. The values of k_1 can be obtained from the slope of the linear plot of log (q_e-q_t) vs. t.

If the pseudo-first order kinetics does not properly account for the kinetics of the adsorption process, two important discrepancies are usually noticed:

(*a*) $k_1 (q_e - q_t)$ does not represent the number of available sites, and

(*b*) ln q_e is not equal to the intercept of the plot of ln (q_e – q_t) against t.

In most cases, the Lagergren equation does not fit well in the whole range interaction time (Ho and McKay, 1999b).

Pseudo-Second Order Equation

If the rate of adsorption follows a second order mechanism, the pseudo-second order chemisorptions kinetic rate equation is expressed as (Ho and McKay. 1999d; Ho *et al.*, 2001);

$$dq_t / dt = k_2 (q_e - q_t)^2 \tag{10}$$

where k_2 is the second order rate constant. For the boundary conditions, t = 0 to t = t and q_t = 0 to $q_t = q_t$, the integrated form of the equation is written as

$$q_t = t/[(1/ k_2 q_e^2) + t/q_e] \tag{11}$$

or, in the linear form,

$$t/q_t = 1/h + (1/q_e) .t \tag{12}$$

where $h = k_2 q_e^2$ can be regarded as the initial sorption rate as t _ 0. If the pseudo second order kinetics is applicable, the plot of t/q_t vs. t gives a linear relationship, which allows computation of q_e, k_2 and h.

Elovich Equation

For the energetically heterogeneous solid surfaces, Elovich Equation (Ho and McKay, 1998b; Ho and McKay, 2002b) is also used successfully to describe second order kinetics. The equation is generally expressed as

$dq_t / dt =$ _ exp (-_ q_t) (13)

Assuming __t >>1, and q_t = 0 at t = 0 and $q_t = q_t$ at t = t, the linear form of the equation (12) is given by (Chien and Clayton, 1980; Ho and Mckay, 1998c):

$q_t =$ _ ln (__) + _ ln t (14)

where _ and _, known as the Elovich coefficients, represent the initial sorption rate (mg g^{-1} min^{-1}) and the desorption constant (g mg $^{-1}$) respectively. The Elovich coefficients could be computed from the plots of q_t vs. ln t.

Intra-particle diffusion model

In the batch adsorption study, adsorbate species can be transported from aqueous solution to the solid surface of adsorbent and there is a possibility of diffusion of adsorbate species into the interior of the pores of the adsorbent due to rapid stirring (Singh and Tiwari, 2003), which is likely to be a slow process. The intra-particle diffusion rate constant (k_i) is given by the equation (Weber and Morris, 1963):

$$q_t = k_i.t^{0.5} \quad (15)$$

When intra-particle diffusion plays a significant role in controlling the kinetics of the adsorption process, the plots of q_t vs. $t^{0.5}$ yield straight lines passing through the origin and the slope gives the rate constant, k_i.

Liquid film Diffusion Model

When the transport of the solute molecules from the liquid phase up to the solid phase boundary plays the most significant role in adsorption, the liquid film diffusion model (Boyd *et al.*, 1949) may be applied:

$$\ln(1 - F) = -\, kfdt \quad (16)$$

where F is the fractional attainment of equilibrium ($F = q_t/q_e$), k_{fd} is the adsorption rate constant. A linear plot of –ln (1 – F) vs. t with zero intercept would suggest that the kinetics of the adsorption process is controlled by diffusion through the liquid film surrounding the solid adsorbents.

Thermodynamic study

The thermodynamic parameters for the adsorption process, ΔH, ΔS and ΔG, were evaluated using the equation (Abou-Mesalam, 2003):

$$\ln K_d = \Delta S/R - \Delta H/RT \quad (17)$$

where K_d, known as the distribution coefficient of the adsorbate, is equal to (q_e/C_e). The plot of ln K_d vs. 1/T is linear with the slope and the intercept giving values of ΔH and ΔS. These values could be used to compute ΔG from the Gibbs relation, ΔG = ΔH - TΔS at constant temperature. All these relations are valid when the enthalpy change remains constant in the temperature range.

Results and Discussions

Surface area and Cation Exchange Capacity of the clays

Determination of the specific surface area of kaolinite (K) and montmorillonite (M) used in this work yielded values of 3.8 m^2g^{-1} and 19.8 m^2g^{-1} respectively. The results show that montmorillonite has a surface area almost five times larger than that of kaolinite. The surface area of kaolinite was reported as 5 to 25 m^2g^{-1} (Volzone *et al.*, 1999). Ravichandran and Sivasankar (1997), have reported the surface area of montmorillonite as 19.0 m^2g^{-1}. The values of surface area obtained in the present study are quite close to these reported results.

CEC values of kaolinite (K) and montmorillonite (M) were measured as 11.3 Cmol Kg^{-1} and 153.0 C mol Kg^{-1} respectively, in agreement with the reported values (Grim, 1968). These values indicate a much higher cation exchange capacity for montmorillonite compared to that of kaolinite.

Adsorption of heavy metals

Effects of pH

The pH of the aqueous solution is an important controlling parameter in the adsorption process (Nuhoglu and Oguz, 2003; Chen and Wang, 2004). In the present work, the pH of the solution was maintained at a particular value by addition of 0.01 N NaOH or 0.01 N HNO_3 as required.

Adsorption of Pb(II) on the clay adsorbents was studied

over the pH range of 1.0 to 6.0 for a constant clay amount of 2 gL^{-1} and Pb(II) concentration of 50 mgL^{-1} at 303 K for 180 min. The adsorption increased almost linearly up to pH 6. The experiments could not be continued at pH > 6 due to the low solubility of Pb(II) hydroxide (Jain and Ram, 1997; Krishnan and Anirudhan, 2002). As the acidity of the medium decreased, the amount of Pb(II) adsorbed per unit mass of clay (q_e) increased almost linearly (Fig. 1a) for both kaolinite and montmorillonite, but the amount adsorbed on montmorillonite at any pH was more than 5 times of the amount adsorbed on kaolinite.

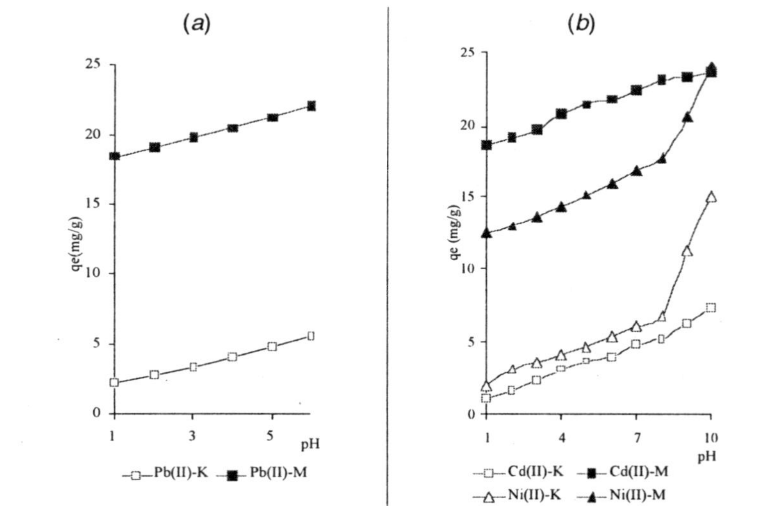

Fig. 1 : Amount of metal ion adsorbed per unit mass (q_e) on the clays at 303 K at different pHs (K kaolinite, M montmorillonite).

Adsorption of Cd(II) could be studied over the pH range of 1.0 to 10.0 (clay 2 gL^{-1}, Cd(II) 50 mgL^{-1}, 303 K, 240 min) without any abrupt changes in q_e due to precipitation of Cd(II)-hydroxide (Fig. 1b). The increase was more rapid for Cd(II)-kaolinite system (q_e increased from 1.08 to 7.38 mg g^{-1}) than the corresponding Cd(II)-montmorillonite system (the increase was from 18.68 to 23.63 mg g^{-1} in the pH range). The amount of Cd(II) adsorbed on montmorillonite was almost 17 times that adsorbed on kaolinite at pH 1.0, but with increase in pH, this came down to ~3 times only at pH 10.0. With Ni(II), the situation was different (Fig. 1b). The amount of Ni(II) adsorbed on unit mass for both kaolinite and montmorillonite (pH 1.0 to 10.0, clay 2 gL^{-1}, Ni(II) 50 mg L^{-1}, 303 K, 180 min) varied linearly with pH till pH crossed over to the alkaline side and then, the amount adsorbed changed rapidly from pH 8.0. This might be attributed to processes other than surface adsorption, viz., precipitation of Ni(II)-hydroxide. Another interesting feature is that kaolinite takes up more Ni(II) than Cd(II) while the situation is reversed in case of montmorillonite.

The changes in adsorption pattern with variation of pH could be explained as follows. At very low pH, the number of H_3O^+ ions exceeds that of the metal ions several times and the metal ions can hardly compete with H_3O^+ ions for the binding sites on the clay adsorbents. The surface remains covered with H_3O^+ ions and the metal ions are compelled to remain in the liquid phase. With an increase in pH, the concentration of H_3O^+ ions decreases and some of the sites become available to the metal ions. As the acidity decreases, more and more H_3O^+ ions on clay surface are replaced by metal ions (Taty-Costodes *et al.*, 2003) through exchange mechanism (H^+/Pb^{+2}, H^+/Cd^{+2}, H^+/Ni^{+2}) (Singh *et al.*, 1993; Krishnan and Anirudhan, 2002). As the pH turns towards alkaline side, precipitation of the insoluble metal-hydroxides may add to higher metal ion removal from solution (Yu *et al.*, 2001; Bayramglu *et al.*, 2003). This happens at a comparatively lower pH (~6.0) for Pb(II) while the adsorption could be safely carried out to pH ~10.0 for Cd(II) (Mathialagan and Viraraghavan, 2002) and Ni(II) (Padmavathy *et al.*, 2003). The sudden rapid increase in adsorption of Ni(II) at pH > 8.0 was most likely to be due to onset of precipitation of the hydroxide with Ni^{2+} and $NiOH^{+}$ being the dominating species (Bayat, 2002).

It is also significant that the active sites on the clay surface are weakly acidic in nature and with increase in pH, they are gradually deprotonated making available more and more sites for metal ion uptake (Dimitrova, 1996). The oxygen atoms present on the clay surface interact with water in an acidic medium forming some aqua complexes (Mathialagan and Viraraghavan, 2002), which result in positive charge formation as follows:

$$-MO + H-OH \xrightarrow{H^+} M-OH_2{}^{+} + OH^{-}$$

This surface charge is responsible for preventing metal ions from approaching the surface and explains the smaller extent of adsorption at low pH. In an alkaline medium, the clay surface becomes negatively charged favouring M^{+2} uptake:

$$-MOH + OH^{-} \rightleftharpoons -MO^{-} + H_2O$$

$$-MO^{-} + M^{2+} \rightleftharpoons -M-O^{-} \cdots\cdots M^{2+}$$

Effects of interaction time and kinetics of adsorption

To establish an optimum interaction time between clay adsorbents and metal ions, adsorption capacities of the metal ions were measured as a function of time. For all the three metal ions, adsorption was very fast initially and within 40 min, maximum uptake was recorded. This can be seen from Fig. 2. The equilibrium is then approached very slowly and it was observed that Pb(II)-clay and Ni(II)-clay interactions reach equilibrium in about 180 min while Cd(II)-clay interactions approach equilibrium only after 240 min. Saravanane *et al.* (2002) have reported that Pb(II) adsorption on rice husk and saw dust reach equilibrium within 60-180 min; whereas about 270 min is the equilibrium time for adsorption of Pb(II) on lignite (Balasubramanian and Jafar Ahmed, 1997). Lakshmi and Srinivasan (2004) have found an equilibration time of 240 min for Pb(II) removal by waste cotton seed. Jain and Ram (1997), have reported that a quasi-stationary state is obtained within 45 min of shaking river bed sediments with Pb(II). Tran *et al.* (1999), have reported 60 – 70 % Cd(II) uptake on silica gel within 50 min although equilibration required 135 min more. Similar, observations have been reported by other authors (Bayat, 2002; Kadirvelu and Namasivayam, 2003). In case of Ni(II) adsorption on activated carbon made from almond husk (Hasar, 2003) and IRN77 cation-exchange resin (Rengaraj, 2002) showed that equilibrium could be obtained in almost 3 h. In the present work, the pH did not show any measurable change even after the equilibrium was attained.

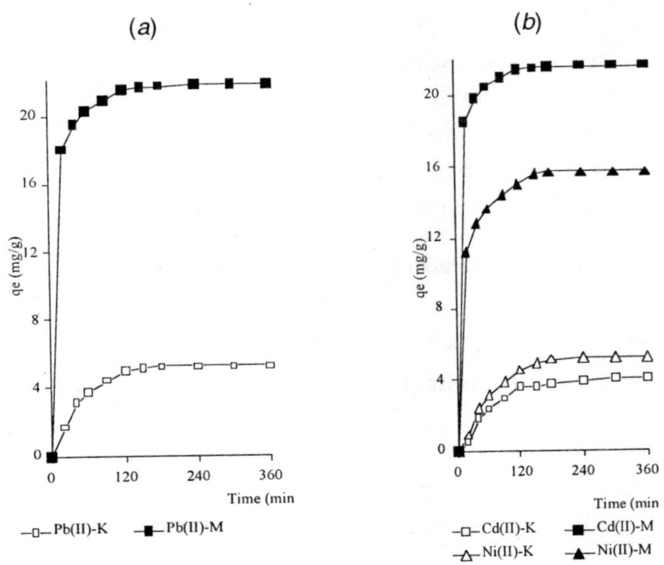

Fig. 2 : Amount of metal ion adsorbed per unit mass (q_e) on the clay adsorbents at 303 K for different time intervals (K kaolinite, M montmorillonite)

The experimental results show that montmorillonite stands apart due to its large adsorption capacity with respect to all the three metals. With a bare surface initially, the available surface area is very large compared to the density of metal ions in the aqueous phase and consequently, the rate of adsorption is very high. However, with increasing coverage, the fraction of the bare surface rapidly diminishes and the metal ions have to compete among themselves for the adsorption sites. This results in a slowing down of the interactions and the rate now becomes predominantly dependent on the rate at which metal ions are transported from the bulk liquid phase to the adsorbent-adsorbate interface. The kinetics of the interactions is thus, likely to be dependent on different rate processes as the interaction time increases (Yu *et al.*, 2000).

Table 1: First order rate constant (min^{-1}) and second order rate constant ($g\ mg^{-1} min^{-1}$) for adsorption of metal ions on clays at 303 K (clay 2 g L^{-1}, initial metal concentration 50 mg L^{-1}, pH 5.7 for Pb(II), 5.5 for Cd(II), 5.7 for Ni(II), K kaolinite, M montmorillonite)

Metal-ion	Clay	Pseudo first order		Pseudo second order	
		k_1 x 10^2 (min^{-1})	**R**	**k_2 x 10^2 ($g\ mg^{-1} min^{-1}$)**	**R**
Pb(II)	K	3.10	0.99	3.5	0.99
	M	2.78	0.99	8.4	0.99
Cd(II)	K	1.86	0.98	4.0	0.99
	M	1.91	0.74	3.0	0.99
Ni(II)	K	2.64	0.97	2.2	0.99
	M	3.08	0.97	5.3	0.99

The rates of adsorption were first tested with the pseudo first order mechanism of Lagergren by plotting log ($q_e - q_t$) vs. t (min) (Fig. 3). The regression coefficients and the first order rate constants obtained from these plots are given in Table 1. All the plots are linear showing that the interactions might be following first order mechanism and that the rate is dependent on initial concentration. The first order rate constants (1.86×10^{-2} to 3.10×10^{-2} min^{-1}) show that the interactions of Pb(II), Cd(II) and Ni(II) with kaolinite and montmorillonite proceed at comparable speeds. Pb(II) uptake by kaolinite is slightly faster than that by montmorillonite, while with respect to Cd(II) and Ni(II), montmorillonite has a faster rate of uptake than kaolinite. Similar first order rate mechanisms have been reported by Ho and McKay (1999a), for adsorption of Pb(II) on peat.

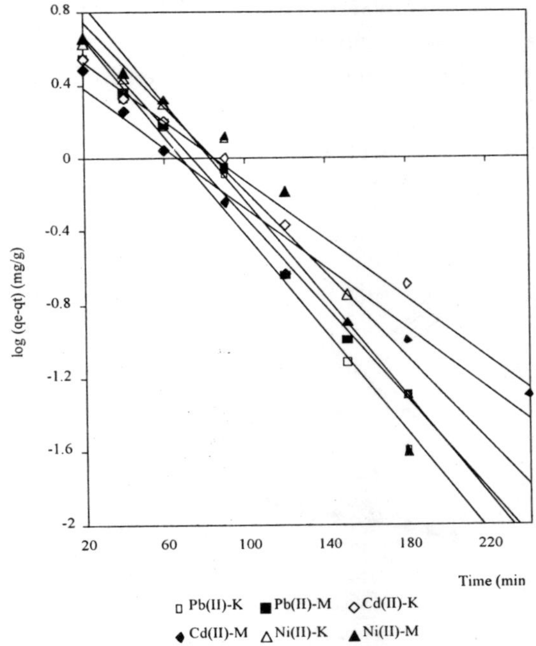

Fig. 3: Lagergren pseudo first order plots for metal ions adsorbed on clays at 303 K (K kaolinite, M montmorillonite).

However, the above results suffer from the major deficiency that q_e values obtained from the Lagergren plots compare poorly with the experimental q_e values (Table 2) in all the cases. There are both positive and negative deviations with minimum and maximum deviations being 19.2 and 83.9 %. Thus, good linearity of the Lagergren plots was no guarantee that the interactions will follow first order kinetics. Almost, similar results have been observed in case of other two metals.

In order to find a more reliable description of the kinetics, second order kinetic equation was applied to the adsorption data by plotting t/q_e vs. t (Fig. 4). Thus, the second order plots for Pb(II)-clay systems are linear (R ~ 0.99) and the rate constant, k_2 varied from 3.5×10^{-2} to 8.4×10^{-2} g mg^{-1} min^{-1} for kaolinite and montmorillonite respectively. Cd(II) and Ni(II) also yielded good linear plots (R ~ 0.99) with better linearity than the Lagergren plots. The second order rate constants for all the three metals are given in table 1.

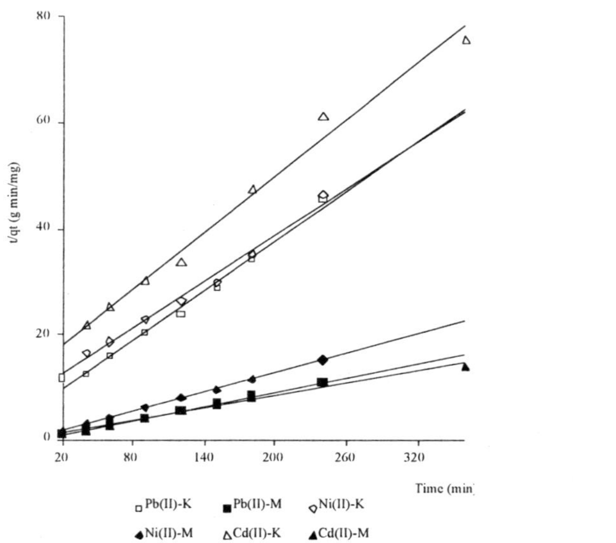

Fig. 4: Second order plots for metal ions adsorbed on clays at 303 K (K kaolinite, M montmorillonite).

A comparison of q_e values (experimental and those obtained from the slopes of the second order plots) for the three metal ions shows much better agreement (deviations from 0.0 to 24.5 %, Table 2). Montmorillonite gave the least deviation for Pb(II) and Ni(II), while kaolinite showed 100 % agreement for interactions with Cd(II). The deviations still existing might be due to the uncertainty inherent in obtaining the experimental q_e values and also due to the actual process being not in conformity with simple first order or second order kinetics.

Table 2: Experimental and computed q_e values from Lagergren and second order plots for adsorption of metal ions on clays at 303 K (clay 2 g L^{-1}, initial metal concentration 50 mg L^{-1}, pH 5.7 for Pb(II), 5.5 for Cd(II), 5.7 for Ni(II), K kaolinite, M montmorillonite)

Metal-ion	Clay	q_e (mg g^{-1})			Deviation (%)	
		Expt.	Lagergren	Second order	Lagergren	Second order
Pb(II)	K	5.25	8.50	6.43	+ 61.9	+ 22.4
	M	21.73	7.45	22.27	– 65.7	+ 2.5
Cd(II)	K	3.98	4.86	3.98	+ 22.1	0
	M	21.60	3.50	18.18	– 83.8	–15.8
Ni(II)	K	5.18	6.85	6.46	+32.2	+ 24.5
	M	15.70	12.69	16.52	– 19.2	+ 5.2

Interactions of Pb(II), Cd(II) and Ni(II) with kaolinite and montmorillonite also yielded good, linear Elovich plots (q_t vs. ln t, Fig. 5) with correlation coefficients of ~ 0.98 to 0.99

(Table 3). The Elovich equation describes predominantly chemical adsorption on highly heterogeneous adsorbents, but the equation does not propose any definite mechanism for adsorbate-adsorbent interaction (Ho and Mckay, 1998b) while predicting that metal ions are held strongly to the clay surface by chemisorptive bonds. The constants depended significantly

Table 3: Elovich coefficients for adsorption at 303 K (clay 2 g L^{-1}, initial metal concentration 50 mg L^{-1}, pH 5.7 for Pb(II), 5.5 for Cd(II), 5.7 for Ni(II), K kaolinite, M montmorillonite)

Metal ion	**Clay**	**Elovich coefficient**		
		α (g mg^{-1} min^{2})	β (mg g^{-1} min^{-1})	R
Pb(II)	K	14.8×10^{-3}	1.50	0.98
	M	29.4×10^{-3}	1.57	0.98
Cd(II)	K	36.8×10^{-4}	1.29	0.98
	M	93.9×10^{-4}	1.12	0.98
Ni(II)	K	23.4×10^{-4}	1.80	0.99
	M	382.8×10^{-4}	1.94	0.99

on the amount of adsorbent with the adsorption rate constant, γ, being much more sensitive. β is considered to represent the initial rate of adsorption and it is seen that with all the three metal ions, montmorillonite had a much higher initial rate of uptake than kaolinite. This might be due to very high surface area and CEC of montmorillonite compared to those of kaolinite. Similar, results are also obtained by Ho and McKay (2002a) for adsorption of Cu(II) on peat.

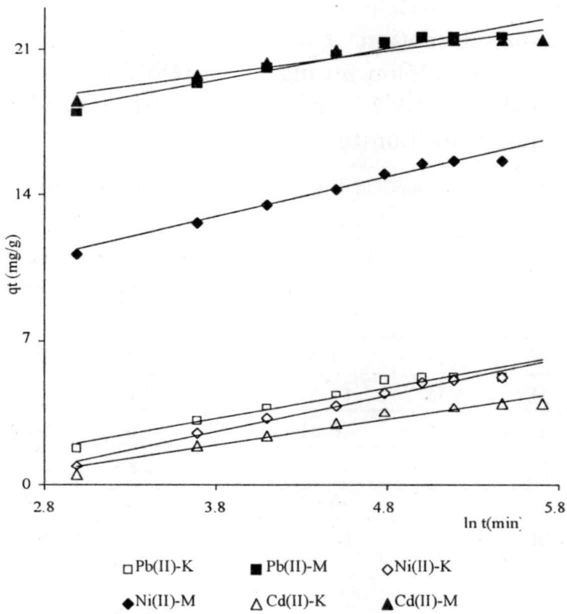

Fig. 5 : Elovich plots for metal ions adsorbed on clays at 303 K (K kaolinite, M montmorillonite)

In adsorption from solution, diffusion from the solid-liquid interface to the interior of the solid particles plays a very important role. Whether the process of adsorption is controlled by this type of intraparticle diffusion, is tested by plotting q_t vs. $t^{0.5}$ (Fig. 6) as in equation (15). The plots were linear with regression coefficient of 0.93 for Pb(II), 0.88 and 0.92 for Cd(II) and 0.95 for Ni(II) adsorption. The diffusion rate constants are given in Table 4 and the values indicate substantial diffusion of metal ions into the pores of the clay adsorbents. Significantly, however, the plots do not have zero intercept (varies from – 0.99 to 18.47) as proposed by the equation (15). Thus, intra-particle diffusion may not be the sole controlling factor in determining the kinetics of the process.

Table 4: Intra-particle and liquid film diffusion coefficients for adsorption at 303 K (clay 2 g L^{-1}, initial metal concentration 50 mg L^{-1}, pH 5.7 for Pb(II), 5.5 for Cd(II), 5.7 for Ni(II), K kaolinite, M montmorillonite)

Metal ion	Clay	Intra-particle diffusion			Liquid film diffusion		
		k_i x 10^{-1} (mg g^{-1} $min^{-0.5}$)	Intercepts	**R**	k_{fd} x 10^{-2} (min^{-1})	**Inter-cepts**	R
Pb(II)	K	3.18	1.04	0.93	3.21	-0.54	0.99
	M	3.33	17.30	0.93	2.77	1.08	0.99
Cd(II)	K	2.50	0.21	0.92	1.87	-0.20	0.99
	M	2.12	18.47	0.88	1.89	1.83	0.98
Ni(II)	K	**3.88**	**-0.99**	0.95	2.64	-0.60	0.98
	M	**4.17**	**10.06**	0.95	2.99	0.26	0.97

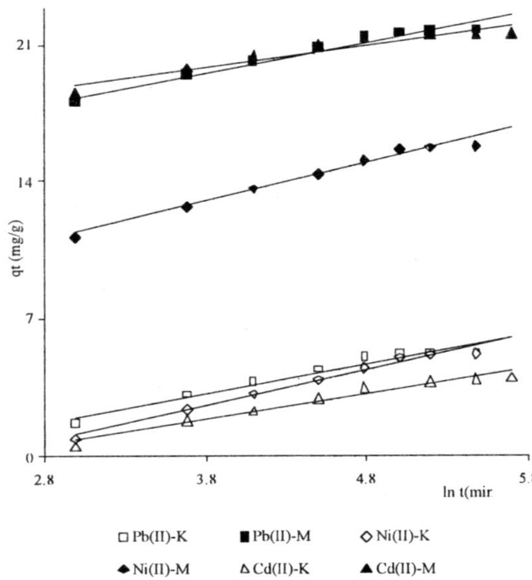

Fig. 6 : Intraparticle diffusion plots for metal ion adsorbed on clays at 303 K (K kaolinite, M montmorillonite).

Diffusion from the bulk liquid phase to the surface of the adsorbent might also play an important role in determining the rate processes. The plots of –ln (1 – F) vs. t (Fig. 7) in accordance with the liquid film diffusion model yield linear plots (R: 0.97 to 0.99) for all the three systems (Table 4). However, the plots differ from the theoretical predictions of the equation (16) by yielding non-zero intercepts in all the cases and thus, although diffusion across the liquid film cannot be ignored, the kinetics of the interactions cannot be solely accounted for by this model.

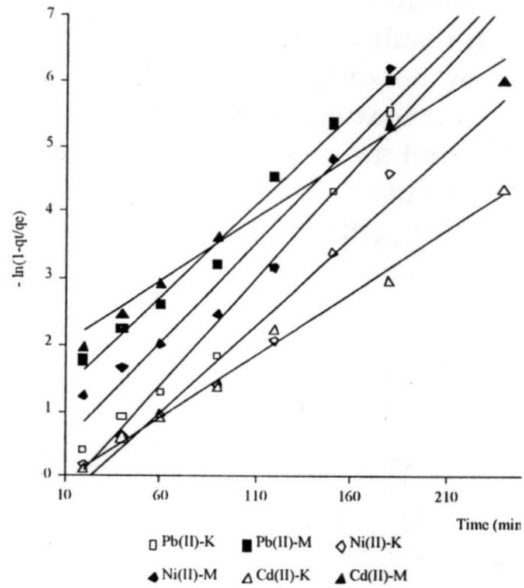

Fig. 7 : Liquid film diffusion plots for metal ions adsorbed on clays at 303 K (K kaolinite, M montmorillonite)

The above discussion therefore makes it clear that the kinetics of interaction of Pb(II), Cd(II) and Ni(II) with the clay surfaces does not follow any simple model suggesting that several mechanisms may be effective simultaneously.

Effects of adsorbent amount

A separate batch of experiments was carried out where the amount of clay was varied from 2 to 6 gL^{-1} keeping the initial metal ion concentration fixed at 50 mg L^{-1}. The interactions were carried out at 303 K for 180 min with Pb(II), 240 min with Cd(II) and 180 min with Ni(II) at the natural pH of aqueous solution of each metal ion. In each case, the extent of adsorption (%) increases with an increase in the adsorbent amount, but the amount adsorbed per unit mass decreases (Fig. 8). Similar results have been obtained by other workers (Yu *et al.*, 2000). The decrease in adsorption density may be due to two different reasons: (i) a large adsorbent amount effectively reduces the unsaturation of the adsorption sites and correspondingly, the number of such sites per unit mass comes down resulting in comparatively less adsorption at higher adsorbent amount, and (ii) higher adsorbent amount creates particle aggregation, resulting in a decrease in the total surface area and an increase in diffusional path length both of which contribute to decrease in amount adsorbed per unit mass (Sukla *et al.*, 2002).

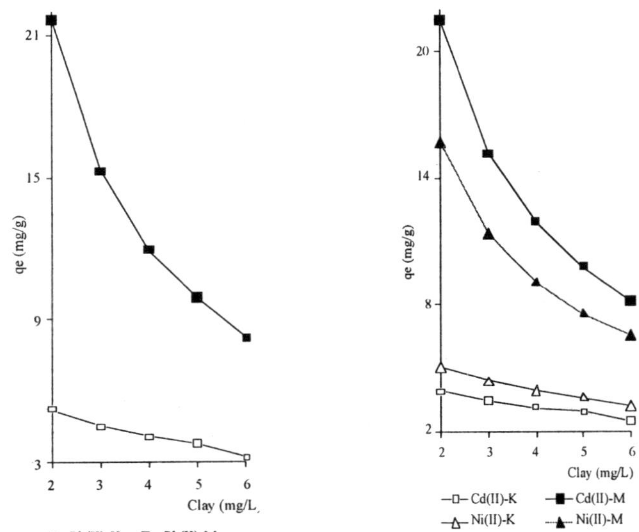

Fig. 8: Amount of metal ions adsorbed per unit mass (q_e) for five different clay amounts (2, 3, 4, 5, 6 gL^{-1}) at 303 K (K kaolinite, M montmorillonite)

Effects of initial metal ion concentration

When the interactions were carried out at 303 K with a constant clay amount of 2 gL^{-1} while the initial metal ion concentration was varied (10, 20, 30, 40, 50 mgL^{-1}) the extent of adsorption (%) decreased with an increase in metal ion concentration (Pb(II): 180 min, pH 5.7; Cd(II): 240 min, pH 5.5, and Ni(II): 180 min, pH 5.7). The amount adsorbed per unit mass (q_e) showed an increasing trend (Fig. 9). At low initial metal ion concentration, the ratio of the number of metal ions to the number of available adsorption sites is small and consequently the adsorption is independent of the initial concentration (Saravanane *et al.*, 2002), but as the concentration of metal ions increases, the situation changes and the competition for adsorption sites becomes fierce. As a result, the extent of adsorption comes down considerably, but the amount adsorbed per unit mass of the adsorbent rises.

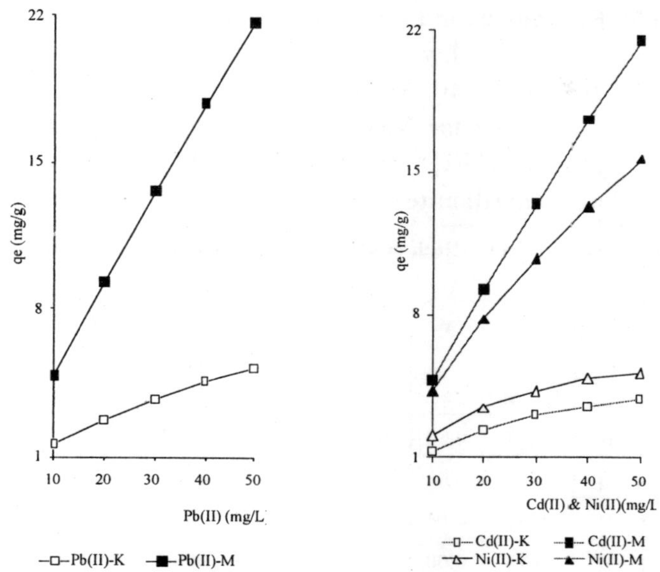

Fig. 9 : Amount of metal ions adsorbed per unit mass (q_e) at 303 K for five different initial metal ion concentrations (10, 20, 30, 40, 50 mg L^{-1}) at 303 K (K kaolinite, M montmorillonite)

Similar results have also been reported for the removal of Pb(II) by treated tea leaves (Singh *et al.*, 1993) and white-rot fungus Bayramoglu *et al.*, 2003). The removal of Cd(II) by chitin (Benguella and Benaissa, 2002) and Ni(II) by bagasse fly ash (Gupta *et al.*, 2003) showed similar adsorption trends.

Adsorption isotherm

The adsorption data followed the empirical Freundlich isotherm (R: 0.99) (Fig. 10). This isotherm does not yield any concrete information about the mechanism of adsorption, but is applicable to non-specific adsorption on heterogeneous solid surfaces. The Langmuir isotherm, applicable strictly to chemisorptive monolayer formation, also yielded linear plots (Fig. 11) (R: 0.98 to 0.99). The values of the adsorption coefficients for both the isotherms are given in Table 5.

Table 5: Freundlich and Langmuir coefficients for adsorption at 303 K (clay 2 g L^{-1}, initial metal concentration 10, 20, 30, 40, 50 mg L^{-1}, pH 5.7 for Pb(II), 5.5 for Cd(II), 5.7 for Ni(II), time 180 min for Pb(II), 240 min for Cd(II), 180 min for Ni(II), K kaolinite, M montmorillonite).

Metal ion	Clay	Freundlich coefficients			Langmuir coefficients			
		K_f mg$^{1-1/n}$ L$^{1/n}$ g^{-1}	n	R	b (L g^{-1})	q_m (mg g^{-1})	R_L	R
Pb(II)	K	0.37	0.72	0.99	20.70	11.52	0.0021	0.99
	M	7.32	0.68	0.99	30.96	31.06	0.0014	0.98
Cd(II)	K	0.37	0.64	0.99	32.30	6.78	0.0013	0.99
	M	6.76	0.60	0.99	29.58	30.67	0.0014	0.99
Ni(II)	K	0.94	0.49	0.99	70.14	7.05	0.0007	0.99
	M	3.40	0.53	0.99	137.74	21.14	0.0003	0.99

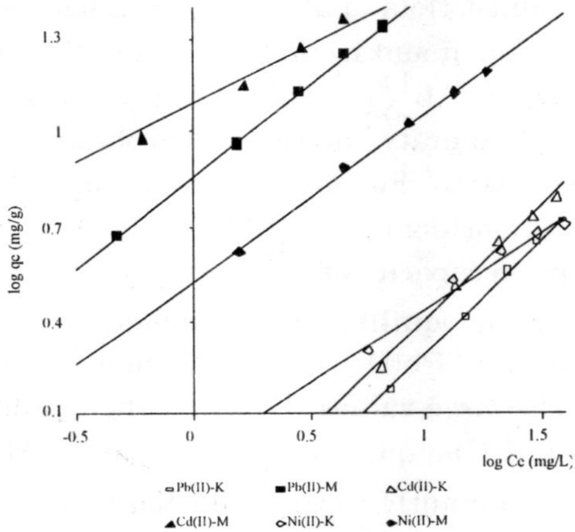

Fig. 10 : Freundlich plots for metal ions adsorbed on clays at 303 K (initial metal ions 10, 20, 30, 40, 50 mg/L) (K kaolinite, M montmorillonite)

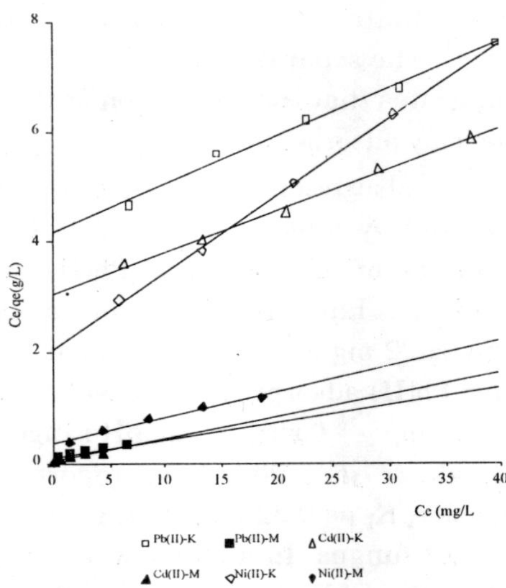

Fig.11 : Langmuir plots for metal ions adsorbed on clays at 303 K (initial metal ions 10, 20, 30, 40, 50 mg/L) (K kaolinite, M montmorillonite)

The Freundlich plots in all the three cases, yielded values for the coefficients, n and K_f, in the ranges of 0.49 to 0.72 and 0.37 to 7.32 $mg^{(1-1/n)} L^{1/n} g^{-1}$. Adsorption intensity given by n should be less than unity and the values obtained in this work conform to the same. For all the metal ions, the higher K_f values for montmorillonite compared to kaolinite indicate the higher adsorption capacity of the former one.

The Langmuir equilibrium coefficient, b, has values of 20.70 (kaolinite·······Pb(II)) to 137.74 (montmorillonite ······· Ni(II)) Lg^{-1}. The large values show that the equilibrium, Clay (solid phase) + M(II) (aqueous phase) = Clay·······M(II) is shifted predominantly to the right hand side, i.e. towards the formation of the adsorbate-adsorbent complex. The largest value for montmorillonite indicate that the interactions were the strongest between Ni(II) and montmorillonite. The Langmuir monolayer capacity, q_m, is appreciably large with values of 6.78 (kaolinite·······Cd(II)) to 31.06 (montmorillonite ·······Cd(II)) mg g^{-1}. The separation factor, R_L (values 0.0003 to 0.0021), also indicates that the adsorption of the metal ions is favoured on the clay adsorbents.

Values of the adsorption coefficients in similar ranges have been reported by other workers. Taty-Costodes *et al.* (2003) from studies of adsorption of Pb(II) and Cd(II) on sawdust, found the Langmuir adsorption capacity, q_m, between 8.45 to 22.22 mg g^{-1} in the pH range 7.0 to 4.0 (R^2 = 0.91 to 0.99) for Pb(II) adsorption. In case of Cd(II), q_m was from 6.72 to 15.27 mg g^{-1} for the same pH range (R^2 = 0.93 to 0.99). Bayramoglu *et al.* (2003) have reported Freundlich adsorption capacity, K_f as 0.32 to 1.29 L g^{-1} for adsorption of Pb(II) on white-rot fungus. In another work, Al-subu (2002), studied the adsorption of Pb(II) on decaying leaves of cypress, cinchona, and pine and reported the Freundlich adsorption capacity as 0.416, 1.347 and 0.019 L g^{-1} and that of n as 1.027, 1.652 and 0.634 respectively.

Values of the adsorption coefficients in similar ranges have also been reported for adsorption of Ni(II) on fly ash n between 0.40 to 0.80 and K_f between 2.05 to 3.01 L g^{-1} for the pH range of 1.0 to 6.0 at 303 K (Kanon, 1991). Chen *et al.* (2001), have reported q_m of 28.26 mg g^{-1} (R = 0.999) and K_f of 5.321 L g^{-1} (R = 0.962) for adsorption of Ni(II) on peat. Similarly, Ho and McKay (1999e) studied the competitive adsorption of Ni(II) with Cu(II) on peat and reported q_m for Ni(II) in the range 5.53 to 8.52 mg g^{-1} for different pH ranges. These values are quite close to the values found in the present work.

Thermodynamic studies

The effect of adsorption temperature on uptake of metal ions by the clay adsorbents was carried out in the temperature range 303 to 313 K. For both Pb(II) and Ni(II), increase in the temperature resulted in a decrease in the

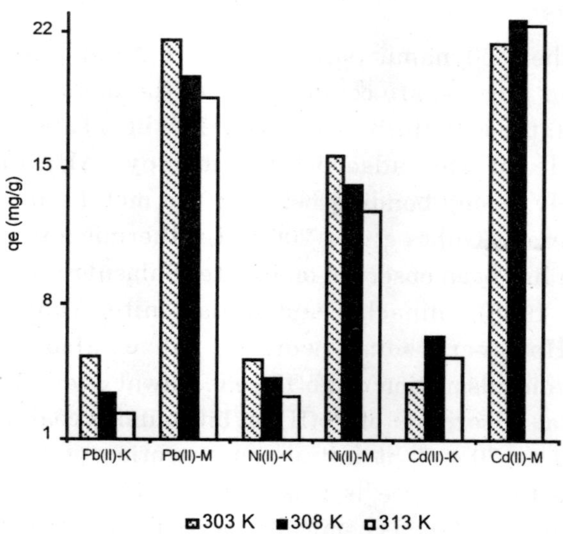

Fig.12 : Effect of temperature on amount of metal ions adsorbed on clays at 303 K (K kaolinite, M montmorillonite)

amount of metal adsorbed per unit mass of clay (Fig. 12), showing the interactions to be exothermic. Thus, the adsorbate ions have a tendency to escape from the solid phase to the bulk solution phase with the rise in temperature (Echeverria *et al.*, 2003). The possible increase in the metal ion solubility and/or damage to the adsorption sites in the clay minerals due to increase in temperature may also be considered in accounting for the decrease in uptake of the metal ions at higher temperature (Othman and Amin, 2003).

The effect of increasing temperature was quite different in case of Cd(II), where increase of temperature from 303 to 308, K was found to enhance the amount of Cd (II) adsorbed per unit mass of the clays, but the trend was reversed between 308 and 313 K (Fig. 13). The process is controlled by the adsorbate-adsorbent and adsorbate-adsorbate forces and it is clear from the results that the first one becomes weak in comparison to the latter as the temperature increases (Ajmal *et al.*, 1998).

The thermodynamic parameters, ΔH, ΔS and ΔG, for the adsorption process, are computed from the plots of ln K_d vs. 1/T. All these values are given in the (Table 6). The magnitude of the adsorption enthalpy, ΔH, indicates moderately strong bonding between the metal ions and the clay minerals (Gupta *et al.*, 2001). Exothermic adsorption of Pb(II) ion has been observed on lignite (Balasubramanian and Ahamed, 1998), chinaclay and wollastonite (Yadava *et al.*, 1991). However, some workers have also reported endothermic adsorption of Pb(II), e.g. Rawat *et al.* (1991) has shown that adsorption of Pb(II) on bituminous coal increases from 29.1 to 70.4 % at initial concentration of 100 mg L^{-1} when the temperature is raised from 313 to 333 K. The adsorption of Pb(II) on chemically treated tea leaves (Singh *et al.*, 1993) and peat (Ho and McKay, 1999d) have also been reported as endothermic.

Table 6: Thermodynamic data for adsorption at 303 K (clay 2 g L^{-1}, initial metal concentration 10, 20, 30, 40, 50 mgL^{-1}, pH 5.7 for Pb(II), 5.5 for Cd(II), 180 min for Ni(II), time 180 min for Pb(II), 240 min for Cd(II), 180 min for Ni(II), K kaolinite, M montmorillonite).

Metal ion	Clay	ΔH (kJ mol^{-1})	ΔS (J K^{-1} mol^{-1})	-ΔG (kJ mol^{-1})		
				303 K	308 K	313 K
Pb(II)	K	- 58.9	- 209.7	63.5	64.6	65.6
	M	- 31.5	-116.3	35.2	35.8	36.4
Cd(II)	K	25.0	66.3	20.0	20.4	20.7
	M	46.2	147.3	44.6	45.4	46.1
Ni(II)	K	- 37.9	- 118.2	41.9	42.6	43.2
	M	- 45.1	- 146.4	44.4	45.1	45.9

The endothermic interaction of Cd(II) on bagasse fly ash (Gupta *et al.*, 2003) and kaolinite (Angove *et al.*, 1998) have been reported earlier. But Singh *et al.* (1998) and Ajmal *et al.* (1998) reported exothermic nature of Cd(II) adsorption on hematite and mangifera indica seed shell respectively.

The exothermic nature of Ni(II) adsorption have been observed by (Abou-Mesalam, 2003) using synthesized silico-antimonate ion exchanger as an adsorbent. Endothermic adsorption of Ni(II) on canola meal has also been reported (Al-Asheh and Duvnjak, 1999).

For Pb(II) and Ni(II) adsorption, entropy decreased during the process, leading to a stable configuration. Since stability is associated with an ordered arrangement, it is obvious that Pb(II) and Ni(II) ions in aqueous solution are in much more chaotic distribution than they are in the adsorbed state. Thus,

Pb(II) and Ni(II) will have strong affinity towards the adsorbent material (Echeverria *et al.*, 2003). But the positive ΔS values for Cd(II) adsorption indicate that the interactions do not involve a considerable change in surface configuration. Entropy increase accompanying the process illustrates increased randomness at the solid-solution interface supporting strong affinity of the adsorbent for Cd(II) (Abou-Mesalam, 2003; Ghosh, 2003).

Spontaneity of the adsorption processes are demonstrated by the decrease in Gibbs energy for all the three systems.

Thermodynamic data on metal adsorption on clays are scarce. Yuvaz *et al.* (2003) have found that ΔH, ΔS and ΔG for adsorption of Cu(II) on Turkish kaolinite are 39.52 kJ mol^{-1}, 11.7 J K^{-1} mol^{-1} and 4.61 kJ mol^{-1} respectively. Echeverria *et al.* (2003) have reported that ΔH, ΔS and ΔG for adsorption of Ni(II) on illite have values of +16.8 kJ mol^{-1}, + 58 J $mol^{-1}K^{-1}$ and –1.04 kJ mol^{-1}, respectively. ΔH, ΔS and _G for Cu(II) adsorption on surfactant-modified montmorillonite were reported 7.05 kJ mol^{-1}, 9.09 J K^{-1} mol^{-1} and – 9.66 kJ mol^{-1} respectively (Lin and Juang, 2002). All these values were compared well with the values obtained in the present work.

Conclusions

The following conclusions have been drawn from this study

1. Both kaolinite and montmorillonite are capable of removing metal ions [Pb(II), Cd(II) and Ni(II)] from aqueous solution. Being 2:1 clay type, montmorillonite has high surface charges resulting from the spread of isomorphous substitution in tetrahedral and octahedral sheets, whereas 1:1 layered kaolinite has little isomorphous substitution. This explains the higher capacity of montmorillonite to adsorb cations.

2. Adsorption increases with pH till the metal ions are precipitated out at highly alkaline solution.
3. The rate of uptake of the metal ions by the clays is very high initially followed by a slow rate indicating entry of the metal ions into the interior of the adsorbent particles as the interactions proceed. The interactions are very close to second order kinetics but other mechanisms are also likely to be acting simultaneously. The intra-particle diffusion and the liquid film diffusion mechanisms play significant role in the adsorption process, but no single model could account for the complex metal-clay interactions.
4. Both Langmuir and Freundlich isotherms yield good fits and the adsorption coefficients agree well with the conditions supporting favorable adsorption.
5. All the three metal-clay interactions are thermodynamically favorable and are accompanied by decrease in Gibbs energy.

References

Abou-Mesalam, M. M. (2003) Sorption kinetics of copper, zinc, cadmium and nickel ions on synthesized silico-antimonate ion exchanger, Colloids and Surfaces A: Physicochem. Eng. Aspects, 225 : 85 –94.

Ajmal, M., Mohammad, A., Yousuf, R., and Ahmad, A., (1998) Adsorption behavior of cadmium, zinc, nickel and lead from aqueous solutions by Mangifera indica seed shell, Indian J. Environ. Hlth., 40 : 15-26.

Al-Asem, S., Duvnjak, Z., (1999) Sorption of heavy metals by canola meal. Water Air Soil Pollut., 114 : 231 – 276.

Al-subu, M.M. (2002) The interaction effects of cypress (Cupressus sempervirens), cinchona (Eucalyptus longifolia) and pine (Pinus halepensis) leaves on their efficiencies for lead removal from aqueous solutions. Advances in Environ. Res., 6 : 569-576.

Alvarez-Ayuso, E. and Garcia-Sanchez, A., (2003) Removal of heavy metals from wastewaters by natural and Na-exchanged bentonites. Clay Miner., 51 : 475-480.

An, H.K., Park, B.Y. and Kim, D.S. (2001) Crab shell for the removal of heavy metals from aqueous solution. Water Res., 35 : 3551–3556.

Angove, M.J., Johnson, B.B. and Wells, J.D. (1998) The influence of temperature on the adsorption of cadmium (II) and cobalt (II) on kaolinite. J. Colloid Interface Sci., 204 : 93-103.

ATSDR, (1999a) Toxicological profile for lead. US Department of Health and Human Services, Public Health Services (Agency for Toxic Substances and Disease Registry), Atlanta, Georgia.

ATSDR (1999b) Toxicological profile for cadmium, US Department of Health and Human Services, Public Health Services (Agency for Toxic Substances and Disease Registry), Atlanta, Georgia.

ATSDR (2003) Draft Toxicological profile for nickel, US Department of Health and Human Services, Public Health Services (Agency for Toxic Substances and Disease Registry), Atlanta, Georgia.

Balasubramanian, M. and Jafar Ahamed, A. (1997) Adssorption dynamics – Removal of lead by lignite- Langmuir model. Indian J. of Environ. Pollut, 17 : 601 – 604.

Balasubramanian, N., Jafar Ahmed, A. (1998) Adsorption dynamics – determination of activation parameters for the adsorption of lead(II) onto lignite material., Pollut. Res., 17 : 341–345.

Bassett, J., Denney, R.C., Jeffery, G.H, and Mendham, J. (Revised), (1978) *In: Vogel's Textbook of Quantitative Inorganic Analysis,* 4th edn., ELBS, Longman, pp., 370–376.

Bayat, B., (2002) Comparative study of adsorption properties of Turkish fly ashes I. The case of nickel(II), copper(II) and zinc(II). J. Hazard. Mater., B95 : 251–273.

Bayramoglu, G., Bekta, S. and Arica, M.Y. (2003) Biosorption of heavy metal ions on immobilized white-rot fungus Trametes versicolor. J. Hazard. Mater., B101 : 285–300.

Benguella, B. and Benaissa, H. (2002) Cadmium removal from aqueous solution by chitin: kinetic and equilibrium studies. Water Res. 36 : 2463–2474.

Bergaya, F. and Vayer, M., (1997) CEC of clays: Measurement by adsorption of a copper ethylendiamine complex. Applied Clay Sci., 12 : 275–280.

Boyd, G.E., Adamson, A.M. and Myers, L.S. (1949) The exchange adsorption of ions from aqueous solutions on organic zeolites, Kinetics II. J. Am. Chem. Soc., 69 : 2836-2842.

Chantawong, V., Harvey, N.W. and Bashkin, V.N. (2003) Comparison of heavy metal adsorptions by thai kaolin and ballclay. Water Air Soil Pollut., 148 : 111–125.

Chen, B., Hui, C.W., and McKay, G. (2001) Film-pore diffusion modeling for the sorption of metal ions from aqueous effluents onto peat. Water Res., 35 : 3345–3356.

Chen, J.P. and Wang, X.Y. (2004) Characterization of metal adsorption kinetic properties in batch and fixed-bed reactors. Chemosphere, 54 : 397–404.

Chien, S. and Clayton, W.R. (1980) Application of Elovich equation to the kinetics of phosphate release and sorption in soils, Soil Sci. Soc. Am. J., 44 : 265 - 268.

Chiron, N., Guilet, R. and Deydier, E., 2003, Adsorption of Cu(II) and Pb(II) onto a grafted silica: isotherms and kinetic models. Water Res., 37 : 3079–3086.

De Leon, A.T., Nunes, D.G. and Rubio, J. (2003) Adsorption of Cu ions onto a 1:10 phenanthroline – grafted Brazilian bentonite. Clay Miner., 51 : 58 – 64.

Deer, W.A., Howie, R.A. and Zussman, J. (1985) An introduction to the rock-forming minerals, ELBS Longman, Essex, England, pp., 250-274.

Dimitrova, S.V., (1996) Metal sorption on blast-furnace slag. Water Res., 30 : 228 – 232.

Echeverria, J., Indurain, J., Churio, E. and Garrido, J., (2003) Simultaneous effect of pH, temperature, ionic strength, and initial concentration on the retention of Ni on illite. Colloids and Surfaces A: Physicochem. Eng. Aspects, 218 : 175–187.

Echeverria, J.C., Churio, E. and Garrido, J. (2002) Retention mechanisms of Cd on illite, Clay Miner., 50 : 614 – 623.

Espantaleon, A.G., Nieto, J.A., Fernandez, M. and Marsal, A., (2003) Use of activated clays in the removal of dyes and surfactants from tannery waste waters. Applied Clay science, 24 : 105 – 110.

Galiatsatou, P., Metaxas, M., and Kasselouri-Rigopoulou, V., (2002) Adsorption of zinc by activated carbons prepared from solvent extracted olive pulp. J. Hazard. Mater., B91 : 187–203.

Gharaibeh, S.H., Abu-El-Sha'r, W.Y., and Al-Kofahi, M.M., (1998) Removal of selected heavy metals from aqueous solutions using processed solid residue of olive mill products. Water Res., 32, 498–502.

Ghosh, D. (2000) Immobilization of pollutants on clay surface, Ph. D Thesis (unpublished), Gauhati University, Assam, India.

Grim, R.E. (1968), *Clay Mineralogy,* 2nd Edn., McGraw Hill, New York, pp., 583.

Gupta, V.K., Jain, C.K., Ali, I., Sharma, M. and Saini, V.K., (2003) Removal of cadmium and nickel from wastewater using bagasse fly ash—a sugar industry waste. Water Res., 37 : 4038–4044.

Gupta, V.K., Gupta, M., Sharma, S. (2001) Process development for the removal of lead and chromium from aqueous solutions using red mud-an aluminium industry waste. Water Res., 35 : 1125-1134.

Hasar, H. (2003) Adsorption of nickel(II) from aqueous solution onto activated carbon prepared from almond husk. J. Hazard. Mater., B97 : 49–57.

Ho, Y.S. (2003) Removal of copper ions from aqueous solution by tree fern, Water Res., 34 : 2323 – 2330.

Ho, Y.S. and McKay, G. (1998a) Sorption of dye from aqueous solution by peat. Chemical Engineering J., 70 : 115 – 124.

Ho, Y.S. and McKay, G. (1998b)A comparison of chemisorption kinetic models applied to pollutant removal on various sorbents, Trans. ChemE, 76B : 332 – 339.

Ho, Y.S. and McKay, G. (1998c) Kinetic models for the sorption of dye from aqueous solution by wood, Trans. Chem E., 76B : 183 – 191.

Ho. Y.S. and McKay, G. (1999a) Competitive sorption of copper and nickel ions from aqueous solution using peat. Adsorption, 5 : 409 – 417.

Ho, Y.S. and McKay, G., (1999b) The sorption of lead(II) ions on peat. Water Res., 33 : 578–584.

Ho, Y.S. and McKay, G. (1999c) Pseudo-second order model for sorption processes. Process Biochemistry, 34 : 451– 465.

Ho, Y.S. and McKay, G. (1999d) Batch lead (II) removal from aqueous solution by peat: Equilibrium and Kinetics, Trans. Chem E., 77B : 165-173.

Ho, Y.S. and McKay, G. (1999e) Competitive sorption of Copper and Nickel ions from aqueous solution using Peat. Adsorption, 5 : 409–417.

Ho, Y.S. and McKay, G. (2002) Application of Kinetic Models to the Sorption of Copper(II) on to Peat. Adsorption Science Technol., 20 : 797–815.

Ho, Y.S., Ng, J.C.Y. and McKay, G. (2001) Removal of lead(II) from effluents by sorption on peat using second-order kinetics. Separation Science Technol., 36 : 241-261.

Ho, Y.S., Huang, C.T. and Huang, H.W. (2002a) Equilibrium sorption isotherm for metal ions on tree fern. Process Biochemistry, 37 : 1421- 1430.

Ho, Y.S., Porter, J.F. and McKay, G. (2002b) Equilibrium isotherm studies for the sorption of divalent metal ions onto peat: copper, nickel and lead single component systems. Water Air Soil Pollut., 141 : 1–33.

Jain, C.K. and Ram, D. (1997) Adsorptions of lead and zinc on bed sediments of the river kali. Water Res., 34 : 154 –162.

Jeon, C. and Holl, W.H. (2003) Chemical modification of chitosan and equilibrium study for mercury ion removal. Water Res., 37 : 4770–4780.

Kadirvelu, A. and Namasivayam, C. (2003) Activated carbon from coconut coirpith as metal adsorbent: adsorption of Cd(II) from aqueous solution. Advances in Environ. Res., 7 : 471 – 478.

Kannan, N. and Umamathi, T. (2003) Studies on the EDTA assisted removal of cadmium(II) ions by adsorption onto mixed adsorbents. Indian J. Environ. Prot., 23 : 41 – 46.

Kannan, N. (1991) A study on removal of Nickel by adsorption on flyash. Indian J. Environ. Prot., 11 : 514 – 518.

Kara, M., Yuzer, H., Sabah, E. and Celik, M.S. (2003) Adsorption of cobalt from aqueous solutions onto sepiolite. Water Res., 37 : 224-232.

Keskinkan, O., Goksu, M. Z. L., Basibuyuk, M., Forster, C. F. (2004) Heavy metal adsorption properties of a submerged aquatic plant (*Ceratophyllum demersum*). Bioresource Technology, 92 : 197–200.

Kiff, R.F. (1987) General inorganic effluents, In: Surveys industrial wastewater treatment manufacturing and chemical industries, Vol 3. Longman, New York.

Ko, D.C.K., Cheung, C. W., Choy, K. K. H., Porter, J. F. and McKay, G. (2004) Sorption equilibria of metal ions on bone char. Chemosphere, 54 : 273–281.

Krishnan, A. and Anirudhan, T.S. (2002) Removal of lead (II) in the presence of organic ligand from aqueous solution using activated carbon. Indian J. Environ. Prot., 22 : 52–59.

Lakshmi, N. and Srinivasan, K. (2004) Lead removal in aqueous medium by agricultural waste cotton seed (Ciba pentradra). Indian J. Environ. Prot., 24 : 379–384.

Lin, S-H., Juang, R.S. (2002) Heavy metal removal from water by sorption using surfactant-modified montmorillonite. J. Hazard. Mater., B92 : 315–326.

Marino, P.E, Franzblau, A and Lilis R. (1989) Acute lead poisoning in construction workers: The failure of current protective standards. Arch Environ Health, 44 : 140–145.

Marshall, C.E. (1935) Layer lattice and base-exchange clays. Z. Krist., 91 : 433 –449.

Mathialagan, T. and Viraraghavan, T. (2002) Adsorption of cadmium from aqueous solutions by perlite. J. Hazard. Mater., 2879 : 1–13.

Mellah. A. and Chegrouche. S., 1997, The removal of zinc from aqueous solutions by natural bentonites.Water Res., 31 : 621-629.

Nuhoglu, Y., Oguz, E. (2003) Removal of copper(II) from aqueous solutions by biosorption on the cone biomass of Thuja orientalis. Process Biochemistry, 38 : 1627–1631.

Othman, M.R., Amin, A.M. (2003) Comparative analysis on equilibrium sorption of metal ions by biosorbent. Tempe. Biochemical Engineering J., 16 : 361–364.

Padmavathy, V., Vasudevan, P. and Dhingra, S.C. (2003) Biosorption of nickel(II) ions on Baker's yeast. Process Biochemistry, 38 : 1389- 1395.

Pan, S.C., Lin, C.C. and Tseng, D.H. (2003) Reusing sewage sludge ash as adsorbent for copper removal from wastewater. Resources, Conservation and Recycling, 39 : 79–90.

Pauling, L. (1930) The structure of chlorites. Proc. Natl. Acad. Sci., 16 : 578–582.

Pinnavaia, T.J. (1983) Intercalated clay catalysts. Science, 220 : 365–371.

Poulsen, I.F. and Hansen, H.C.B. (2000) Soil sorption of nickel in presence of citrate or arginine. Water Air Soil Pollut., 120 : 249–259.

Ravichandran, J. and Sivasankar, B. (1997) Properties and catalytic activity of acid-modified montmorilonite and vermiculite. Clays Clay Miner., 45 : 854-858.

Rawat, N.S., Ranjana and Singh, D. (1991) Characteristic adsorption of aqueous Pb(II) on bituminous coal. Indian J. Environ. Prot., 13 : 193 – 197.

Rengaraj, S., Yeon, K-H., Kang, S-Y., Lee, J-U., Kim, K-W. and Moon, S-H. (2002) Studies on adsorptive removal of Co(II), Cr(III) and Ni(II) by IRN77 cation-exchange resin. J. Hazard. Mater., B92 : 185–198.

Rummo J. H., Routh D. K. and Rummo N.J. (1979) Behavioral and neurological effects of symptomatic and asymptomatic lead exposure in children. Arch Environ. Health, 34 : 120-125.

Saravanane, R., Sundararajan, T. and Reddy, S. (2002) Efficiency of chemically modified low cost adsorbents for the removal of heavy metals from wastewater: A comparative study. Indian J. Environ. Hlth., 44 : 78 – 87.

Sarma, Y.C., Prasad, C. and Rupainwar, D.C. (1991) Managing the Cd(II) rich hazardous waste. J. Indian Assoc. Environ. Management, 18 : 100-102.

Sears, G. (1956) Determination of Specific Surface Area of Colloidal Silica by Titration with Sodium Hydroxide. Anal. Chem., 28 : 1981–1983.

Shawabkeh, R.A. and Tutunji, M.F. (2003) Experimental study and modeling of basic dye sorption by diatomaceous clay. Applied Clay Sci., 24 : 111–120.

Shukla, A., Zhang, Y-H., Dubey, P., Margrave, J.L. and Shukla, S. S. (2002) The role of sawdust in the removal of unwanted materials from water. J. Hazard. Mater., 2884 : 1–16.

Singh, D.K., Tiwari, D.P. and Saksena, D.N. (1993) Removal of lead from aqueous solutions by chemically treated tealeaves. Indian J. Environ. Hlth., 35 : 169 –177.

Singh, D.B., Rupainwar, D.C., Prasad, G. and Jayaprakas, K.C. (1998) Studies on the Cd (II) removal from water by adsorption. J. Hazard. Mater., 60 : 29–40.

Singh, A.K. and Tiwari, P.N. (2003) Removal of basic dye from industrial wastewater by adsorption. Indian J. Chemical Technol., 10 : 211 – 216.

Singh, K.K., Singh, N.L. and Hassan, S.H. (2004) Removal of copper from wastewater by agricultural waste wheat bran. Indian J. Environ. Prot., 24 : 499 – 505.

Strawn, D.G., Palmer, N.E., Furnare, L.J., Goodell, C., Amonette, J.E. and Kukkadapu, R.K. (2004) Copper sorption mechanisms on smectites. Clay Miner., 52 : 321 – 333.

Tanabe, K. (1981) Solid Acid and Base Catalysis, *In: Catalysis Science and Technology,* (Eds. J. R. Anderson and M. Boudart) Springer Verlag, New York, pp., 231.

Taty-Costodes, V.C., Faudue, H., Porte, C. and Delacroix, A. (2003) Removal of Cd(II) and Pb(II) ions, from aqueous solutions, by adsorption onto sawdust of Pinus sylvestris. J. Hazard. Mater., B105 : 121–142.

Theng, B.K.G. (1979) Formation and properties of clay polymer complexes. Elsevier, New York, pp., 1-12.

Tran, H.H., Roddick, F.A. and O'Donell, J.A. (1999) Comparison of chromatography and desiccant silica gels for the adsorption of metal ions-I. Adsorption and Kinetics. Water Res. 33 : 2992-3000.

Ulmanu, M., Maranon, E., Fernandez, Y., Castrillon, L., Anger, I. and Dumitriu, D. (2003) Removal of copper and cadmium ions from diluted aqueous solutions by low cost and waste material adsorbents. Water Air Soil Pollut., 142 : 357–373.

Volzone, C., Thompson, J.G., Melnitchenko, A., Ortiga, J. and Palethorpe, S.R. (1999) Selective gas adsorption by amorphous clay-mineral derivatives. Clay Miner., 5 : 647–657.

Wang, Y.H., Lin, S.H. and Juang, R.S. (2003) Removal of heavy metal ions from aqueous solutions using various low-cost adsorbents. J. Hazard. Mater., B102 : 291–302.

Weber, W.J. Jr. (1985) Adsorption Theory, Concepts and Models, *In: Adsorption Technology:* A step-by-step Approach to Process Evaluation and Application (Ed. F.L. Slejko) Marcel Dekker, New York, pp., 1–36.

Weber, W.J. Jr., Mc Ginley, P. and Katz, M.L.E. (1991) Sorption phenomena in subsurface systems: concepts, models and effects on contaminant fate and transport. Water Res., 25 : 499–528.

Weber, W.J. and Morris, J.C. (1963) Kinetics of adsorption of carbon from solutions. J. Sanit. Engg. Div. Am. Soc. Civ. Engg., 89 : 31–63.

Yadava, K.P., Tyagi, B.S. and Singh, V.N. (1991) Effect of temperature on the removal of lead (II) by adsorption on china clay and wallastonite, J. Chem. Technol. Biotechnol., 51 : 47– 60.

Yavuz, O., Altunkaynak, Y. and Guzel, F. (2003) Removal of copper, cobalt and manganese from aqueous solution by kaolinite. Water Res., 37 : 948-952.

Yin, J. and Blanch, H. W. (1989) A bio-mimetic cadmium adsorbent: design, synthesis and characterization. Biotech. Bioengg. 34 : 180 - 188.

Yu, B., Zhang, Y., Shukla, A., Shukla, S. S. and Dorris, K. L., (2000) The removal of heavy metal from aqueous solutions by sawdust adsorption-removal of copper. J. Hazard. Mater., B80 : 33–42.

Yu, B., Zhang, Y., Shukla, A., Shukla, S.S. and Dorris, K. L., (2001) The removal of heavy metals from aqueous solutions by sawdust adsorption — removal of lead and comparison of its adsorption with copper. J. Hazard. Mater., B84 : 83–94.

Yu, L.J., Shukla, S.S., Dorris, K.L., Shukla, A., Margrave, J.L. (2003) Adsorption of chromium from aqueous solutions by maple sawdust. J. Hazard. Mater., B100 : 53–63.

CHAPTER 2

MANAGEMENT OF FLYASH MENACE THROUGH AGRICULTURAL USE : PROBLEMS AND ALTERNATIVES

Ramesh Chandra Parida

Department of Chemistry, College of Basic Science & Humanities, Orissa University of Agriculture & Technology, Bhubaneswar-751003 (Orissa).

ABSTRACT

Flyash emerging from coal based thermal plants and other sources has become a cause of serious concern to environmentalists all over the world. Its management through utilization in various fields ranging from filling the abandoned mines and low lands, construction of roads upto making cement bricks and other building materials has not lessened the burdens of this obnoxious solid waste. Even its much-advertised utilization as a soil-amending agent may not be of much help in the long run. Therefore, with growing industrialization and increasing consumption of power, the menace is bound to accelerate unless new alternatives for its management are found.

Key Word : Flyash, Agricultural use.

Introducion

With rapid industrialization and explosion of population, our energy need is accelerating necessitating an addition of about 10000 to 12000 MW every year for the next 10 years and even higher thereafter. Since coal is the prime source of energy all over the world including India, dependence on it is bound to grow year after year. Known as "black diamond", not only it is directly used as a fuel in many industries and house holds but also, in thermal power stations to churn out electricity, which are the major consumers of coal and producers of flyash. According to an estimate (Sharma *et al.*, 1989), a modern 200 MW capacity generation unit produces 2 tonnes of flyash every minute.

Coal ash consists of two fractions - the heavier bottom ash (about 20%) and the lighter fly ash (about 80%). The later having particle size from micron to several microns is considered highly hazardous to health and environment (Page *et al*, 1979; Terman, 1978; Tuner *et al.*, 1978; Vaughan *et al.*, 1978). Not only it has the potential to get airborne and cause air pollution but also, can contaminate sea or river water damaging aquatic life cycles. Slurry disposal lagoons/settling tanks can serve as the breeding grounds for mosquitoes and bacteria. Besides, it can also contaminate soil and ground water resources with traces of toxic metals present in it. Flyash, both in air as well as in water, is potentially dangerous to public health. While in air, it can cause various respiratory related problems and in water, metal toxicity.

Dimension of the Problem

In India there are 75 coal-fired thermal power stations, with and estimated thermal power capacity of about 70,000 MW per annum. Those consume about 250 million tonnes of coal and generate more than 90 million tonnes of ash (Parida *et al.*, 1997), which is expected to increase to 110 and 148 million tonnes by the year 2010 and 2020 respectively (Table 1).

Table 1 : Estimated ash generation in power sector in India

Item	Year				
	1989-90	1996	2000	2010	2020
Thermal power capacity (MW)	30,000	40,000	70,000	98,000	137,000
Coal consumption (Million tonnes)	110	150	250	300	380
Ash Generation (Million tonnes)	38	60	90	110	148

An estimated land requirement for disposal of flyash emerging from the existing thermal power stations of the country in mid-1990s was put as 50,000 acres during its life span of 30 years. The annual expenditure on its road transporation just for dumping was calculated to be about Rs. 50 cores. Considering the annual growth of 10% in power generation through thermal power plants, both these figures need upward revision (Kumar *et al.*, 1998).

Management

Serious efforts to minimize the hazardous effects of this obnoxious solid waste have been made in several countries around the world. A number of technologies have been developed by R & D laboratories and other institutes for gainful utilization of flyash, which ranges from low value added applications like use in road or embankments, minefills, lime-flyash concrete, cement -flyash concrete etc to high value added utilization such as extraction of alumina /magnetite/cenospheres, manufacture of acid resistant bricks/tiles, fire resistant tiles /bricks, lighter aggregates etc. However, the so-called "medium value added utilization", which includes manufacture of flyash bricks, portland pozzolana cement, flyash blocks, sintered flyash, light weight aggregate and concrete etc. have attracted more attention and are considered as more promising.

In spite of the development of all these technologies, large quantities of flyash generated in thermal power plants in the country have remained unutilized (utilization between 3 to 5%), whereas, in certain other countries its gainful utilization vary from 30% to 80%. However, we need not blame ourselves for this predicament considering the fact that only those countries which produce less of it have been able to utilize it to a significant extent (Table 2).

Table 2 : Ash utilization in different countries

Country	Annual Ash production (Million tonnes)	Ash utilisation	
		Amount (m ton)	Percentage of annual production (%)
USA (1991)	71	22	31
China (1991)	90	34	38
Russia (1991)	62	21	34
Germany (1989)	31	1-8	58
U.K. (1989)	12.5	6.1	49
Japan (1989)	4	2	50
Canada (1989)	4.4	1.3	29
Spain (1991)	9.4	1.6	17
Australia (1990)	7.9	0.5	10
France (1989)	2.7	1.55	57
Denmark (1990)	1.0	0.9	90
Italy (1989)	1.4	1.3	92
Netherlands (1991)	0.9	0.94	100
India (1991)	60	2-2.5	3-4

The world-wide utilization of flyash in different areas as estimated in 1990s is given in Table 3. It does not indicate the exact quantity of flyash used in agriculture, because at that time it was not considered important. However, during the last decade the situation has changed dramatically and the promising areas of utilization of flyash have not delivered the desired results. Therefore, attention has been turned to agriculture and many even profess that a new Green Revolution can be brought about by utilizing it for amendment of soil.

Table 3 : Worldwide ash utilization in different areas (1992)

S. No.	Areas	Ash utilization (Million tonnes)
1.	Concrete and cement industries	39
2.	Structural / land fill, embankment	40
3.	Filler for mines, quarries and pits	40
4.	Others	34
	Total	**153 MT**

Total Ash production = 460 MT

% utilization = 33%

Factors Contributing to Soil Amending Properties of Flyash

The physical, mineralogical and chemical properties of flyash depend on the composition of parent coal, conditions during coal combustion, efficiency of emission control devices, storage and handling of by-product and climate. Therefore, those vary widely from sample to sample obtained from different sources. Its mineralogical analysis shows that on an average 70-90% of it consists of minute glasslike particles (particle size 0.01 to 100 mm) with spherical shapes. The rest are quartz (SiO_2), mullite ($3Al_2O_3$, $2SiO_2$), hematite (Fe_2O_3), magnetite (Fe_3O_4) and unburnt carbon (1 to 2%). Besides, it also contains boron phosphate, gypsum, boron arsenide, rhodium boride etc, in smaller quantities. The colour of flyash depends upon its iron oxide content and specific gravity vary from 2.1 to 2.6.

The physico-chemical properties of a typical sample of flyash, as determined by Warmmbhe *et al.*, (1993) are presented in Table 4. It is evident from it that about 61% of flyash has particle size less than 0.25mm and only 29% has size above it. As a result, it has no colloidal properties. Besides, it is light (bulk density <1.41 mg m^{-3}), sparingly soluble in water (about 10%) and has high water-holding capacity (maximum 39.85%). Therefore, when applied to heavy soil, it makes it porous and less compact, improves its drainage and aeration and increases water infiltration as well as retention even below 30 cm of soil (Plank *et al.*, 1974). Although, poor in major soil nutrients like nitrogen and phosphorus, it contains useful quantities of potash, calcium, magnesium iron and zinc (Sikka, *et al.*, 1994). All these factors weigh favourably in making flyash an ideal soil amending agent.

Table 4 : Physico-chemical Properties of Flyash

S. No.	Properties	Content / Values
A.	**Physical properties**	
i)	Moisture (%)	0.45
ii)	Bulk density (Mg m^{-3})	1.41
iii)	Maximum water holding capacity (%)	39.85
iv)	Solubility (%)	0.26

Contd.

v)	Particle size composition (%)	
	(*a*) More than 0.25 mm	39
	(*b*) Less than 0.25 mm	61
B.	**Chemical properties**	
vi)	pH	7.55
vii)	Organic Carbon (%)	0.31
viii)	Total N (%)	0.52
ix)	Available N (%)	0.0037
X)	Total P_2O_5 (%)	0.086
xi)	Available P_2O_5 (%)	0.0021
xii)	Total K_2O (%)	0.172
xiii)	Available K_2O (%)	0.046
xiv)	Total CaO (%)	1.50
xv)	Total MgO (%)	0.83
xvi)	Total Fe (%)	0.33
xvii)	Total Mn (ppm)	187.00
xviii)	Total Cu (ppm)	87.50
xix)	Total Zn (ppm)	100.00
xx)	Total B (ppm) /(M	345.00

Results are expressed on oven-dry basis

A number of research workers have reported beneficial effects of amendment of soil with flyash. Crops like sunflower, groundnut (Patil *et al*., 1993), onion (Kalas, 1995), tomato etc (Khan *et al*., 1996), legumes (Das *et al*., 2000) rice (Sarangi *et al*., 2001) have been beneficially grown in soils amended with flyash.

It is also worth mentioning here that scientists of the Annamalai University have reported that flyash can be an effective pesticide (Narayanswamy, 1997), which adds to the prospects of it playing a more useful role in agriculture. According to it, flyash can kill various crop pests such as, leaffolder, grasshopper, yellow hairy caterpillar and a number of plant juice suckers. It is particularly effective against rice pests.

However, these should not make us over enthusiastic, as prolonged application of flyash in soil is pregnant with a number of potential problems. Those must be adequately addressed before it is handed over to the farmers.

Probable Problems and Alternatives

Flyash contains a number of toxic elements including heavy metals. Particularly, it has significant amounts of nickel, lead, zinc, calcium, chromium, magnesium, and copper. These are known to cause toxicity in certain crops (Cox *et al.*, 1980, Sikka *et al.*, 1994, Barman *et al.*, 1999). Similarly, higher contents of arsenic, mercury, born, sulphur, magnesium, selenium and copper have been found in the vegetative parts of the plants grown on the flyash contaminated soil. Even weeds, algae, dragon-fly nymphs etc. from flyash contaminated ponds contain higher concentrations of selenium, while the aquatic plants accumulate titanium, manganese, arsenic and mercury (Cherry *et al.*, 1997; Baraman *et al.,* 1999). The same possibility cannot be ruled out for food and fodder crops, which can make those toxic enough for consumption. In fact, crop plants like field corn, millet, bean, onion, cabbage, potato grown in flyash amended soil have shown higher contents of many of these toxic elements (Furron *et al.*, 1978). Moreover, some research workers (Sahu, 1996) also claim that flyash contains minor quantities of radioactive substances like thorium and uranium, which adds a new dimension to its potential hazards. Therefore, all these problems must be taken care of before recommending the use of flyash to the farmers.

In order to reduce the toxic load of flyash some research workers (Aitken *et al.*, 1984) have suggested that it should be subjected to leaching, watering and weathering before applying in agricultural fields. No doubt it can remove soluble oxides, including that of potassium, an important plant nutrient and to some extent hydrolyse and solublize many others, but, it will be a time consuming process, needing large storage facilities. Of course, the later part of the problem can be partially solved by using abandoned mines as reservoirs, however, it may give rise to another problem - water pollution, which cannot be ignored.

Similarly, it has also been reported (Sahu, 1997) that when flyash comes in contact with water under certain circumstances a thin layer of zeolite having a large exchangeable capacity is formed on the surface of the ash particles. Those can be modulated to generate exchangeable sites of different sizes (different co-ordinations), suitable to accommodate micro-nutrient heavy metals and macro-nutrient radicals like phosphates, nitrates etc, so that, they can be remobilized and pumped into over growing bio-mass as per requirement. However, the concept needs extensive studies on chemo-dynamic and crystal chemistry of zeolites and their formation on ash particle surface. Therefore, it cannot be accepted as a solution, atleast for the present.

The pH of flyash obtained from different sources vary widely - from acidic to alkaline range. As a result, all types of flyash cannot be applied to all types of soil, which makes the choice limited. Again to reap the benefits, flyash can be applied to the soil only in a limited quantity and not again and again for a prolonged period, which can prove detrimental to the soil and crops (Kaltra *et al.*, 1997; Saxena *et al.*, 1998; Pandeye *et al.*, 2001).

Besides all these, transportation of light weight flyash from industries to croplands is also a practical problem. Under such circumstances, amending flyash infected land, like mines and low lands filled with it and abandoned ash-ponds deserve serious consideration, which can provide better alternatives. As for example, it has been observed that certain plants like yellow sweet clover, sweet clover etc. naturally colonize flyash filled lands in the U.S. Their Indian counterparts can be identified and grown on it. Even plants usually used for green manure can be planted on strips of soil prepared for this purpose on the flyash beds. After sometime those can be mingted with ground by cuftivafion, so that its humus content can increase and in course of time it can harbour other varieties of plants.

Another prospective method of reclaiming flyash filled waste lands is to treat it with organic wastes generated from cities and towns or agricultural farms. On decomposition, these can produce humus rich in organic carbon, nitrogen and other nutrients essential for plants. Such lands can be used for social forestry and even for agriculture. Therefore, not only it will eliminate the necessity of transportation and storage, but also the threat of affecting the soil composition of agricultural land, its ecology and producing food and fodders containing toxic elements, while reclaiming wasteland for forestry and farming.

References

Aitken, R.L, Campbell, D.J. and Bell, L.C. (1984) Properties of Australian flyashes relevant to their agronomic utilization. Aust. J. Soil Res., 22 (4): 443-453.

Barman, S.C., Kisku, G.C. and Bhargava, S.K. (1999) Accumulation of heavy metals in vegetables, pulse and wheat grown in flyash amended soil. J.Environ Bio., 20 (1): 15-18.

Cherry, D.S. and Guthrie, R.K. (1977) Toxic metal in surface waters form coal ash. Water Res. Bull., 20 :1227-1236.

Cox, R.M. and Hutchinson, T. (1980) Multiple metal tolerances in the grass Deschampsia cespitosa. Nature, 279 : 231-233.

Das, R.K., Kumar, V. and Singh, R.S. (2000) lmpact of flyash pond effluent on selected leguminous plants. Eco. Env. Conserv., 6(1): 63-66.

Furr, A.K., Pakinson, T.F., Gutenmann, W.H., Pakkjala, I.S. and Lisk, D.J. (1978) Elemental content of vegetables, grains and forages field-grown on flyash amended soil. J. Agric. Food Chem., 26 : 357-359.

Kalas, K. (1995) Thesis on "Effect of coal flyash on growth, metabolism , cytology and yield of Allium Cepa L." Submitted to Khallikote Autonomous College, Berhampur (Orissa).

Kaltra, N., Joshi, H.C. Choudhury, A. and Sharma, S.K. (1997) Impact offlyash incorporation in soil on germination of crops. Bioresource Technol., 61 (1) : 39-41.

Kumar, V., Sharma, P. (1998) Mission mode, management of flyash : Indian Experience. Workshop on use of flyash for building material by the Orissa Environment of Programme on 11.9.198.

Narayanaswamy, P. (1997) Flyash, a pesticide of tomorrow. Sci. Expr. (22, July 1997): 2.

Page, A.L., Elesewi, A.A. and Strainghn, A. (1979) Physical and chemical properties of flyash from coal fired power-plants with reference to /environmental impact. Residue Rev., 71 : 83-120.

Pandey, D.D., Sinha, M. and Eqbal, A. (2001) Impact of flyash pollution on characteristics of grains of wheat. Env. Eco., 19(1): 237-238.

Parida, A., Panda, De, Mishra, R.N. and Murty, J.S. (1997) Hydraulic stowing with flyash. Paper presented at Workshop on Integrated Solidwaste Management (22-23, April, 1997), Orissa Evn. Prog. (Indo-Norwagian Def. Coop.)., Bhubaneswar.

Patil, C.V., Math, K.K. and Prakash, S.S. (1993) Agric. Col., Hindu (27.1.1993), pp., 4.

Plank, C.O. and Martens, D.C. (1974). Boron availability as influenced by application of flyash to soil. Soil Sci. Soc. Amer. Proc., 38 : 974-977.

Sahu, K.C. (1994) Power plant pollution : Cost of coal combustion. The Hindu Survey of Environment, pp., 47-51.

Sahu, K.C. (1996) Flyash management. Paper presented at Workshop on Integrated Solidwaste Management (22-23), April, 1997), Orissa Env. Prog. (Indo-Norwagian Dev. Coop.), Bhubaneswar.

Sharma, S., Fulker, M.K. and Jayalakshmi, C.P. (1989) Flyash dynamics in soil-water system. Critical Review on Environmental Control, 19 (3) : 251-275.

Sarangi, P.K., Mahakur, D and Mishra, .C. (2001) Soil biochemical activity and growth response of rice (*Oryza sativa L.*) in flyash amended soil. Bioresources Tech, 7(3): 199-205.

Saxena, M., Chauhan, A. and Asokan; P. (1998) Flyash Vermicompost from non-ecofriendly organic waste. Polln. Res., 17 (1) : 5-11.

Sikka, R., Kansal, B.D. (1994) Characterization of thermal power plant flyash for agronomic purposes and to identify pollution hazards. Bioresource Technal., 50(3) : 269-273.

Terman, G.L., Kilmer, V.J., Hunt, C.M., Buchanan, W. (1978) Fluidized bed boiler waste as a source of nutrients and lime. J. Env. Quality, 7 : 147-150.

Turner, F.B. and Strojan, C.L. (1978) Coal combustion, trace element emission and mineral cycles. In: Environ. Chem. and Cycling Process (Eds D.C. Adriano and I.K. Brisbin) Conf. 760429. US Dept. Corn. Springfield VA.

Vaughan, B.E, Abel, K.H. Cataldo, D.A. Hales, J.M. and Wolf, E.G. (1975) Review of potential impact on health and environmental quality from metals entering the environment as a result of coal utilization. Battele Pacific Northw. Lab., Richland Wash

Warambhe, P.E., Kene, D.R., Thakare, K.K., Darange, O.G. and Bhoyar, V.S. (1993). Evaluation of physico-chemical properties of flyash of thermal power station, Koradi (Nagpur) for its likely use in agriculture. J. Soils and Crops, 3(1): 75-77.

CHAPTER 3

BIOSURFACTANT TECHNOLOGY FOR REMEDIATION OF CADMIUM AND LEAD CONTAMINATED SOILS

Asha A. Juwarkar, S. K. Singh and Kirti V. Dubey

Environmental Biotechnology Division,
National Environmental Engineering Research Institute (NEERI),
Nehru Marg, Nagpur – 440020, India.

ABSTRACT

Contamination of soil with heavy metals poses serious threat to soil ecosystem and its health. It has become constraining factor in remediation of wide range of contaminated sites. Present practice of remediating metal contaminated sites have been excavation and disposal in landfills or capping of the contaminated soils site. These methods actually do not remediate the soils. Alternative ecofriendly methods must be investigated for reduction in volume, toxicity or mobility of metal contamination. Application of rhamnolipid biosurfactant produced by Pseudomonas aeruginosa stain BS2 has been explored for bioremediation of heavy metal contaminated soil through column studies using natural soil spiked with toxic concentrations of heavy metals such as Cd SO_4 $8H_2O$ (500 ppm) and $(CH_3COO)_2$ Pb $3H_2O$ (1000 ppm).

Results of comparative analysis on removal of two different heavy metals from the spiked soil by using di-rhamnolipid and tap water has shown high potential of di-rhamnolipid in mobilization and decontamination of contaminated soil. Within 36 hours of leaching study, di-rhamnolipid as compared to tap water facilitated removal of Pb to 8-9 folds. Leaching of Cd was 25 folds higher from the spiked soil. This shows that leaching behavior was different for different metals. Among the two different heavy metals, specificity of biosurfactant towards Cd was higher, indicated by overall 90% removal of Cd, whereas, 86% removal was observed for Pb after 36 hours. This indicates that di-rhamnolipid selectively favours mobilization of metals in the order of Cd>Pb. Biosurfactant specificity observed towards specific metal will help preferential elution of specific contaminant using di-rhamnolipid. Leachates collected from heavy metal spiked soil column treated with di-rhamnolipid solution had low pH (6.60 – 6.78) as compared to that of leachates from heavy metal spiked soil column treated with tap water (pH 6.90-7.25), which showed high dissolution of metal species from the spiked soil, and effective leaching of metals. Treatment of heavy metal spiked soil with 0.1% di-rhamnolipid solution has not decreased the counts of beneficial micro flora. However, it has increased their counts due to mobilization and removal of toxic heavy metals from spiked soil and restored the lost biodiversity.

Key Words : *Pseudomonas aeruginosa* strain BS2, Di-rhamnolipid biosurfactant, Spiked soils, Cadmium, Lead.

Introduction

Rapid developments and increase in mining and industrial activities have gradually redistributed many of the toxic metals from the earth's crust to the environment. This has substantially raised the chances of human exposure to these metals (in excess of their natural levels) through ingestion, inhalation or skin contact. Between 1900 and 1980 a manifold increase in the mine production of many metals e.g. aluminium (114 fold), nickel (35 fold), chromium (18 fold), copper (5 fold) and zinc (4 fold) were recorded (Athar and Vohora, 1995). All metals that are mined will be dissipated into the environment, thereby endangering the health of ecosystem. As metals cannot be degraded further to non-toxic products, their deleterious effects tend to be permanent unless measures are taken to recover the metals economically from the contaminated site.

Metal contamination of soil represents a potential environmental hazard in terms of toxicity to animals (IPCS, 1992) and inhibition of microbial processes (Babich and Stotsky, 1985). According to USEPA, survey of 395 remedial action sites, it is revealed that heavy metals were most prevalent class of contaminants (USEPA, 1984). Soils are described as sinks for metals. The latter being immobile in soils, accumulate in the topsoil, thus endangering crops and vegetables and microflora. Soil has complex functions which are beneficial to man and other living organisms. It acts as a filter, buffer, storage and transformation system and thus protects the global ecosystem against the adverse effects of environmental pollutions. These functions can be performed effectively only if the normal soil properties are preserved and natural balance is not unduly disturbed (Athar and Vohora, 1995).

In contaminated sites, heavy metal concentrations may be high enough to inhibit microbial activity. Soil micro-organisms may be critical to plant growth because they encourage development of stable soil structure, release required nutrients in inorganic forms by mineralization and produce growth regulating substances. Soil micro-organisms also contribute to plant growth by immobilizing heavy metal in soil. The direct effects of Cd, Cu, Zn and Pb on soil micro-organisms are generally understood. Heavy metal contamination of soil decreases microbial activity, microbial numbers, and microbially mediated soil processes such as nitrification, denitrification and decomposition of organic matter (Chang and Broadbent, 1981; Nordgren *et al.,* 1988; and Doelman and Haanstra, 1979).

Attempts to remediate metal contaminated soil have involved soil washing strategies or pump and treat strategies for subsurface environments. However, slow desorption kinetics necessitate extended washing or pumping periods in order to displace soil bound metals (Miller, 1995). Washing strategies can be greatly enhanced by the use of an agent that can increase the desorption of soil bound metals and facilitate their transport through the soil matrix. An ideal complexing agent is one that is soluble in water, chemically stable under environmental conditions, not strongly bound to soil particles, and has a high affinity for complexing metals (Chang *et al.,* 1981). Chang *et al.* (1981) described the use of water-soluble bacterial exopolymers (MW - 10^6) to mobilize soil-bound metals in sand materials. Recently, it has been shown that rhamnolipid biosurfactant (MW - 500) can complex heavy metals and is effective in removing soil bound cadmium, zinc and lead (Herman *et al.,* 1995; Tan *et al.,* 1994).

One of the alternative strategies currently being explored is soil flushing with pump and treat technologies for *in-situ* remediation. Unfortunately, the single reactants capable of mobilizing all metal contaminants are either toxic or destructive to the physical, chemical or biological structure of the soil. Anionic surfactants have also shown potential as soil washing agents due to their ability to solubilize metals within micelle. Biosurfactants have advantages over their chemical counterparts because they are not petroleum based, are less toxic and are biodegradable. Extensive research is needed to evaluate the potential effectiveness of environmental compatible, biological agents such as biosurfactants for soil flushing of metal contaminated soil.

In this chapter, the potential of di-rhamnolipid biosurfactant produced from *Pseudomonas aeruginosa* strain BS2 for removal of Cd^{2+} and Pb^{2+} sorbed on soil matrix are reported.

Material and Methods

The column studies were carried out at bench scale at National Environmental Engineering Research Institute (NEERI), Nagpur (India) to evaluate the effectiveness of the di-rhamnolipid biosurfactant towards removal of heavy metals such as Cd^{2+} and Pb^{2+} from soil matrix.

- ***Physico-chemical and Microbiological Characterization of Soil***

The soil used for column study was analyzed for physico-chemical parameters using as per the method of Piper (1994) and Black *et al.* (1965) Microbes such as bacteria, fungi, actinomycetes and nitrogen fixing strains of *Rhizobium* and *Azotobacter* were analyzed by following standard methods for soil microbial populations and were expressed in terms of colony forming units ($CFUg^{-1}$) (Black *et al.*, 1965; Page *et al.*, 1982).

- ***Production of Di-rhamnolipid Biosurfactant***

Pseudomonas aeruginosa strain BS2, a potential di-rhamnolipid biosurfactant producing culture that was isolated from an oily sludge was used for di-rhamnolipid production (Dubey and Juwarkar, 2001).

- ***Preparation of Heavy Metals Spiked Soil***

The natural soil was spiked with toxic concentrations of heavy metals such as $3Cd\ SO_4\ 8\ H_2O$ (500 ppm) and $(CH_3COO)_2\ Pb\ 3H_2O$ (1000 ppm). Spiking was done to increase the concentration of different metal in the soil. Ratio of 1 kg of soil/liter of solution was used based on the hydraulic conductivity of the spiked soil. Soil was shaken for 3 days on the rotatory shaker, then spread in plastic trays for air-drying and sieved through 200 mesh. The soil was allowed to mature for 2 months at room temperature to reach stabilization.

- ***Column Experiment***

A column study was conducted to study the feasibility to remove the heavy metals from soil matrix using di-rhamnolipid biosurfactant. 50 g of heavy metals spiked soil was filled in 3 glass columns with internal diameter of 2.0 cm and length of 15 cm and into the fourth column of same dimensions; 50 g of natural soil was filled. From the top of the columns (I – IV), washing solutions were applied and total volume of each washing solution was kept constant i.e. 200 ml (Table 1).

Table 1 : Details of the different treatments screened under column experiments

Treatments No.	Column Details	Washing Solution
I	Natural Soil (Uncontaminated)	Tap Water
II	Heavy Metals Spiked Soil	Tap Water
III	Natural Soii (Uncontaminated)	0.1% Di-rhamnolipid Biosurfactant
IV	Heavy Metals Spiked Soil	0.1% Di-rhamnolipid Biosurfactant

- ***Collection and Characterization of Leachate Samples from Column Experiment***

Collection of first leachate samples from all the four columns was feasible within 2-3 hours. Thereafter, leachates were collected regularly after 12 h of time interval. 1 ml of leachates were acidified with 5 ml of concentrated HNO_3 and digested in a sand bath and the volume was reduced to $1/4^{th}$ These digested samples were diluted to 100 ml and the concentration of heavy metals was analyzed using ICP-AES as per the standard method (APHA, 1975). 0.1 % biosurfactant solution and tap water were also similarly digested to determine the presence of heavy metal contaminants.

Result and Discussion

- ***Physico-chemical and Microbiological Characteristics of Soils***

Natural soil used to spike specified toxic concentrations of heavy metals such as $3Cd\ SO_4\ 8H_2O$ (500 ppm) and $(CH_3COO)_2\ Pb\ 3H_2O$ (1000 ppm) is characterized for its physico-chemical and microbiological characteristics. The results depicted in Table 2 showed that the bulk density of natural soil was 1.16g cm^{-3}. After metal spiking, it increased slightly to 1.28g cm^{-1}. Water holding capacity and porosity of natural soil was 60.20 % and 51.60 % which decreased slightly to 56.20 % and 49.10 % after addition of metals. There was no variation observed in textural class of the soils. Due to mixing, metal contaminated particles decreased soil aggregation, thereby decreasing soil porosity or void areas and increased the bulk density (Power *et al.,* 1975).

Addition of metals, reduced the pH of the natural soil which ranged from 7.70 to 6.30. There was improvement in the electrical conductivity of soil from 0.19 ms cm^{-1} to 0.29 ms cm^{-1} after metal spiking. The cation exchange capacity (CEC) of soil decreased from 73.27 meq $100g^{-1}$ to 66.20 meq$100g^{-1}$. Similarly, the organic carbon content of metal spiked soil marginally reduced to 0.38 % from 0.45 %, while the nutrient status of the natural soil i.e. nitrogen, phosphorous and potassium after metal spiked varied from 0.044 to 0.030 %, 0.072 to 0.052 % and 0.157 to 0.170 % respectively. The total heavy metal content of the soil after metal spiked resulted enrichment of respective metals in the soil while concentrations of rest of the metals remained almost the same.

Microbiological characteristics of natural soil and spiked soil with heavy metals are presented in Table 2. Results showed that the total counts of bacteria, fungi and actinomycetes in natural soil were $17x10^5$, $26x10^3$, $43x10^3$ $cfug^{-1}$ respectively, while the nitrogen fixers viz. *Azotobacter* and *Rhizobium* were 23 $x10^3$ and $21x10^3$ $cfug^{-1}$, respectively. Spiking of natural soil with toxic concentrations of heavy metals was found to drastically lower the counts of these micro flora. The total counts of bacteria, fungi and actinomycetes in heavy metal spiked soil reduced to $58x10^4$, $42x10^2$, $18x10^1$ $cfug^{-1}$ respectively while the nitrogen fixers viz. *Azotobacter* and *Rhizobium* reduced to $17x10^1$ and $16x10^2$ $cfug^{-1}$, respectively.

Table 2: Physico-chemical and Microbiological Characteristics of natural soil and heavy metal spiked soil

Parameters	Natural Soil	Heavy Metal Spiked Soil
Physical Properties		
Bulk density, g cm^{-3}	1.16	1.28
Maximum water holding capacity, %	60.20	56.20
Porosity, %	51.60	49.10
Sand, %	27	28
Silt, %	26	27
Clay, %	47	45
Textural Class	Clay	Clay

Contd.

Chemical Properties		
pH	7.70	6.30
EC, mS cm^{-1}	0.19	0.29
Cation Exchange Capacity (CEC), meq $100g^{-1}$	73.27	66.20
Organic Carbon, %	0.45	0.38
Nitrogen, %	0.044	0.030
Phosphorous, %	0.072	0.052
Potassium, %	0.157	0.170
Total Heavy Metals, mg kg^{-1}		
Cadmium	16.5	435.4
Lead	118.6	905.4
Microbial Properties, $CFUg^{-1}$		
Bacteria	17×10^5	58×10^4
Fungi	26×10^3	42×10^2
Actinomycete	43×10^3	18×10^1
Azotobacter	23×10^3	17×10^1
Rhizobium	21×10^3	16×10^2

- ***Effect of Di-Rhamnolipid Biosurfactant on Removal of Cd and Pd from Heavy Metal Spiked Soil***

Results have shown that use of rhamnolipid biosurfactant has enhanced the removal of heavy metal from the spiked soil. Pattern of cadmium removal from spiked soil using di-rhamnolipid biosurfactant solution is presented in Fig. 1. Results indicated that di-rhamnolipid biosurfactant readily mobilizes Cd because in the first leachate sample 2 folds higher Cd is removed which amounted to 8% of the total Cd present in the spiked soil used in the column study as compared to the mobilization and removal of Pb. Leachate analysis at 24 hours, 30 hours and 36 hours showed 20% removal of Cd. Di-rhamnolipid biosurfactant had facilitated almost 25 folds higher leaching and removal of Cd as compared to tap water. Cd removal with tap water from metal spiked soil and natural soil was very low which ranged from 0.12-0.8%. This indicated strong binding of cadmium with soil particles. These results showed the efficiency of di-rhamnolipid in mobilization of Cd, which is strongly binded to soil.

Results presented in Fig. 2 shows that removal of lead from heavy metal spiked soil facilitated almost 9-10 folds higher on using di-rhamnolipid biosurfactant as compared to tap water as an eluant. Initially, at the time of first leachate collection, 4% removal of Pb was obtained, followed by 8% at 6 hours, 12% at 12 hours and 20% at 24 hours. Later on, Pb removal remained constant up to 22% at 30 and 36 hours respectively. This comparative analysis between removal of Pb from spiked soil by the virtue of biosurfactant and tap water revealed the positive indication for its use in bioremediation of Pb contaminated soil.

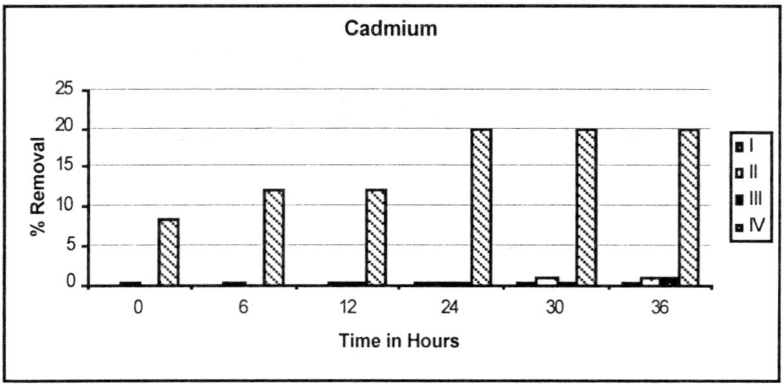

Fig. 1 : Effect of time on removal of Cadmium from the heavy metal spiked soil using Di-rhamnolipid biosurfactant

Treatments Details:

I-Garden Soil Treated with Tap water

II -Heavy Metal Spiked Soil Treated with Tap water

III-Garden Soil Treated with 0.1% Dirhamnolipid Biosurfactant

IV-Heavy Metal Spiked Soil Treated with 0.1% Dirhamnolipid Biosurfactant

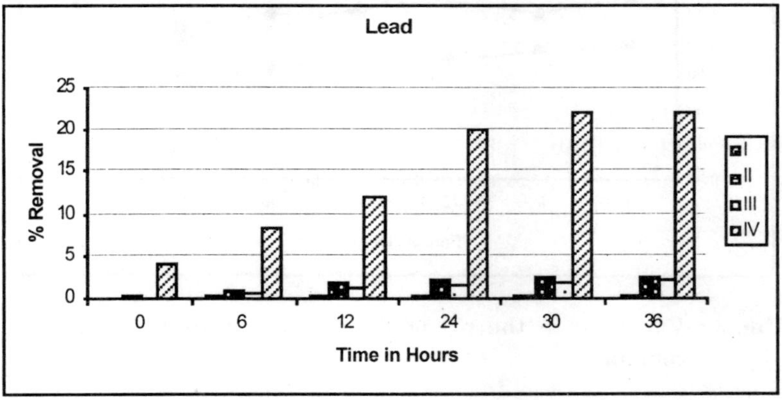

Fig. 2 : Effect of time on removal of Lead from the heavy metal spiked soil using Di-rhamnolipid biosurfactant

Treatments Details:

I - Garden Soil Treated with Tap water

II - Heavy Metal Spiked Soil Treated with Tap water

III - Garden Soil Treated with 0.1% Dirhamnolipid Biosurfactant

IV - Heavy Metal Spiked Soil Treated with 0.1% Dirhamnolipid Biosurfactant

- ***Variation in pH of the Leachate***

Leachates collected from soil columns I – IV were also monitored for the changes in pH along with the concentrations of heavy metals. The pH gives an indication for the extent of metal removal because retention/mobilization mechanism is strongly pH dependent. Results presented in

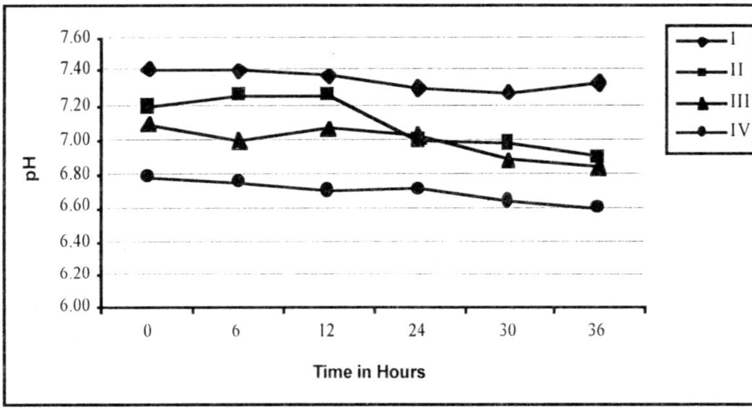

Fig. 3 : Variation in the pH of the leachate collected from soil columns

Treatments Details:

I - Garden Soil Treated with Tap water

II - Heavy Metal Spiked Soil Treated with Tap water

III - Garden Soil Treated with 0.1% Dirhamnolipid Biosurfactant

IV - Heavy Metal Spiked Soil Treated with 0.1% Dirhamnolipid Biosurfactant

Fig. 3 indicated that leachates collected from column having natural soil treated with tap water (column I) had the pH above neutral ranging 7.28 - 7.42 which was almost equal to pH of natural soil. Leachate colleted from heavy metal spiked soil treated with tap water i.e. column II had comparatively lower pH ranging from 6.90 – 7.26, which was due to the treatment with tap water that removes /leaches heavy metals in the range of 0.4-2.4%. Leachates from column III which was having natural soil treated with di-rhamnolipid had pH in 6.84 – 7.10 wherein pH of 6.84 coincided with high concentrations of heavy metals *viz.* Pb (2%) and Cd (0.8%) in the leachate which are comparatively higher as compared to the concentrations of these metals present in the leachates from column I in which tap water was used as eluant instead of di-rhamnolipid. In case of leachates collected from heavy metal spiked soil treated with biosurfactant solution (column IV) pH range was the lowest i.e. between 6.60-6.78 indicating high dissolution of metal species from the simulated soil and effective leaching with the aid of di-rhamnolipid biosurfactant which amounted to 4 - 26%. Lowest pH of 6.60 recorded at 36 hours of leachate collection coincided with the highest leaching of Pb (22%) and Cd (20%) each.

- ***Changes in Physico-chemical Characteristics of Soils***

Results depicted in Table 3 showed that the bulk density, maximum water holding capacity and porosity of the natural soil before and after treatment with di-rhamnolipid biosurfactant increased from 1.16 to 1.18 g cm^{-3}, 60.20 to 62.50% and 51.60 to 52.10% respectively. There was not much variation observed in sand, silt and clay particles of the natural soil. This indicated that the di-rhamnolipid biosurfactant had no much effect on textural class of the uncontaminated soil. The bulk density, maximum water holding capacity and porosity of the heavy metal spiked soil before and after treatment with di-rhamnolipid biosurfactant varied from 1.28 to 1.24 gcc^{-1}, 56.20 to 55.20 % and 49.10 to 50.10 % respectively. Similarly, sand, silt and clay particles of the natural soil varied from 28 to 30 %, 27 to 28 % and 45 to 42 %, respectively.

Table 3: Physico-chemical characteristics of natural soil and heavy metal spiked soil before and after treatment with Di-rhamnolipid biosurfactant

Parameters	Natural Soil		Heavy Metal Spiked Soil	
	Before Treatment	After Treatment	Before Treatment	After Treatment
Physical				
Bulk density, g cm^{-3}	1.16	1.18	1.28	1.24
Maximum water holding capacity, %	60.20	62.50	56.20	55.20
Porosity, %	51.60	52.10	49.10	50.10
Sand, %	27	27	28	30
Silt, %	26	27	27	28
Clay, %	47	46	45	42
Textural Class	Clay	Clay	Clay	Clay
Chemical				
pH	7.70	8.02	6.30	6.80
EC, mS cm^{-1}	0.19	0.22	0.29	0.27
Cation Exchange Capacity (CEC), $mg100g^{-1}$	73.27	74.34	66.20	72.34
Nutrients				
Organic Carbon, %	0.45	0.46	0.38	0.42
Nitrogen, %	0.044	0.049	0.030	0.040
Phosphorous, %	0.072	0.079	0.052	0.075
Potassium, %	0.157	0.168	0.170	0.240
Total Heavy Metals, mg kg^{-1}				
Cadmium	16.5	13.4	435.4	40.5
Lead	118.6	108.6	905.4	120.5

Results depicted in Table 3 showed that the pH, EC and CEC of the natural soil before and after treatment with di-rhamnolipid biosurfactant varied from 7.70 to 8.02, 0.19 to 0.22 mS cm^{-1} and 73.27 to 74.34 mg100g^{-1} respectively. Similarly, the pH, EC and CEC of the heavy metal spiked soil before and after treatment with di-rhamnolipid biosurfactant changed from 6.30 to 6.80, 0.29 to 0.27 mS cm^{-1} and 66.20 to 72.34 mg 100g^{-1} respectively. This indicates that di-rhamnolipid biosurfactant leaches the heavy metal ions from the metal spiked soil and reduced the acidity of soil to a large extent as compared with tap water. Also, the organic carbon and nutrient status with respect to nitrogen, phosphorous and potassium of the natural soil before and after treatment with di-rhamnolipid biosurfactant varied from 0.45 to 0.46% and 0.044 to 0.049%, 0.072 to 0.079% and 0.157 to 0.168%, respectively.

Similarly, the organic carbon and nutrient status with respect to nitrogen, phosphorous and potassium of the heavy metal spiked soil before and after treatment with di-rhamnolipid biosurfactant varied from 0.38 to 0.42% and 0.030 to 0.040%, 0.052 to 0.075% and 0.170 to 0.240% respectively. The changes in organic carbon and nutrients status of the heavy metal spiked soil is due to the changes in pH from slightly acidic to neutral. Thus, the treatment of heavy metal spiked soil with 0.1% di-rhamnolipid biosurfactant solution had enabled the soil to regain its lost fertility.

The results presented in Table 3 showed that the total heavy metal content with respect to Cd and Pb in the natural soil before and after treatment with di-rhamnolipid biosurfactant varied from 18.5 to 8.9 mg kg^{-1} and 120.6 to 50.6 mg kg^{-1} respectively. Similarly, the total heavy metal content with respect to Cd and Pb in the heavy metal spiked soil before and after treatment with di-rhamnolipid biosurfactant varied from 435.4 to 40.5 mg kg^{-1} and 905.4 to 120.5 mg kg^{-1} respectively. This indicated that di-rhamnolipid biosurfactant mediated the removal of toxic metals i.e. Cd and Pb that were inhibitory and toxic to the soil microflora.

Changes in Microbiological Characteristics of Soils

Results presented in Table 4 showed the microbiological characteristics of metal spiked soil samples from glass columns after treatment with tap water and di-rhamnolipid biosurfactant solution. Results indicated high counts of different microbial groups such as bacteria; fungi, actinomycetes and nitrogen fixers are present in control soil i.e. treated with plain tap water. The total counts of bacteria, fungi and actinomycetes in natural soil were 19 x 10^5, 31 x 10^3, 45 x 10^3 c.f.u.g^{-1} respectively while the nitrogen fixers viz. *Azotobacter* and *Rhizobium* were 28 x10^3 and 33 x 10^3 c.f.u.g^{-1}, respectively. These counts were nearly similar to the counts of different microbial groups estimated before running with tap water. Spiking of natural soil with toxic concentrations of heavy metals was found to drastically lower the counts of these micro floras, which is evident from the Table 4. However, after treatment with plain tap water, there was reduction in the concentration of heavy metals due to leaching which facilitated marginal improvements in the counts of different microbial groups. Results also showed that treatment of natural soil with 0.1% di-rhamnolipid biosurfactant solution was not observed to affect the counts of bacteria, fungi, actinomycetes and nitrogen fixers which indicated that 0.1% di-rhamnolipid can be safely used for bioremediation of heavy metal contaminated soil without disturbing the integrity of soil micro flora. Marked improvements in the counts of bacterial, fungi, actinomycetes and nitrogen fixers (almost equal to the counts found in natural soil) was observed in the heavy metal spiked soil after treatment with 0.1% di-rhamnolipid biosurfactant solution. This was mainly attributed to di-rhamnolipid mediated removal of the toxic heavy metals such as cadmium and lead from the spiked soil, which were inhibitory and toxic to the soil microflora. Thus, the treatment of heavy metal spiked soil with 0.1% di-rhamnolipid biosurfactant solution has enabled soil to regain its lost fertility.

Table 4 : Microbiological Characteristics of natural and heavy metal spiked soil samples from glass columns after treatment with Di-rhamnolipid biosurfactant solution

Glass Column with specifications of soil treatments	**Bacteria ($c.f.u.g^{-1}$)**	**Fungi ($c.f.u.g^{-1}$)**	**Actinomycetes ($c.f.u.g^{-1}$)**	***Azotobacter* ($c.f.u.g^{-1}$)**	***Rhizobium* ($c.f.u.g^{-1}$)**
Control					
I. Natural Soil Treated with Tap Water	19×10^5	31×10^3	45×10^3	28×10^3	33×10^3
II. Heavy Metal Spiked Soil Treated with Tap Water	64×10^4	47×10^2	24×10^1	21×10^1	20×10^2
Experimental					
III. Natural Soil Treated with 0.1 % Di-rhamnolipid Biosurfactant	23×10^5	29×10^3	51×10^3	24×10^3	41×10^3
IV. Heavy Metal spiked soil treated with 0.1 % Di-rhamnolipid Biosurfactant	10×10^5	26×10^3	13×10^3	21×10^3	20×10^3

Conclusions

Metal contamination of soil represents a potential environmental hazard in terms of toxicity to animals and inhibition of microbial processes. In this context, usefulness of a natural product i.e. di-rhamnolipid biosurfactant has been proposed to solve environmental hazards posed due to the presence of heavy metals such as cadmium and lead in the contaminated sites. This type of approach will not only minimize the use of chemical agents such as synthetic surfactants which act to mobilize or increase the availability of different contaminants such as heavy metals, but also complex and mobilize heavy metals in soil so as to facilitate their recovery. The results obtained from column studies are encouraging and promising and present an ecofriendly approach for removing the heavy metals from contaminated soils, metal sludge's and even from wastewaters.

Acknowledgement

The authors acknowledge Dr. Sukumar Devotta, Director, NEERI for his encouragement and valuable suggestions.

References

APHA (1978) *Standard Methods for the Examination of Water and Wastewater*. American Public Health Association, Washington, DC 20036.

Athar, M. and Vohora, S.B. (1995) *In: Heavy metals and environment*. Man and Environment Series, (Editor P.K. Ray) New Age International Publishers Limited, Wiley Eastern Ltd., New Delhi, India.

Baath, E. (1989) Effects of heavy metals in soil on microbial processes and populations (a review). Water, Air, Soil Pollution, 47: 335 – 379.

Babich, H. and Stotsky, G. (1985) Heavy metal toxicity to microbe-mediated ecologic process – A review and potential application to regulatory policies. Environ. Res., 36: 111 – 137.

Black, C.A., Evans, D.D., White, J.L., Ensminger, L.E. and Clark, F.E. (ed.) (1965) *In: Methods of Soil Analysis. Chemical and Microbiological Properties*. Agronomy-9, Part II, ASA, Madison, Wisconsin, USA.

Chang, F.H. and Broadbent, F.E. (1981) Influence of Trace Metals on Carbon dioxide evolution from a Yolo soil. Soil Sci. 132: 416 – 421.

Doelman, P. and Haanstra, L. (1979) Effect of lead on soil respiration and dehydrogenase activity. *Soil Biol. Biochem.*, 11 : 475 – 479.

Dubey, K. and Juwarkar, A. (2001) Distillery and curd whey waste as viable alternative to synthetic medium for biosurfactant production and pollution abatement of these wastes. W. Microbiol. Biotech; 17: 61-99

Herman, D.C., Artiola, J.F., Miller, R.M. (1995) Removal of Cd, Pb and Zn from Soil by Rhamnolipid Biosurfactant. Environ. Sci. Technol., 29: 2280 – 2285.

ICPS (International Programme on Chemical Safety), Environmental Health Criteria 135, Cadmium-environmental Aspects, World Health Organization, Geneva, 1992

Miller, R.M. (1995) *In: Bioremediation: Science and Application,* (Eds. H. Skipper and R. Turco) Soil Science Society of America, Madison, W.I., pp., 33-52

Nordgren, A, Baath, E., Soderstorn, B. (1988) Evaluation of soil respiration characteristics to assess heavy metal effect on soil microorganism using glutamic acid as a substrat. Soil Biol. Biochem., 20: 949 – 954.

Page, A.L., Miller, R.H. and Keeney, D.R., (1982) *In: Method of Soil Analysis:* Chemical and Microbiological Properties, Agronomy 9, Part II, ASA, SSSA, Medison, Wiscosin, USA.

Piper, C. S. (1996) *Soil and Plant Analysis. Hanns Publication,* Bombay, pp. 401.

Power, J. F., and J. W. Doran. (1988) Role of crop residue management in nitrogen cycling and use. p. 101-113. In cropping strategies for efficient use of water and nitrogen. ASA- CSSA- SSSA, special publication # 51.

Tan, H., Champion, J.T., Artiola, J.F., Brusseau, M.L. and Miller. R.M. (1994) Complexation of Cadmium by a Rhamnolipid Biosurfactant. Environ. Sci. Technol., 28: 2402 – 2406.

U.S. Environmental Protection Agency (USEPA), Summary Report: Remedial Response at Hazardous Waste Sites; EPA-540/2-84- 002a; U.S. EPA: Washington, DC, March, 1984.

CHAPTER 4

MITIGATION STUDIES ON UTILIZATION OF BIOLOGICALLY TREATED DISTILLERY WASTEWATER THROUGH HIGH RATE TRANSPIRATION SYSTEM

S.K. Singh, A.A. Juwarkar, P.S. Rao and P.R. Thawale

Environmental Biotechnology Division
National Environmental Engineering Research Institute NEERI,
Nehru Marg, Nagpur – 440020, India.

ABSTRACT

Land application through High Rate Transpiration System (HRTS) for treatment of wastewater has been considered as a low cost, low-tech method for improving its quality for potential reuse. The disposal of distillery wastewater posing problem of increasing importance throughout the World. In countries like India, most of the distilleries are molasses based and generate spent wash which is treated in conventional anaerobic followed by aerobic biological treatment process. Even after the treatment, biologically treated distillery effluent (BTDE) contains intense colour, high total dissolved solids (TDS), chemical oxygen demand (COD) and biochemical oxygen demand (BOD). These characteristics of BTDE makes it unfit for disposal on land and other water bodies and if disposed, the impact of distillery wastewater on the environment will be more serious in the near future. Looking into the various pollution problems of distillery wastewater, it is urgent to develop a low cost zero discharge technology for utilizing the distillery wastewater for resource conservation vis-vis managing the pollution load of BTDE. The objective of the investigation was to evaluate the performance of HRTS for treatment and disposal of BTDE through forestry using column lysimeter. Two experiments (Bench & Pilot Scale) were conducted using column lysimeter indicate that a properly designed land treatment system *(High Rate Transpiration System)* having coconut husk as a bedding material could successfully treat the BTDE with a hydraulic load of 200 $m^3ha^{-1}day^{-1}$ and 500 $m^3ha^{-1}day^{-1}$ with an average COD load of 0.686 and 2.88 ton $ha^{-1}day^{-1}$ during post and pre monsoon periods respectively. The organic constituents of BTDE could be stabilized in the soil, as there was no significant increase in the organic carbon of the soil irrigated with BTDE. The characteristics of leachate produced under optimal conditions indicate that the magnitude of different pollutants in the leachates were within the prescribed limit for the drinking water sources. The results also indicated that 99 to 100% colour removal, BOD and COD from BTDE was possible to treat through HRTS planted with *Dendrocalamus stricutus.*

Key Word : BTDE, Column lysimeter, *Dendrocalamus strictus*, HRTS, Land application, Reuse

Introduction

Due to rapid industrial developments during the last two decades in India, the disposal of industrial effluents has become a major problem. The water pollution caused by the disposal of untreated and inadequately treated effluents into fresh and marine water bodies are gradually becoming a major threat. In recent years, considerable attention has been paid to industrial wastes, which are usually discharged on land or into the sources of water (Kaur and Singh, 2002). It is anticipated that the industrial activities will accelerate within the pace of development. The use of industrial effluents in irrigation is a recent phenomena with scientific attention towards this being focused only after 1940 when the problem of fresh water pollution due to effluents disposal became particularly acute. A large number of wastes viz. dairy waste (Scott, 1962), food processing waste (Fisk, 1964), pulp and paper mill waste (Billing, 1959: Lumbely, 1977; Juwarkar *et al.*, 2003), meat processing waste (Cohen, 1982) and Distillery waste (Chhonkar *et al.*, 2000) etc. have been successfully used for irrigation of crops with and without treatment. Several studies based on column lysimeter or field experiment have been carried out to evaluate the performance of HRTS with different types of wastewater under different experimental condition showed a significant result (Juwarkar *et al.*, 2003; Hansen *et al.*, 1980).

In India, so far no systematic studies have been carried out to utilize distillery effluent for crop irrigation or for forestry development without any ground water pollution. Presently, there are about 285 distilleries that rapidly sprang up in India. The distillery generated waste water after the biological treatment unit contains very high solids, COD and BOD in order of several thousands. The direct disposal of this biologically treated distillery effluent on land results in various environmental problem not only due to presence of high TDS, COD and BOD but because of the dark brown colour. The sound technology for the complete treatment of various effluents and bringing them to the desired standards is yet to develop for large number of wastes and the available techniques for the treatment of wastewater is continue to be cost prohibitive. Thus, the successful treatment and disposal of distillery effluent is still a challenging task before the scientific world. Most of the distillery units in India are treating the effluent with rudimentary lagooning methods, with very little success in BOD and solids reduction. Precisely, this situation has forced most of the distilleries to dispose the treated effluent on land for irrigation instead of discharging into the water bodies but the problem of colour remains a major problem which may lead to the pollution of ground water quality of the nearby region.

Keeping in view, the different problems encountered with disposal of effluent on land, the present investigations were carried out to evaluate the performance of HRTS for treatment and disposal of BTDE through column lysimeters to utilize the potential of biologically treated distillery effluent for forestry development with a properly designed land treatment system without any ground water contamination. The HRTS consists of especially designed ridges and furrows for treatment of distillery effluent with suitable laid filter media in the furrows to arrest and stabilize pollutants, is one of the eco-friendly technology developed by National Environmental Engineering Research Institute (NEERI), and can be used for safe disposal of distillery effluent on to the land.

Different approaches may be used for such type of studies. Batch experiments are frequently used to establish retention equilibrium under laboratory conditions. Nevertheless, because of the mixing and the high solution to soil ratios used, these experiments typically fail to reproduce well field conditions. These can be approximately more closely by column experiment that additionally allows the evaluation of some relevant transport parameters. Also, the partition coefficients or the isotherm parameters may be obtained from the corresponding break through curves. In this sense, this work deals with the study of optimization of bedding material, hydraulic and organic load of BTDE. In a subsequent paper, a model is applied to the results to study the retention phenomena as well as solid-liquid contact efficiency in the columns.

Materials and Methods

The laboratory studies were carried out at the National Environmental Engineering Research Institute (NEERI), Nagpur in Maharashtra state of India representing hot semi arid climate.

Installation and Operation of Lysimeter

The lysimeters are simulated soil reactor systems packed with soil as per the soil profiles that exist at actual effluent disposal site and used for investigations in order to ascertain the extent of stabilization of the pollutants in the soil using suitable plant species, changes in the soil physico-biochemical characteristic due to application of biologically treated distillery effluent with reference to physicochemical and microbiological parameters to assess the pollution potentiality of leachates produced due to application of the wastewater. In the present investigation lysimeter experiments were conducted for evaluating the feasibility of application of HRTS for stabilization of biologically treated distillery effluent and growth of the value added plants through forestry. The biologically treated distillery effluent contained intense colour, high magnitude of TDS and high concentrations of residual COD and BOD. Therefore, the feasibility studies on utilization of biologically treated distillery effluent through HRTS were undertaken on bench scale and pilot scale with *Dendrocalamus strictus* plant in order to ascertain some of the important parameters required for scale up at the field level.

Bench Scale Experiments

Two bench scale lysimeters made up of high density polyethylene (HDP) were designed, fabricated and installed for selection of bedding material for pilot scale studies. These lysimeters were packed with the soil as per the soil profile in the field. The two different bedding material viz. cocunut

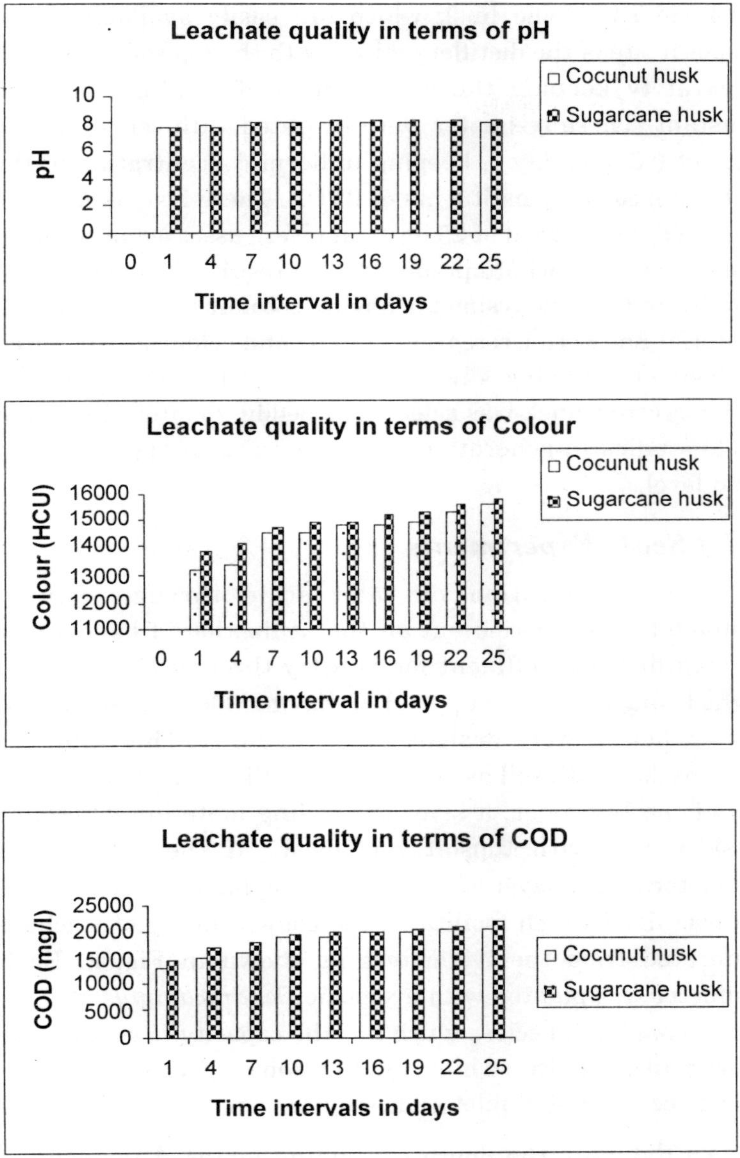

Fig. 1 : Effect of different bedding materials in terms of pH, colour and COD in the leachate collected from the lysimeters

huskand sugarcane husk which are easily available at the disposal site of the distillery mixed with the top soil were used separately keeping the depth (5cm) of bedding material constant. These lysimeter were irrigated with constant flow rate of 0.320 L day^{-1}, keeping uniform concentration of the COD and colour constituents of BTDE. These lysimeters were operated for a period of 25 days and were assessed in terms of the quality of leachate produced. The results depicted in Fig. 1 indicate that the lysimeter having coconut husk as bedding material had better retention of COD and colour as compared to lysimeter having sugarcane husk as bedding material. Thus, coconut husk was selected as bedding material for pilot scale studies to generate data for large-scale application at field level.

Pilot Scale Experiments

The investigation on pilot scale through column lysimeters was carried out on the utilization of biologically treated distillery effluent for forestry through HRTS. Total eight lysimeters made up of HDP having 30cm diameter and 200cm height were designed and installed. The lysimeter were packed with soil as per the soil profile in the field. At the top of the lysimeter, a layer of bedding material of coconut husk mixed with topsoil was used. At the bottom the lysimeter, mixed layer of gravel and sand having a depth of 20 cm was fixed which facilitated the easy draining of leachate generated from the lysimeters as shown in Fig. 2. Each lysimeter was planted with a specific *Dendrocalamus strictus* (Bamboo) plant species, which has the capacity to sustain the growth in presence of high total dissolved solids. The main objectives covered in pilot scale studies were to:

- Evaluate the depth of bedding material in order to ascertain the retention of different pollutants present in the biologically treated distillery effluent,

- Assess the optimal hydraulic load to the lysimeter to generate data for large scale application,
- Ascertain/select the optimal pollutant load of the effluent to the lysimeter at optimal hydraulic load, and
- Performance evaluation of lysimeter at optimal conditions in different seasons in order to ascertain the quality of leachate produced, characteristics of BTDE irrigated soil and its effect on the growth of the plant species.

Treatment Details

Different depths of the bedding material used in lysimeters

Lysimeters No.	Treatment Details
A	Control, without bedding material (Treated with plain water)
B	Control, without bedding material (Treated with 100 mg L^{-1} BOD of biologically treated distillery effluent)
C	5 cm depth of Coconut husk (Treated with 100 mg L^{-1} BOD of biologically treated distillery effluent)
D	7.5 cm depth of Coconut husk (Treated with 100 mg L^{-1} BOD of biologically treated distillery effluent)
E	10 cm depth of Coconut husk (Treated with 100 mg L^{-1} BOD of biologically treated distillery effluent)
F	15 cm depth of Coconut husk (Treated with 100 mg L^{-1} BOD of biologically treated distillery effluent)
G	15 cm depth of Coconut husk (Treated with 500 mg L^{-1} BOD of biologically treated distillery effluent)
H	15 cm depth of Coconut husk (Treated with 1000 mg L^{-1} BOD of biologically treated distillery effluent)

Wastewater and soil samples were collected and subjected for the analysis of various physico-chemical parameters. The wastewater samples used for HRTS and percolate samples were analyzed as per standard methods for the examination of water and wastewater (APHA, 1978). Plant height was measured periodically and soil samples before and after application of distillery wastewater were collected from HRTS were analysed by Standard technique (Black, 1965; Jackson, 1973; Piper, 1966).

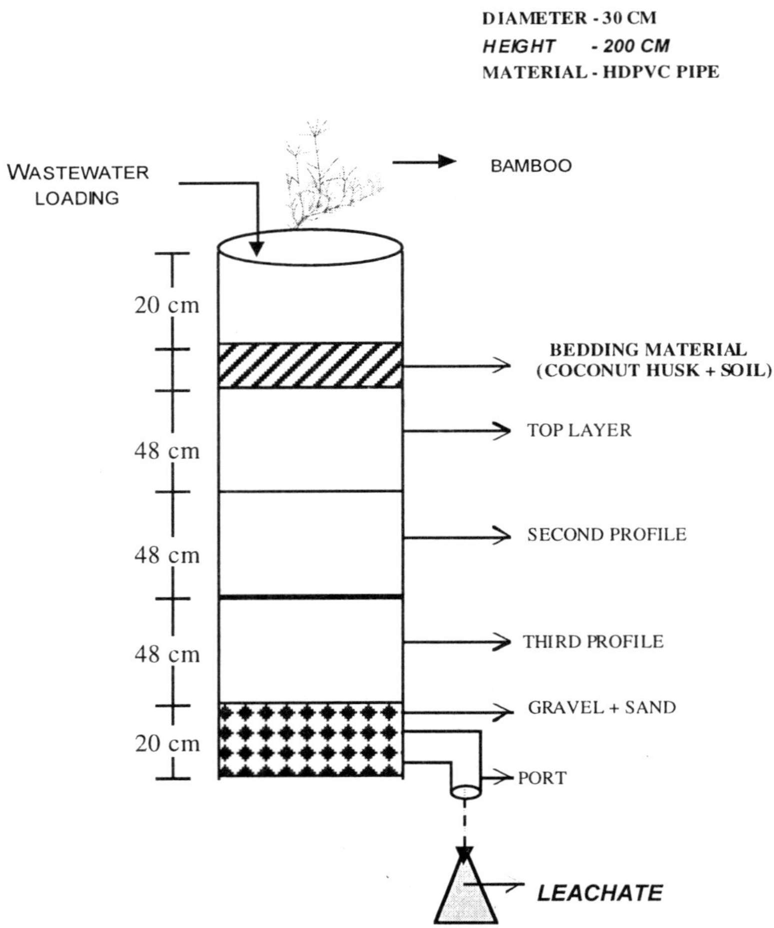

Fig. 2 : Schematic diagram of column lysimeter

Results and Discussions

The results depicted in Table 1 indicated that the effluent comprised of high BOD (4000 – 4200 mgL^{-1}), COD (30,400 – 36,432 mgL^{-1}), TDS (37,332 – 39,200 mgL^{-1}). The inadequate disposal of such effluent on the land may affect the soil productivity. The effluent was dark brown in colour in the range of 72,000 to 75,000 (Hazen Coloúr Unit) and inadequate disposal is of great environmental concerns as it may lead to ground water pollution through leaching. The effluent belongs to the irrigation water group *"Moderate to Severe restriction on use"* with respect to salinity and specific ion toxicity (Kandiah, 1987).

Table 1 : Characteristics of the biologically treated distillery effluent samples

Physico-chemical Properties					
S. No.	**Parameters**	**Samples**			
		1st Magnitude*	**2nd Magnitude***	**3rd Magnitude***	**Standards for Industrial Effluent on land for irrigation**
Physico-chemical Parameters					
1.	pH	8.52	8.62	8.30	5.5-9.0
2.	EC, $mS\ cm^{-1}$	18.97	19.05	23.00	-
3	Colour, Hz	75000	73200	72000	-
4.	TSS, mgL^{-1}	4900	5200	5800	200
5.	TDS, mgL^{-1}	38642	37332	39200	2100
6.	BOD, mgL^{-1}	4200	4000	3900	100

Contd.

7.	COD, mgL^{-1}	33846	36432	30400	-
8.	Chloride, mgL^{-1}	923	900	915	600
Microbiological Properties ($CFUml^{-1}$)					
1.	Bacteria	$30x10^5$	$25x10^5$	$30x10^5$	-
2.	Fungi	$40x10^2$	$50x10^2$	$50x10^2$	-
3	Actinomycetes	$20x10^2$	$20x10^2$	$10x10^2$	-
4.	Azotobacter	ND	ND	ND	-
5.	Rhizobium	ND	ND	ND	-

ND - Not detected

CFU - Colony forming unit

* Magnitude 1, 2 and 3 indicate composite samples collected during different seasons

The effluent also contains considerable amount of bacterial, fungal and actinomycetes populations which varied in the range of 25 – 30 x 10^5, 40 – 50 x 10^2 and 10 – 20 x 10^2 $CFUml^{-1}$, respectively. Nitrogen fixer's viz. *Rhizobium* and *Azotobacter* were totally absent.

The physico-chemical and microbiological characteristics of Soil are presented in Table 2 showed that the soil was clay in texture. The bulk density ranged from 1.10 to 1.20 gm cm^{-3}. The soil had good maximum water holding capacity and porosity and which varied from 48.53 to 62.16% and 45.80 to 54.19%, respectively. The organic carbon content of the soil ranged from 0.33 to 0.46%. The CEC of the soil ranged from 60.58 to 75.57 [Cmol(p+)kg^{-1}]. The total and available nutrients with respect to N, P and K were also present in appreciable amounts in the soil.

Table 2 : Characteristics of soil profile samples

Physico-chemical Properties		Depth of the soil samples		
		0 – 100 cm	100 – 200 cm	200 – 300 cm
Physical Properties				
1.	Bulk density (gm cm^{-3})	1.18	1.20	1.10
2.	Maximum water holding capacity (%)	62.16	57.25	48.53
3	Pore space (%)	53.92	54.19	48.53
4.	Sand (%)	26	39	8
5.	Silt (%)	26	30	39
6.	Clay (%)	48	31	52
7.	Textural Class	Clay	Clay Loam	Clay
Chemical Properties				
1.	pH	8.80	8.99	8.60
2.	EC, $mScm^{-1}$	0.200	0.210	0.190
3.	CEC, $(Cmol(p^{+})kg^{-1})$	75.57	72.14	60.58
4.	Organic carbon (%)	0.46	0.38	0.33
Total nutrients (%)				
1.	Nitrogen	0.045	0.016	0.055
2.	Phosphorous	0.074	0.057	0.077
3.	Potassium	0.160	0.150	0.230
Total nutrients (%)				
1.	Nitrogen	3.90	2.48	3.40
2.	Phosphorous	5.5	4.5	5.4
3.	Potassium	20.4	10.4	30.0
Microbiological Properties ($CFUg^{-1}$)				
1.	Bacteria	$20x10^{5}$	$50x10^{4}$	$24x10^{5}$
2.	Fungi	$6x10^{3}$	$3x10^{3}$	$48x10^{3}$
3	Actinomycetes	32x10	$15x10^{3}$	$17x10^{3}$
4.	Azotobacter	$11x10^{3}$	$30x10^{2}$	$70x10^{2}$
5.	Rhizobium	$10x10^{2}$	$13x10^{3}$	$15x10^{3}$

Assessment of Depth of Coconut Husk as Bedding Material

Lysimeter were installed with different depths of bedding material mixed with top soil *(5 to 15cm)* for ascertaining the optimal depth of bedding material, except lysimeters A and B. The lysimeter A and B were operated as control *(without bedding material)* using plain water and biologically treated distillery effluent. The lysimeter B to F were operated continuously for a period of 14 days with a total volume of 9800 ml of biologically treated distillery effluent having a uniform concentration of BOD (100 mgL^{-1}) at the rate of 100 $m^3ha^{-1}day^{-1}$. The biologically treated distillery effluent proposed to be utilized for forestry through HRT system should lead to the generation of minimal leachate, otherwise there is a possibility of ground water contamination. The result shows that the lysimeter having a depth of 15cm bedding material did not generate any leachate during the operation of 14 days as shown in Fig. 3. This indicates that the lysimeter F having 15 cm depth of bedding material facilitates the better transpiration and effective evaporation of biologically treated distillery effluent.

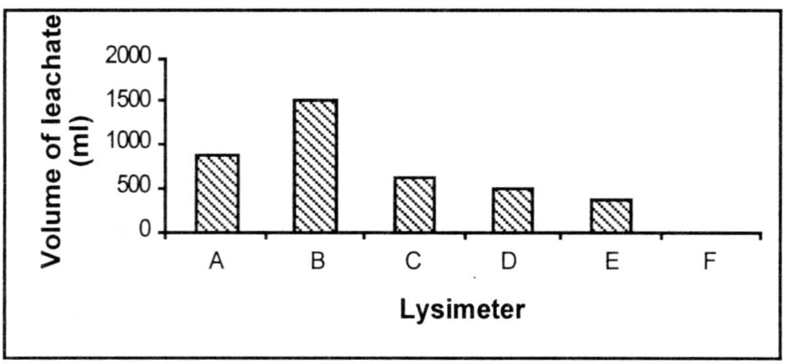

Fig. 3 : Total volume of leachate collected from different lysimeters irrigated with hydraulic loading of $100m^3$ ha^{-1} day^{-1}

Assessment of Optimal Hydraulic Load

The lysimeter packed with 15 cm depth of bedding material of coconut husk was operated at different hydraulic loading, keeping the characteristic of biologically treated distillery effluent constant *(100 mgL^{-1} of BOD)*. The hydraulic loading varied from 100 m^{3}ha^{-1}day^{-1} to 250 m^{3}ha^{-1}day^{-1} and the leachate produced was assessed with reference to colour, pH, EC, COD, BOD and TDS and microbiological characteristics (viz. Bacteria, Fungi, Actinomycetes, *Azotobacter* and *Rhizobium)*.

As ground water forms the potential source for supply of drinking water to the community, the characteristics of the leachate produced upto the hydraulic load of 200 m^{3}ha^{-1}day^{-1} with reference to magnitude of different constituents were well below the prescribed limits for drinking water sources as depicted in Figure 4a and 4b. This study was carried during post monsoon season and hence the hydraulic loading of 200 m^{3}ha^{-1}day^{-1} is selected as optimal during post monsoon season.

However, the characteristics of the leachate produced upto the hydraulic load of 500 m^{3}ha^{-1}day^{-1} applied to lysimeter G with reference to magnitude of different constituents were well below the prescribed limits for drinking water sources and is optimal during pre-monsoon season.

Selection of Pollution Load of Biologically Treated Distillery Effluent to the Lysimeter at Optimal Hydraulic Load

The three lysimeters F, G and H with 15 cm depth of bedding material were operated with different TDS, BOD and COD loading at optimal hydraulic load of 200 m^{3}ha^{-1}day^{-1} during post monsoon in order to ascertain the maximum load of biologically treated distillery effluent that could be stabilized in the system with minimal production of leachates and less magnitude of pollutants.

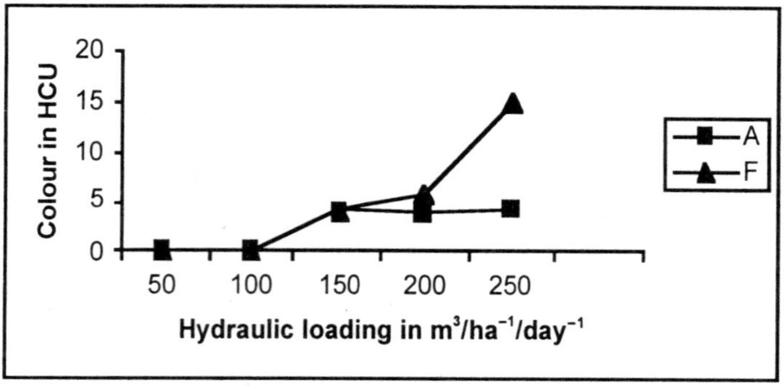

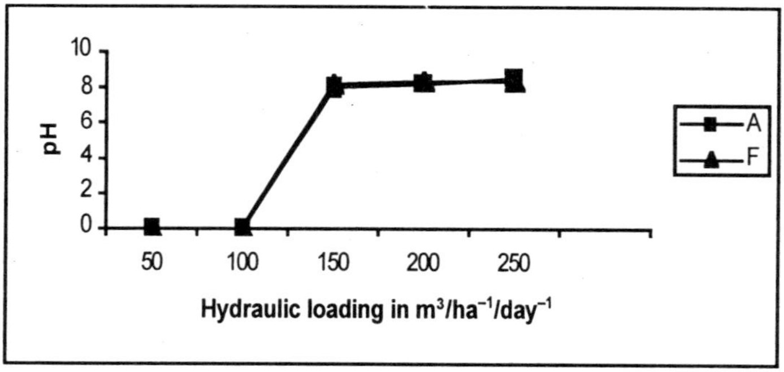

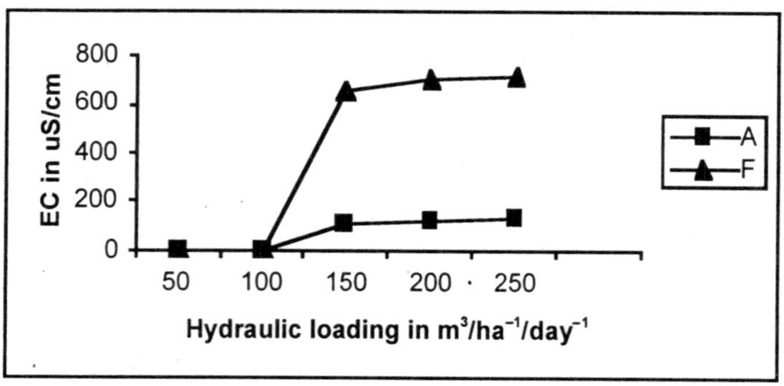

Fig. 4(a) : Levels of Colour, pH and EC in the leachates of the lysimeters during the application of Biologically Treated Distillery Effluent at various Hydraulic Loadings during post - monsoon

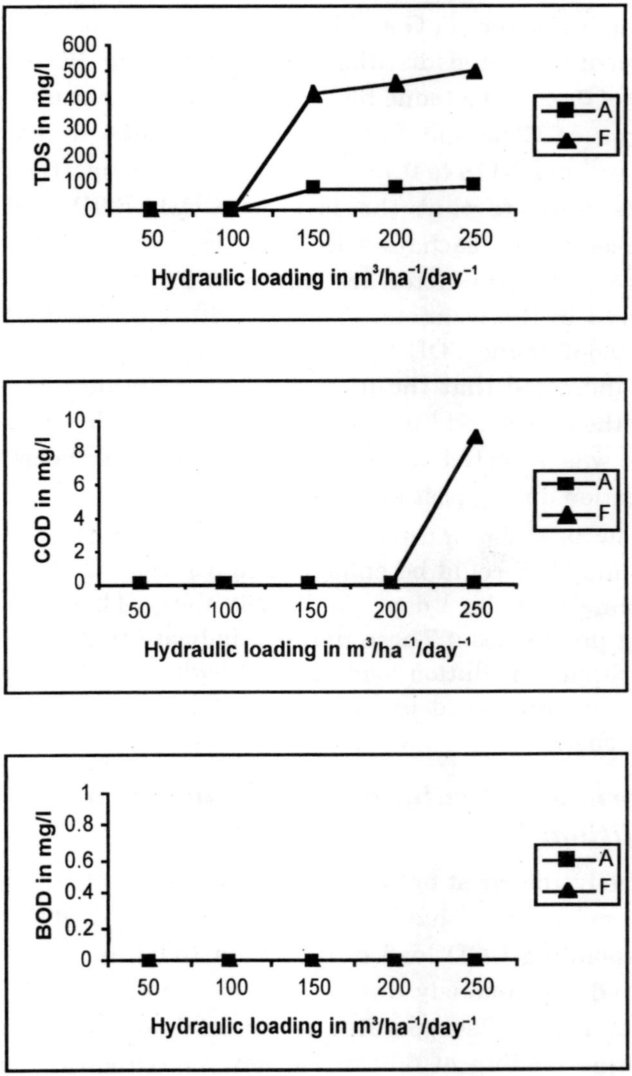

Fig. 4(b) : Levels of TDS, COD and BOD in the leachates of the lysimeters during the application of Biologically Treated Distillery Effluent at various Hydraulic Loadings during post - monsoon

The lysimeters F, G and H were irrigated separately with biologically treated distillery effluent having BOD in the range of 0.02 to 0.2 tonne $ha^{-1}day^{-1}$, while corresponding load in terms of COD and TDS ranged from 0.686 to 3.4 tonne $ha^{-1}day^{-1}$and 0.178 to 0.758 tonne $ha^{-1}day^{-1}$ respectively. The results indicate that the level of COD, BOD and TDS increases in the leachate with increase in the pollution load applied to the lysimeter are shown in Fig. 5. The leachate produced in the lysimeter operated with 0.02 ton BOD ha^{-1} day^{-1} 0.686 tonne COD ha^{-1} day^{-1} and 0.178 tonne TDS ha^{-1} day^{-1} indicated that the magnitude of pollutants were well below the prescribed limits for the drinking water sources and hence was selected as a optimal loading for large scale application during post monsoon.

However, the optimal substrate load in terms of BOD, COD and TDS could be enhanced to 0.100 ton BOD/ha/day, 2.8 tonne COD ha^{-1} day^{-1} and 0.438 tonne TDS ha^{-1} day^{-1} during premonsoon. These findings indicate that the rate of application of pollution load keeping hydraulic load constant is greatly influenced by environmental and meteorological conditions.

Performance Evaluation of Lysimeter at Optimal Condition:

The lysimeter at optimal conditions with a hydraulic load of 200 $m^3ha^{-1}day^{-1}$ having BOD of 100 mgL^{-1} of BTDE with corresponding COD load of 0.638 ton COD ha^{-1} day^{-1} was operated continuously during post monsoon. Similarly, the lysimeter was also operated at optimal conditions with a hydraulic loading of 500 $m^3ha^{-1}day^{-1}$ having BOD of 500 mgL^{-1} of BTDE with a COD load of 2.8 tonne COD ha^{-1} day^{-1} continuously in pre-monsoon. The performance of the lysimeters at optimal conditions was evaluated through monitoring of characteristics of produced leachate, characteristics of soil and response of the plant growth.

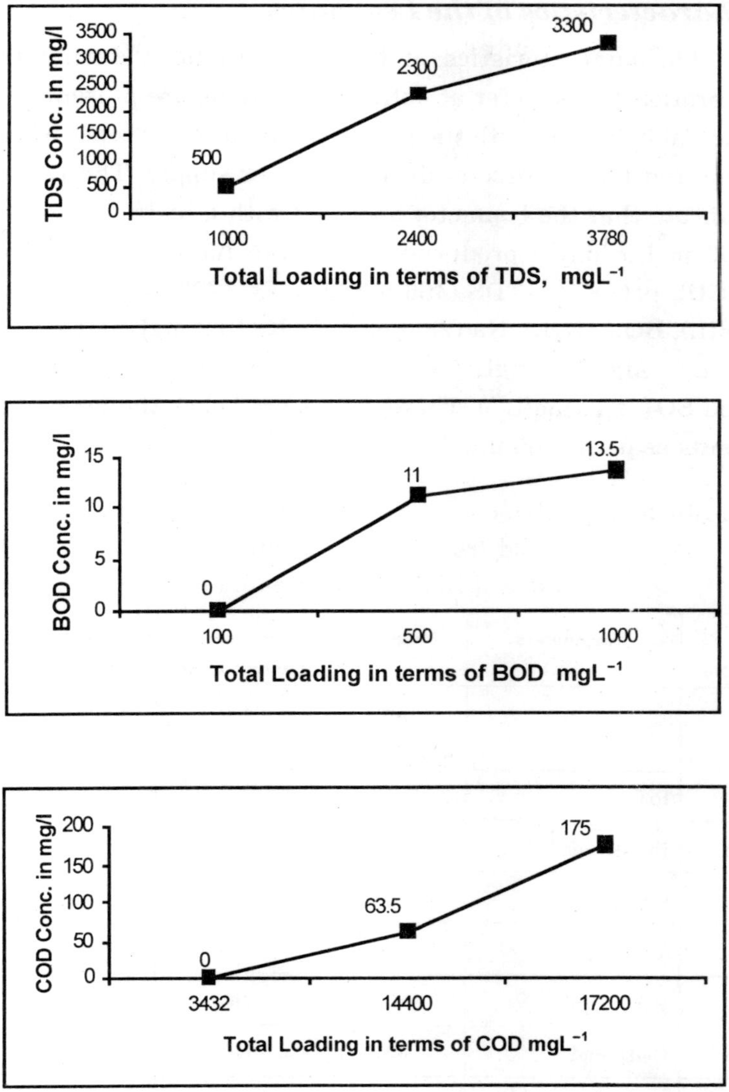

Fig. 5. Magnitude of TDS, BOD and COD of the leachates produced at various TDS, BOD and COD loading at optimal hydraulic loads (200 $m^3 ha^{-1} day^{-1}$)

Characteristics of the Leachates

The characteristics of leachate produced during the operation of lysimeter at optimal conditions are presented in the Table 3 along with the prescribed limit of the constituents required for a source of drinking water supply. The results indicate that the lysimeter operated with a hydraulic load of 200 $m^3ha^{-1}day^{-1}$ produced a leachate having Colour (5.0 HCU), pH (8.13), TDS (465 mg L^{-1}), EC (700 µS cm^{-1}). COD (NIL), BOD (NIL), Na (28.5 mgL^{-1}), K (10.2 mgL^{-1}), Ca (56.8 mgL^{-1}), Mg (29.4 mgL^{-1}), Cl (85.2 mgL^{-1}), HCO_3 (183.0 mgL^{-1}) and SO_4 (24.7 mgL^{-1}). These values are below the prescribed limits as per Kandiah (1987).

Table 3 : Physico-chemical Characteristics of the leachate collected from lysimeter with different hydraulic loadings of Biologically Treated Distillery Effluent

S. No.	Parameters	Magnitude of constituents in the leachate at Optimal hydraulic loadings		
		200 $m^3 ha^{-1} day^{-1}$ *	500 $m^3 ha^{-1} day^{-1}$ **	Standards for Drinking water
1.	PH	8.13	NG	6.5-8.5
2.	EC, µS cm^{-1}	700	NG	-
3.	Colour, Hz	5.0	NG	10
4.	TDS, mgL^{-1}	465	NG	-
5.	BOD, mgL^{-1}	NIL	NG	-
6.	COD, mgL^{-1}	NIL	NG	-
7.	Chloride, mgL^{-1}	85.2	NG	250
8.	Bicarbonate, mgL^{-1}	183.0	NG	-

Contd.

9.	Sulfate, mgL^{-1}	24.7	NG	150
10.	Sodium, mgL^{-1}	28.5	NG	–
11.	Potassium, mgL^{-1}	10.2	NG	–
12.	Calcium, mgL^{-1}	56.8	NG	75
13.	Magnesium, mgL^{-1}	29.4	NG	30

NG: No generation of leachate

* Post-monsoon

** Pre-monsoon (There is no generation of leachate at this loading)

Physico-Chemical and Microbiological Characteristics of Soil

Soil samples irrigated with BTDE with a BOD load of 0.02ton BOD/ha/day and at optimal hydraulic load of 200 $m^3ha^{-1}day^{-1}$ were collected at different depths as per soil profile from the lysimeter and were analyzed for physico-chemical properties viz. water holding capacity (WHC), bulk density, pH, electrical conductivity, water soluble cations and anions, exchangeable cations, organic carbon, available and total nutrients etc. The results are presented in Table 4. The continuous application of BTDE affects the bulk density of the soil, which in turn influences the porosity of soil and ultimately WHC of the soil. Further, application of BTDE at optimal conditions does not indicate substantial increase in the organic carbon content of the soil. This indicates that the soil in the lysimeter has a capacity to stabilize the organic constituents of the BTDE through different microbial communities present in the soil. Trivedi and Shinde (1983), also reported fast degradation of organic matter in distillery waste water irrigated soil.

Table 4 : Characteristics of BTDE Irrigated soil profile of the samples collected from lysimeters at optimal conditions

Physical Properties

S. No.	Depth (cm)	Bulk Density (g cm^{-3})	Pore space (%)	Maximum Water Holding Capacity (%)
1	0 – 48	1.20	51.20	73.03
2	48 – 96	1.19	63.56	72.32
3	96 – 144	1.18	57.18	72.13

Chemical Properties

S. No.	Depth (cm)	pH	EC ($mScm^{-1}$)	Water Soluble Ions ($meqL^{-1}$)							Organic Carbon (%)
				Ca	Mg	K	Na	CO_3^-	HCO_3^-	Cl^-	
1	0 – 48	8.25	1.26	6.1	11.5	12.1	11.0	-	24.0	35.4	0.49
2	48 – 96	8.22	0.63	4.2	9.0	8.3	8.4	-	18.0	34.8	0.41
3	96 – 144	8.14	0.62	4.1	8.7	8.3	8.5	-	17.2	24.5	0.34

C ontd.

Microbiological Properties

S. No.	Depth (cm)	Bacteria ($CFUg^{-1}$)	Fungi ($CFUg^{-1}$)	Actinomycetes ($CFUg^{-1}$)	*Rhizobium* ($CFUg^{-1}$)	*Azotobacter* ($CFUg^{-1}$)
1	0 – 48	86×10^{5}	69×10^{3}	34×10^{3}	84×10^{2}	96×10^{2}
2	48 – 96	85×10^{5}	68×10^{3}	28×10^{3}	76×10^{2}	89×10^{2}
3	96 – 144	88×10^{5}	74×10^{3}	22×10^{3}	71×10^{2}	87×10^{2}

Treatment : 100 mgL^{-1} BOD of BTDE (FM – 15cm)

FM – Filter Media of Coconut husk

The microbiological analysis of the soil at different depths of the lysimeter was carried out to ascertain the colony-forming units (CFUs) for the population of the bacteria, fungi, actinomycetes, *rhizobium* and *azotobacter*. The bacterial population of the soil through out the lysimeter is maximum as compared to other microbial communities. Further, the soil has developed *rhizobium* and *azotobacter,* which are potential nitrogen fixers. This result is in confirmity with findings reported by Trivedy and Shinde (1983) and Rajjanan and Oblisami (1979).

Response of Plant Growth at Optimal Conditions of Operation of the Lysimeters

The growth of the plant species *Dendrocalamus strictus* (Bamboo) planted in the lysimeters showed good response towards BTDE irrigation. Increase in height of the plant irrigated with BTDE was better as compared to the height of the plant observed with the plain water application. This is due to the addition of nutrients through the biologically treated distillery BTDE. The percent increase in height of the plant was 233.33%. Similar findings were reported by Raja and Vijaykumari (2003), Thawale *et, al.* (1999), Chhonkar *et al.* (2000), Trivedy and Shinde (1983) and Yakunshenku *et al.* (1971).

Conclusions

The studies revealed that the distillery effluent is characterized by intense colour, high BOD, TDS and COD levels and also contains high percentage of organic and inorganic materials. The conventional methods in plant treatment of distillery effluent even upto secondary biologically treatment unit does not provide an environmentally compatible solution to effluent management for its disposal in surface water and onto the land. Based on lysimeter investigations on pilot scale, it was observed that a well designed land system with HRTS having a bedding material of coconut husk with a depth of 15cm could treat the BTDE at a hydraulic loading of 200 $m^3ha^{-1}day^{-1}$ having BOD of 100 mg L^{-1} with a corresponding COD load of 0.686 ton $ha^{-1}day^{-1}$ during post-monsoon. During pre-monsoon, the BTDE could be treated effectively through application of HRTS by growing specific *Dendrocalamus strictus* (Bamboo) species with an optimal hydraulic load of 500 $m^3ha^{-1}day^{-1}$ having BOD of 500 mgL^{-1} with a corresponding COD load of 2.8 tonne $ha^{-1}day^{-1}$. The pilot scale data generated using BTDE through column lysimeter will be helpful for its application at field level. Thus, the laboratory studies proved that with optimal hydraulic and organic load, the BTDE could be safely disposed onto the land without any harm to the soil and water sources.

Acknowledgement: The author's are thankful to Dr. R. N. Singh, Former Director, NEERI to undertake the activities. Thanks are also due to Dr. S. Devotta present Director, NEERI, for his valuable suggestions and finally author thank to M/s Jubilant Organosys Limited for providing the financial support and assistance to carry out the studies.

References

Anderson, A (1979) Disposal of an Integrated Pulp and Paper Mill Effluent by Irrigation, Tech. Rep. No. EPA-600/2-79-633, EPA Cincinnati, Ohio.

APHA (1978) *Standard Methods for the Examination of Water and Wastewater*. American Public Health Association, Washington, DC 20036.

Black, CA (1965) *Methods for Soil Analysis*. Am. Soc. Agro. Inc., Publ. Madison, Wisconsin, USA.

Chhonkar, P. K., Dutta S. P., Joshi H. C. and Pathak H. (2000) Impact of Industrial effluent on soil health and agriculture – Indian Experience Part –I : Distillery and paper mill effluent, J. of Scientific and Industrial Research, 59 : 350-361.

Hansen, E. A., Dawson, H. D. and Tolsfed, N. D. (1980) Irrigation of Intensively Cultured Plantation with Paper Mill Effluent, Tappi, 63 (11) : 139.

Jackson, M.L. (1973) *Soil Chemical Analysis*, Publ. Prantice Hall of India Ltd, New Delhi.

Juwarkar A. S., Thawale P. R., Juwarkar A. A, Singh S. K. (2003) An ecofriendly approach treatment and disposal of Pulp and Paper Mill Wastewater through Land Management: A Case Study, Souvenier & Abstract IEAM National Conference, New Delhi.

Juwarkar, A.S., and Subrahamanyam, P.V.R. (1987) Impact of Pulp and Paper Mill Wastewater on Crop and Soil. *Wat. Sci. Tech*. 19 : 693.

Kandiah A., (1987) Water Quality in Food Production. Water Quality Bulletin. F.A.O., Rome.

Kaur, Samanpreet and Singh Mandeep (2002) Soil Aquifer Treatment (SAT) system : A Case Study, Indian J. of Environmental Health, 44 (3) : 242-246

Lumbely W. G. (1977) The simplest effluent permit, Pulp and paper, Int. 12, 165.

McCormic, L.L. (1959) Effect of Paper Mill Wastewater on Cattle, Crop and Soil, Bull.La. *Agric. Stn*., 529.

Piper, C.S. (1966) *Soil and Plant Analysis*. Univ. Adelaide, Australia.

Rajanan, G. and Oblisami, G. (1979) Effect of Paper Factory Effluents on Soil and Crop Plants'. Indian J. Environ. Hlth., 21(2) : 120-130.

Raza H. and Vijayakumari (2003) Impact of distillery effluent spent wash on Seed Germination, Morphological character, Yield and Pigment cocentration of *Trigonella Foenumgraecum* L. Poll. Res, 8(3) : 109-116

Thawale, P.R., Juwarkar, A.S., Kulkarni, A.B. and Juwarkar, A.A. (1999) Lysimeter Studies for Evaluation of Changes in Soil Properties and Crop Yield using Wastewater. *Intern. J.Trop. Agric.,* 17 (1-4) : 231-244.

Trivedi R. K. and Shinde D. B. (1983) Effect of distillery waste irrigation on soil characteristics. Pollution Research 2(2) : 71-76

Yukunshenku, I.A., Kazantav and Ovsyannikava, V. G. (1971) Wastewater from Sulphate Pulp Production and their Use for Irrigation. Chem Abstr. 74, 196 79305n

CHAPTER 5

AN ECO-FRIENDLY APPROACH FOR TREATMENT AND DISPOSAL OF PULP AND PAPER MILL WASTEWATER THROUGH LAND MANAGEMENT - A CASE STUDY

A.S. Juwarkar, P.R. Thawale. P. Rao, S.K. Singh and Asha. A. Juwarkar

Environmental Biotechnology Division, National Environment Engineering Research Institute (NEERI), Nehru Marg, Nagpur-440020, India

ABSTRACT

The pulp and paper mill wastewater generated from Kraft bleaching process poses problem with respect to salinity and chlorides even after treatment and contaminates the soil and the ground water of the nearby region. Therefore, long-term discharge of such wastewater causes irreversible disturbances in the ecosystem equilibrium. The conventional physico-chemical method significantly reduces the pollutants (except chlorides) in the wastewater to meet the standard limits prescribed by regulatory agencies though the problem of colour in pulp and paper mill wastewater, which is imparted by lignin remains. Thus, for safe disposal of treated coloured pulp and paper mill wastewater on land, high rate transpiration system (HRTS), one of the ecofriendly technologies, was designed and developed which consists of specially designed ridges, planted with suitable plant species and furrows laid with filter media for treatment of wastewater. After making laboratory evaluation of the system, HRTS was implement at field level for the first time at the Orient paper Mills, Amlai at Madhya Pradesh, on an area of 80 hectares of land in the vicinity of effluent treatment plant to treat 18,000 - 20, 250 m^3 day^{-1} of coloured wastewater. The results of field trial showed no appreciable built up of salts concentration in the furrows, when the wastewater was applied at a rate of 150 $m^3 ha^{-1} day^{-1}$. The underground water quality monitored through well water samples was satisfactory with respect to salt and metal concentrations and the colour of well water samples was sparkingly clear. The results showed that HRTS provides cost effective and environmentally acceptable solution to manage the problem of coloured wastewater and also minimize the impacts on ground water quality. Besides this, the system also promoted development of forest and green belt and created much-required sink potential for absorption of green house gases.

Key Words: Pulp and paper mill wastewater, colour, HRTS, Forestry.

Introduction

Land application is considered to be the most acceptable and cost effective method of pulp and paper mill wastewater management as soil provides physical, chemical, and biological treatment to wastewater and removes 100% of the colour (Anderson, 1979 and Thawale *et al,* 1999) besides helping to grow the crops (Yakunshenko *et al.*, 1971; Lumbely, 1977; Hansen *et al.*, 1980; Juwarkar and Subrahamanyam, 1987; Anonymous, 1994). Presently, in India there are 305 paper mills with an installed capacity of 1.9×10^6 tonnes per annum (TPA). Paper mills consume large quantity of water, which varies from 300-450 m^3 t^{-1}, of which 220-350 m^3 of water per tonne of paper produced is discharged as wastewater. The wastewater comprises; high suspended solids (SS - 290-1115 mg L^{-1}), Biochemical Oxygen Demand (BOD - 100-1070 mg L^{-1}), Chemical Oxygen Demand (COD - 600-4760 mg L^{-1}) and dark brown colour due to lignin (82-700 mg L^{-1}).

In the process of pulp and paper manufacturing, large quantity of water is required. One of the largest integrated pulp and paper mill in India, Orient Paper and Industries Limited has established on the West bank of Sone River at village Amlai in Shahdol district of Madhya Pradesh which started its production in February 1965 and on an average, about 190 m^3 water is required to produce 1 MT of paper. These pollutants create problems in disposal of wastewater in water bodies. The conventional wastewater treatment method reduces SS, BOD, and to some extent COD but colour remains more or less unchanged, because of no biodegradability of lignin. Available treatment methods for colour removal i.e. use of adsorbents (activated carbon), coagulants (lime and alum) and as bleaching agent (ozone), are not so effective.

In this view extensive R&D in laboratory scale has been carried out to tackle the problem of colour of pulp and paper mill wastewater, and developed an ecofriendly technology, i.e. High Rate Transpiration System (HRTS), a unique land treatment technology for utilization of pulp and paper mills wastewater, which has been demonstrated successfully for the first time at Orient Paper Mills, Amlai (M.P.) at full-scale level on an area of 80 hectares in the vicinity of the plant to treat 18,000 - 20,250 m^3 day^{-1} of the wastewater.

The present paper describes a case study for treatment and safe disposal of all the coloured wastewater for forestry development and eliminate the necessity of discharging the wastewater in river Sone during non-monsoon months with a properly designed land treatment system without any ground water contamination and absorptions of green house gases.

Materials and Methods

Study Area

The laboratory studies were carried out at National Environmental Engineering Research Institute (NEERI), Nagpur and HRTS was installed at Orient Paper Mill, Amlai (Madhya Pradesh), India. The study area comes under hot semi-arid ecoregion and the climate of the area is characterized by hot and dry summers and mild winters. The annual precipitation ranging from 600 to 900 mm, covers 40 to 50% of annual potential evapotranspirative (PET) demand of 1600 to 2000 mm, resulting in gross annual deficit of 800 to 1200 mm.

Plant Species Selected for Plantation in High Rate Transpiration System

The details of the various species of trees and grasses planted in HRTS area is given below:

Acacia	-	*Acacia mangium*
Amaltash	-	*Cassia fistula*
Australian babool	-	*Acacia auriculiformis*
Bamboo	-	*Dendrocalamus strictus*
	-	*Bambusa arundinacea*
	-	*Bambusa vulgaris*
Cassia	-	*Cassia seamea*
Citronella grass	-	*Cymbopogon sp.*
Eucalyptus	-	*Eucalyptus hybrid*
	-	*Eucalyptus camaldulensis*
Grevillea	-	*Grevillea pteridofolia*
Karanj	-	*Pongamia pinnata*
Lemon grass	-	*Cymbopogon flexuosus*
Neem	-	*Azadirachata indica*
Palamorosa grass	-	*Cymbopogon martini*

Siras	-	*Albizia lebbeck*
Vetiver grass	-	*Vetiveria zizaniodes*

High Rate Transpiration System

The treatment and disposal of wastewater through High Rate Transpiration System (HRTS) provides cost effective and environmentally acceptable solution to manage the problem of coloured wastewater. The system also promotes development of environmental forests and green belt and enables creation of much required sink potential for absorption of green house gases.

The high rate transpiration system envisages the use of dynamic, multicomponent soil system as a live filtration device to renovate the wastewater through adsorption, ion exchange, precipitation and stabilization of pollutants through microbial degradation (Fig. 1). Impact network for treatment and disposal of pulp and paper mill wastewater using high rate transpiration system is presented in Fig. 2.

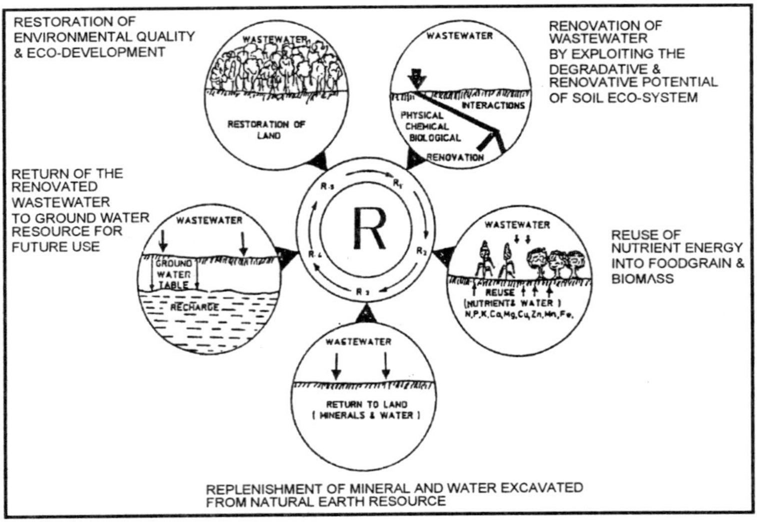

Fig. 1 : 5R Concept of wastewater management and recycling, reuse and eco-development

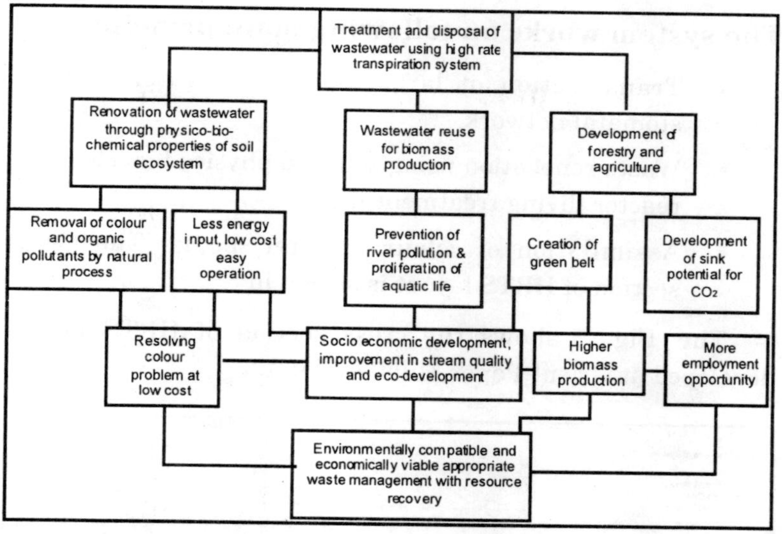

Fig. 2 : Impact network for treatment and disposal of pulp and paper mill wastewater using high rate transpiration system

The high transpiration capacity of plants grown on soil matrix enables the system to serve as biopump. Various plant species like Acacia (*Acacia mangium*), Bamboo (*Bambusa arundinacea*), Neem (*Azadirachata indica*), Shishum (*Dalbergia sis*so) and Eucalyptus (*Eucalyptus hybrid)* transpire water equivalent to 5 to 13 times that of potential evapotranspiration from the soil matrix alone. The soil system works in close conjunction with plants on it that provide a bio-pump through their high transpiration capacity. The filter media provided in the furrows mainly consists of bamboo/saw dust, fly ash and gypsum at the rate of 2-5 tonnes per hectare. Thickness of filter media varies from 5-15 cm depending on the colour intensity of the wastewater, soil texture and permeability of the soil. In addition to this, artificial media and leaf fall from standing plants provides thick mat and forms a filter bed, which is also responsible for retention and assimilation of colour bodies.

The system works on following main principles:

- Transpiration of large amount of water through stomatal network.
- Waste renovation using soil as a physico-bio- chemical reactor (living treatment filter).
- Assimilation of colour in filter media. The Cross section of HRTS layout is shown in

The Fig. 3 shows the cross section of HRTS layout developed at Orient Paper Mills, Amlai.

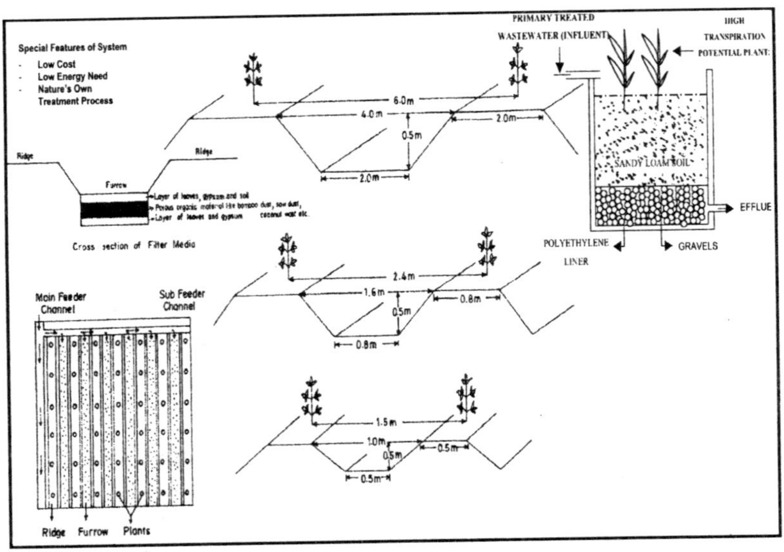

Fig. 3 : Schematic diagram of High Rate Transpiration System for treatment and disposal of pulp and paper mill wastewater at Orient Paper Mills, Amlai

Analysis of Wastewater, Soil and Plants Samples

Wastewater and soil samples from the identified site of M/s Orient Paper Mill, Amlai were collected and subjected for the analysis of various physico-chemical parameters. The wastewater samples used for HRTS and the well water to evaluate the effect on application of wastewater on the soil were analyzed as per standard methods for the Examination of water and wastewater. Plant height were measured periodically and soil samples before and after application of pulp and paper mill wastewater were collected from HRTS were analysed by Standard technique (Black, 1965).

Results and Discussions

Physico-Chemical Characteristics of Pulp And Paper Mill Wastewater (Grade III)

The wastewater samples were collected from anaerobic lagoon outlet during winter and summer seasons to ascertain the wastewater for various physico-chemical parameters as depicted in Table 1. The wastewater was dark brown in colour, which indicated that the application of such highly coloured wastewater to the land may affect the soil characteristics and may also further lead to ground water pollution through leaching. The wastewater was neutral to slightly alkaline in reaction and its pH varied from 6.70 to 7.90. Soluble salt content in the wastewater, expressed as EC (mS cm^{-1}) ranged from 2.26 – 4.50. The sodium absorption ratio of wastewater was low and ranged from 2.78 – 4.56 indicating that, it will not impose sodicity problem. The wastewater also contained considerable chemical oxygen demand (404 to 675 mgl^{-1}) and appreciable quantity of chlorides, which ranged from 15.69 – 23.49 meq L^{-1} and belonged to the class 'Severe Problem'.

Table 1 : Physico-chemical characteristics of pulp and paper mill wastewater (Grade- III)

Sr. No.	Parameters	Magnitude	Standards for Industrial Effluent for irrigation
1.	pH	6.70 – 7.90	5.5 – 9.0
2.	EC, mS cm^{-1}	2.26 – 4.50	-
3	Colour, Hz	Dark Brown	-
4.	TSS, mg L^{-1}	70.0 – 216.0	-
5.	COD, mg L^{-1}	404 – 675	200
6.	Sodium, mg L^{-1}	7.50 – 13.10	-
7.	Potassium, mg L^{-1}	0.32 – 0.95	-
8.	Calcium, mg L^{-1}	9.30 – 15.50	-
9.	Magnesium, mg L^{-1}	0.40 – 8.08	-
10.	Bicarbonate, mg L^{-1}	1.50 – 15.16	-
11.	Chloride, mg L^{-1}	15.69 – 23.49	600
12.	Sodium Absorption Ratio (SAR)	2.78 – 4.56	-

Physico-chemical Characteristics of Soil

The results depicted in Table 2, showed that the soil from the selected field was loamy sand in texture. Bulk density of the soils ranged from 0.78 to 1.28 g cm^{-3}. Maximum water holding capacity varied from 48.60 to 16.4 %. Hydraulic conductivity of the soils was very high which ranged from 3.0 $\times 10^{-2}$ to 2.0 $\times 10^{-2}$ cm sec^{-1}. The soil was slightly acidic to almost neutral in reaction having pH in the range of 6.70 to 7.00. The soluble salt expressed in terms of electrical conductivity of saturation extract of soil were higher in upper layer and decreases with depth and ranged from 2.08 to 1.21 mS cm^{-1}. The cation exchange capacity of the soil in uppermost layer was good as compared to lower layer, which ranged from 30.54 to 7.60 c mol kg^{-1}. The total concentration of nutrients *viz.* nitrogen, phosphorus and potassium ranged from 0.064 – 0.008%, 0.070 – 0.030% and 0.080 – 0.128%, respectively. The concentration of total heavy metals like Ni, Cr, Cd, Zn, Pb and Cu were also present in appreciable amount with high Fe and Mn content in the soil.

Table 2 : Physico-chemical characteristics of soil profile samples collected from the identified site by M/s Orient Paper Mill, Amlai

S. No.	Parameters	Soil Depth, cm		
		0-5	5-15	15-30
1.	Clay, %	-	8.6	8.8
2.	Sand, %	-	9.6	10.4
3.	Bulk Density, g cm^{-3}	0.78	1.21	1.28
4.	Water Holding capacity, %	48.6	24.4	16.4
5.	Hydraulic Conductivity, cm sec^{-1}	0.30	0.218	0.020
6.	Cation Exchange Capacity, c mol Kg^{-1}	30.54	8.40	7.60
7.	pH	6.7	6.8	7.0
8.	ECe, mS cm^{-1}	2.08	1.42	1.21
9.	Organic Carbon, %	3.84	1.40	0.80
10.	Nitrogen, %	0.064	0.020	0.008
11.	Phosphorous, %	0.070	0.043	0.030
12.	Potassium, %	0.080	0.124	0.128

Contd.

13.	Zn, mg kg^{-1}	40.8	20.8	16.8
14.	Cd, mg kg^{-1}	0.40	0.10	0.00
15.	Ni, mg kg^{-1}	8.80	8.70	9.10
16.	Fe, mg kg^{-1}	3094.2	2865.8	3968.2
17.	Mn, mg kg^{-1}	352.4	80.4	40.7
18.	Pb, mg kg^{-1}	2.8	4.9	4.2
19.	Cu, mg kg^{-1}	6.8	6.4	7.0
20.	Cr, mg kg^{-1}	2.4	0.00	0.00

Effects on Wastewater Irrigated Soil

Salt Movement in the HRT System

To study the salt movement in the ridges and furrows irrigated with pulp and paper mill wastewater, soil samples were collected from center and edge of the ridges (2.5 meter wide) in the HRT system and were analyzed for their salt content. The results indicated that upper soil layer of 0-15 cm was moderately acidic, due to decomposition of leaf litter which is acidic in nature, while the soils of lower depth were neutral in reaction. The salt concentration was high in the soil from 0-15 cm depth at the edge of the ridge (EC - 3.76 mS cm^{-1}) as compared to soil from the center portion of the ridge.

The soil from lower depth i.e. 30-90 cm of the ridge showed low salt concentration (EC - 2.16 mS cm^{-1}). The concentration of sodium was higher in all depths (19 to 25 $meqL^{-1}$) followed by calcium and magnesium (Table 3). The chloride concentration was in the range of 16.92 to 33.84 $meqL^{-1}$. The filter media in the furrows showed neutral reaction with electrical conductivity of 2.1 mS cm^{-1}. This indicated that inspite of continuous application of wastewater; there was no appreciable build-up in salt concentration in the furrows because the plants on the ridges created a moisture gradient, which facilitated salt movement along with water from the furrows to the ridges.

Table 3 : Chemical characteristics of soil samples collected from HRTS

Sample Description	Depth, cm	pH	ECe, $mScm^{-1}$	Water Soluble ions, meq L^{-1}					
				Na^+	K^+	Ca^{++}	Mg^{++}	HCO_3^-	Cl^-
Center of the ridge	0 – 15	5.5	2.55	21.0	0.85	4.4	1.2	1.2	25.09
	15-30	6.9	2.50	22.5	0.60	3.4	1.6	1.4	24.25
	30-60	7.4	2.68	22.0	0.40	1.6	1.4	2.0	25.38
	60-90	7.2	2.20	20.0	0.60	2.0	0.6	1.6	19.74
Edge of the ridge	0 – 15	5.8	3.76	25.0	0.60	4.0	1.80	1.6	33.84
	15-30	6.7	2.64	20.0	0.50	4.6	1.2	3.2	23.17
	30-60	7.2	2.16	9.0	0.25	2.0	0.8	1.6	16.92
Filter Media	0-10	7.1	2.10	14.0	0.45	5.4	1.8	4.0	15.22

Physical Properties of Soil

Soil samples were collected from the field irrigated with wastewater since long period. The results, as presented in Table 4, indicated that soil in the irrigated areas was loamy sand in texture with clay and sand content ranging from 13.8-13.9% and 70.8-73.8% respectively. The uppermost (Ao) layer of soil had low bulk density (0.79 g cm^{-1}) due to retention of lignin and leaf litter and it increased with the depth. Ao horizon had maximum water holding capacity of 87% and its hydraulic conductivity was also very high (0.430 cm sec^{-1}). However, the soils at a depth of 5-15 cm and 15-30 cm had low hydraulic conductivity and were in the order of 0.122, 0.033 cm sec^{-1}, respectively.

The cation adsorption capacity of the uppermost soil horizon was high as compared to lower layer (CEC 46.32 C mol kg^{-1}), because of its organic nature. The available moisture content was also high in the upper organic rich layer (11.9%) and it decreased with depth.

Table 4 : Physico-chemical characteristics of wastewater irrigated soil samples collected from HRTS site

S. No.	Parameters	Soil Depth, cm		
		0-5	**5-15**	**15-30**
1.	Clay, %	-	13.8	13.9
2.	Sand, %	-	12.4	15.3
3.	Bulk Density, g cm^{-1}	0.79	1.31	1.58
4.	Water Holding capacity, %	86.9	37.3	27.5
5.	Hydraulic Conductivity, cm sec^{-1}	0.43	0.122	0.033
6.	Cation Exchange Capacity, (C mol kg^{-1})	46.32	12.50	11.33
7.	pH	7.0	7.3	7.4
8.	ECe, mS cm^{-1}	3.03	2.65	2.17
9.	Exchangeable sodium percentage	7.73	13.66	11.85
10.	Organic Carbon, %	17.73	2.59	0.41
11.	Nitrogen, %	0.133	0.011	0.008
12.	Phosphorous, %	0.095	0.060	0.025

Contd.

13.	Potassium, %	0.127	0.195	0.274
14.	Zn, mg kg^{-1}	56.2	24.9	18.0
15.	Cd, mg kg^{-1}	0.6	0.2	0.00
16.	Ni, mg kg^{-1}	15.9	15.3	16.8
17.	Fe, mg kg^{-1}	4592.9	4487.9	7655.0
18.	Mn, mg kg^{-1}	452.5	70.6	53.6
19.	Pb, mg kg^{-1}	4.1	13.1	5.2
20.	Cu, mg kg^{-1}	8.6	6.8	7.6
21.	Cr, mg kg^{-1}	2.6	0.0	0.0

Chemical Properties of Soil

The result presented in Table 4 showed that soil in the existing irrigated area was neutral in reaction (pH 7.0-7.4). The soluble salts expressed in terms of electrical conductivity of saturation extract of soil were higher (3.03 mS cm^{-1}) in upper layer and it decreased in the lower depth and exhibited value of 2.17 mS cm^{-1}. Increase in soluble salt and pH as observed in the present study as a result of pulp and paper mill wastewater application were also reported by Mc Carmic (1959). Juwarkar and Subramanyam (1987), also showed increase in soluble and exchangeable salts due to wastewater irrigation. The exchangeable sodium percentage of the soils was less than 15 and therefore the soils were categorized in non saline-non alkali group.

The organic carbon content in the upper (Ao) layer was high (17.7%) due to continuous accumulation of leaf litter and retention of lignin compounds of organic nature from the wastewater. The increase in organic matter content in soil was due to presence of dissolved lignin in the wastewater applied, which retained in soil. The total nitrogen and phosphorous contents were also high. Rajanan and Obliswami (1979) also reported increase in OM and available N, P, K of soil when irrigated with pulp and paper mill wastewater. Heavy metal concentration in irrigated soil at all the depths were below the toxicity level (Table 4). This might be due to the fact that toxic heavy metal are not used in any stage of process in paper manufacture.

Plant Growth

The various plant species planted in HRT system showed better growth with respect to foliage development (Plate 1). The grasses like lemon, citronella and pamarosa also developed profusely on the ridges (Plate 2). The growth of typha grown in the furrow was also good which encourages its use on large scale in the system.

Plate 1: Eucalyptus and Bamboo Plantation on the Ridges in the HRTS site at Orient Paper Mill, Amlai

Plate 2: Lemon and Citronella grasses planted in the Ridges in the HRTS site at Orient Paper Mill, Amlai

Introduction of aromatic grasses like citronella and lemon in the HRTS helps to improve ambient environment in the following manner:

- in controlling obnoxious odours resulting from evaporation wastewater from the furrows,
- in controlling breeding of mosquitoes and other insects due to astringent and repelling aroma from the grasses,
- effective check on cattle trespassing as cattle do not browse on these grasses thus preventing cattle damage to HRT system, and
- in controlling growth of harmful weeds like parthenium etc.

Nutrient and Heavy Metal Uptake by the Plant Leaves

The leaves of different plants viz. Australian babul, eucalyptus, cassia, prosopis, karanj and bamboo irrigated with pulp and paper mill wastewater were analyzed for nutrient and heavy metal uptake. The leaves were analyzed for calcium, magnesium, sodium and potassium uptake. Results showed variable response with respect to nutrient and heavy metal uptake by different plant species. The uptake of calcium was higher, in the range of 2301-17591 μgg^{-1} followed by magnesium (769.4-1879.40 μgg^{-1}), potassium (87.97-65.80 μgg^{-1}) and sodium (23-115 μgg^{-1}) (Fig. 4). Among different plant species, bamboo and prosopis showed high uptake of iron while high manganese uptake was observed in case of eucalyptus. Uptake of metals like copper, zinc and chromium showed variation with the plant species (Fig. 5). The results indicated that plants differ in their capacity to accumulate nutrients and heavy metals and acts as a sink in removing different types of pollutants from soil matrix.

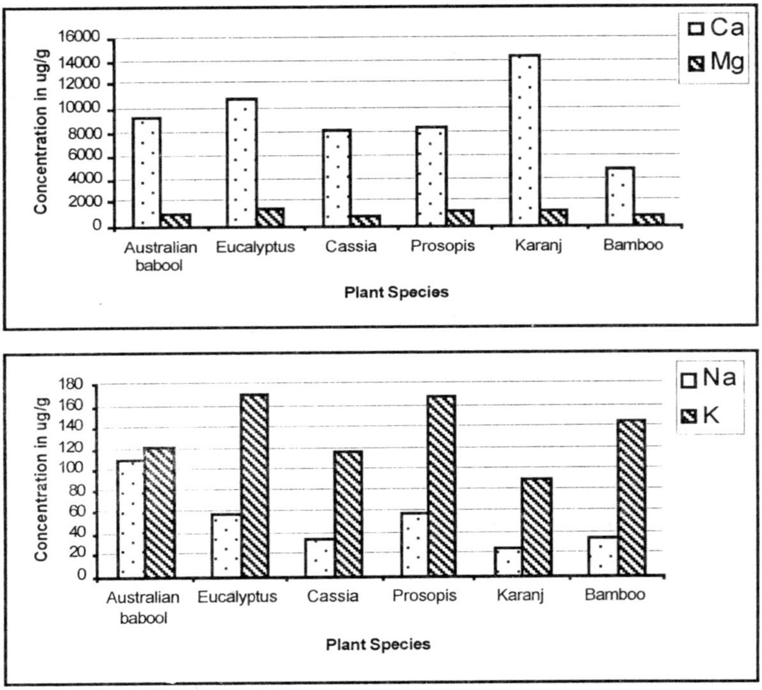

Fig. 4 : Calcium, magnesium, sodium and potassium uptake by different plants species irrigated with pulp and paper mill wastewater

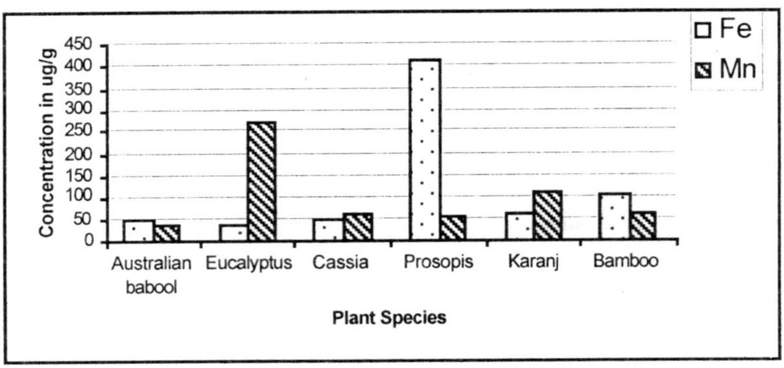

Fig. 5

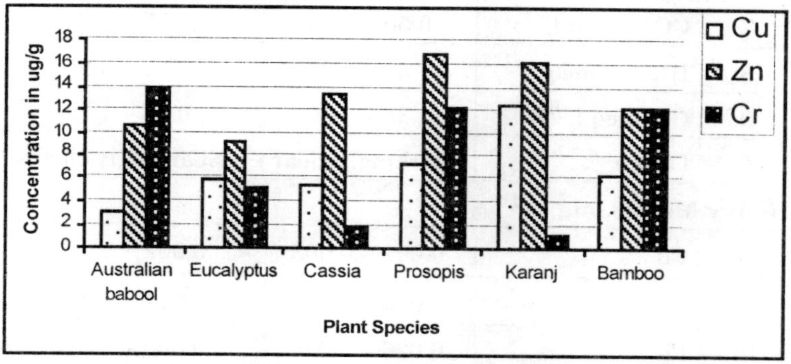

Fig. 5 : Iron, manganese, copper, zinc and chromium uptake by different plants species irrigated with pulp and paper mill wastewater

Effect on Underground Water

Well water samples collected from the wells, located at the distance of 1.0 and 2.0 km from the HRTS were analyzed for chemical properties. The results indicated that the well water was slightly alkaline in reaction and their pH varied from 8.2-8.4 and 8.0-8.2 respectively for the samples collected from 1.0 and 2.0 km respectively (Table 6).

Table 6 : Chemical characteristics of the well water located near HRTS site at M/s Orient Paper Mill, Amlai

S. No.	Parameters	Approximate distance from HRTS	
		1.0 Km	2.0 Km
1.	pH	8.20 – 8.40	8.00 – 8.20
2.	EC (μS cm^{-1})	0.48 – 0.84	0.37 – 0.39
3.	Na (meq L^{-1})	0.67 – 3.80	0.70 – 0.80
4.	K, (meq L^{-1})	0.05 – 0.16	0.10 – 0.13
5.	Ca, (meq L^{-1})	2.76 – 3.20	1.52 – 2.15
6.	Mg, (meq L^{-1})	0.64 – 1.56	0.96 – 1.15

Contd.

7.	CO_3, (meq L^{-1})	0.50 – 1.75	0.55 – 0.86
8.	HCO_3, (meq L^{-1})	1.55 – 3.55	1.32 – 2.35
9.	Cl, (meq L^{-1})	1.38 – 2.50	0.85 – 1.12
10.	Colour	Sparkingly clear	Sparkingly clear
Heavy Metals, mg L^{-1}			
11.	Cd	0.002 – 0.003	0.002 – 0.004
12.	Cu	0.012 – 0.017	0.011 – 0.015
13.	Pb	0.026 – 0.028	0.009 – 0.011
14.	Ni	BDL	0.008 – 0.013
15.	Zn	0.008 – 0.010	0.031 – 0.045
16.	Fe	0.620 – 0.700	0.661 – 0.697

Soluble salt concentration in well water, expressed as EC (mS cm^{-1}), ranged from 0.48-0.84 and 0.37-0.39 in wells at 1.0 and 2.0 km away from HRTS, respectively. The significant observation was that the colour of all well waters was sparkingly clear. The concentration of heavy metals like Cd, Pb, Zn, Fe, Ni and Cu in the well waters were not in appreciable range which indicated that well waters upto a distance of 2.0 km from HRTS area were not contaminated ruling out the possibility of groundwater contamination due to wastewater.

Conclusions

The preliminary experiment through column lysimeter conducted at NEERI, proved that the coloured Paper Mill wastewater could be successfully treated using High Rate Transpiration System. The HRTS proved that the coloured wastewater initially loaded at the rate of 150 m^3 ha^{-1} day^{-1} and gradually increased to 250-275 m^3 ha^{-1} day^{-1} could be successfully treated pulp and paper mill wastewater without any ground water contamination. The HRTS planted with different plant species viz. eucalyptus, bamboo, acacia mangium, cassia, gravellia, lemon grass and citronella grass showed healthy and better growth response and develop forestry which acts as a sink potential for absorptions of green house gases.

Acknowledgements

The authors wish to express their gratitude to the management of M/s Orient Paper Mill, Amlai for their cooperation and assistance during the research work.

References

Anderson, A. (1979) Disposal of an integrated pulp and paper mill effluent by irrigation. Tech. Rep. No. EPA-600/2-79-633, EPA Cincinnati, Ohio.

Anonymous (1989) 'Standard Methods for the Examination of Water and Wastewater, 17th ed. Publ. APHA, AWWA, WPCF, 1015, Washington, DC 20036.

Black, C.A. (1965) *Methods for Soil Analysis*, Am. Soc. Agro. Inc., Publ. Madison, Wisconsin, USA.

Jackson, M.L. (1973) *Soil Chemical Analysis*, Publ. Prantice Hall of India Ltd, New Delhi.

Juwarkar, A.S. and Subrahamanyam, P.V.R. (1987) Impact of pulp and paper mill wastewater on crop and soil. Water Sci. Tech., 19 : 693.

Kandiah A. (1987) Water Quality in Food Production, Water Quality Bulletin. F.A.O., Rome.

McCormic, L.L.: 1959, Effect of paper mill wastewater on cattle, crop and soil, *Bull.La. Agric. Stn.*, 529.

Piper, C.S. (1966) *Soil and Plant Analysis*, Univ. Adelaide, Australia.

Rajanan, G. and Oblisami, G. (1979) Effect of paper factory effluents on soil and crop plants. Indian J. Environ. Hlth., 21(2) : 120-130.

Thawale, P.R., Juwarkar, A.S., Kulkarni, A.B. and Juwarkar, A.A. (1999) Lysimeter studies for evaluation of changes in soil properties and crop yield using wastewater. Intern. J.Trop. Agric., 17 (1-4) : 231-244.

CHAPTER 6

MANAGEMENT OF URBAN WASTES FOR RESTORATION OF SOIL FERTILITY

K.K. Singh[1], Vinod Phogat[2], Gayatri Verma[3] and Alka Tomar[4]

[1] Project Directorate (Research), Agriculture and Soil Survey, Krishi Bhawan, Bikaner (Raj.)

[2] Dept. of Soil Science, C.C.S. Haryana Agricultural University, Hisar (Haryana).

[3] S.M. Degree College, Palidongra, Sonkh, Mathura (U.P)

[4] CMS Environment, Research House, Saket, New Delhi-110017.

ABSTRACT

A review article is presented focusing mainly on growth of urbanization, nature of city wastes, various processes of treatments of sewage & sludge and recycling of garbage, quality of treated wastewater and sewage sludge. Impact of toxic metals and pathogens on soil, plant and human health are discussed. Use of treated sewage wastewater, sludge and garbage in restoration of soil fertility by employing suitable irrigation methods are described.

Key Words : Urban wastes, soil fertility, sewage sludge, heavy metals, ion toxicity, sewage water.

Introduction

Rapid industrialization and population explosion have generated many problems and pollution is one of them. With the country's population having crossed the one billion mark, coupled with unplanned development and urbanization, one thing is certain - an enormous amount of waste is going to be generated. On the other hand, the world population has crossed the six billion mark in 1999. By the year 2025, this will increase by 2 to 3 billion. Most of the projected increase in population (95%) will be in the developing countries. This is because their rate of population growth is much higher than the world's average rate of 1.4 percent per annum (Chandna, 2003). By that time, about 70% of the earth's population will be urban based and the generation of urban wastes will nearly quadruple. A high level of consumption, and generation of solid and liquid wastes, by the concentrated mass of people that an urban place is, will have serious environmental and health repercussions.

On the other hand, to ensure sufficient supply of food for the growing population, the production of food will need to be doubled by 2025 against the present level of food grain production at about 203.9 million tonnes during 1999-2000 (Sanio, 1998; Kanwar, 1997). Since, there is no scope for horizontal expansion of land area to achieve the targeted level of food grain production, the major emphasis has, therefore, been laid on increasing the existing level of productivity of different crops by hybrid and improved varieties of principal crops and increasing the cropping intensity with the help of irrigation facility, use of chemical fertilizers and pesticides, thereby restoring further deterioration of soil quality (Mukhopadhyay, 2005).

The disposal of industrial effluents and sewer waters is becoming a widespread problem in the developing countries due to rapid industrialization and urbanization. The industrial effluents are the source of several heavy metals such as Pb, Ni, Cd and Cr (Leeper, 1978). Moreover, municipal solid waste is having a considerable amount of major nutrients as well as elements like Cd, Cu, Fe, Cr, Zn, Pb and Ni. Chemicals used are widely associated with widespread pollution, mainly depending on the persistence of the chemicals. Disposal of huge amount of ash produced from thermal power plants containing heavy metals, has been cautioned against the further use in agriculture.

Thus, two problems of preservation of urban environment and agricultural productivity have to be dealt with in a unified manner. A prudent management of urban wastes would not only provide a cleaner and safer environment for the urban population but also help maintain the productivity of the vital agricultural land. The urban wastes and the agricultural land - a good proportion of the wastes generated in the urban areas can be recycled and reused to condition and fertilize the arable land. The objective of this chapter is to emphasize the mutually beneficial relationship between the urban wastes and the agricultural land, which would ensure a better urban living environment as well as fertility of the agricultural land.

Urbanization and its growth

In general, urbanization may be characterised as the increase in the points of higher population densities, as also in the population size of these individual points of dense population (Carter, 1982), with growth in urbanization, increase takes place in:

(*i*) the proportion of population living areas, (*ii*) the absolute number of urban dwellers and (*iii*) the rate of growth of number of people living in urban places (Clarke, 1972). The world is poised to experience rapid urbanization in the next couple of decades. By the year 2025, about 61% of the world's population will have been urbanized. Two-thirds of the population of the developed countries, and 41% of the less developed countries, will be urban based. However, despite a lower proportion of urban population, the absolute number of urban people in such countries is much higher than in the developed countries (2.5 billion compared to 0.9 billion in 1995). Moreover, the rate of growth of urban population in the less developed countries (3.7% during 1994-2000) is much higher than in the developed ones where it is only 0.8% (Chandna, 2003).

Urban world is growing so quickly because of the heavy migration of rural people to urban areas. Excessively high pressure on the limited agricultural land and a lack of employment opportunities in the rural areas are amongst the main factors which encourage this migration. One of the essential features of urbanization is the process of metropolitanization. It means that larger cities progressively account for an ever greater proportion of the urban population. Due to urbanization and metropolitanization, the size and density of small towns and large cities is continuously on the rise. This is causing excessive pressure on the urban infrastructure, housing, employment, essential services, as well as sanitation.

Nature of City Wastes

Urban areas are characterized by a high concentration of population per unit area, comparatively higher per capita income levels and, hence, higher consumption of goods and services. A relatively greater level of consumption of food, water and other goods per unit area results into generation of large quantity of solid and liquid urban wastes. Urban or municipal wastes are the wastes that originate from the households, commercial establishments, hotels and restaurants, offices, gardens and the like. Sewage waste water is the liquid urban waste, while the sewage sludge, along with garbage; plastics and metals (recyclables); construction wastes (rubbish) etc., forms the urban solid wastes. Sewage sludge is the solid portion carried by the sewage wastewater and includes faecal matter and other organic matter. Garbage is the organic component of the solid wastes constituted by food residues; vegetable and fruit peelings; garden wastes and droppings of the pet animals. Sewage sludge and garbage are the wastes rich in organic substances and have possibly significant implications on the fertility of arable land.

Composition of urban solid wastes varies from city to city, and within different parts of a city (Table 1). The comparatively poorer cities, or neighbourhoods, generate lesser amount of solid wastes most of which are organic in nature. This is because the poor people have lower buying power, and most of their little income is spent on buying the daily rations of fuel and food supplies only. The prosperous cities like Singapore, on the other hand, generate a vast amount of solid wastes because of high consumption levels (Table 2). The proportion of organic matter in their wastes is comparatively lower because only food quality, and not its quantity, changes with prosperity. The waste stream, from the prosperous cities contains more of paper, metal and plastic items than organic matter like vegetables and wood/cow drug fuel ash. Organic solid waste can be converted into compost, which can then be used for farming purpose, provided that it is free from impurities.

Table 1 : Composition of solid wastes in some selected cities (Percent by weight)

Material Type	Cities					
	Singapore	Lahore	Karanchi	Jakarta	Delhi[1]	Delhi[2]
Combustibles (Paper, Wood)	27	6	2	6	7	4
Recyclables (Metals, plastics)	22	6	1	7	7	6
Others	8	15	1	2	16	15
Compostable (Vegetable, bio-degradables)	43	73	96	85	70	75

Source : UNEP/WRI (1988), ENV (1997) and NEERI (1996)

[1]HIG and [2]LIG & Slum areas of Municipal Corporation, New Delhi.

Table 2 : Solid wastes and their generation rates in some cities

City	Solid wastes generated (tonnes day^{-1})	Solid waste generation rates (kg $person^{-1}$ day^{-1})
Singapore	4564	1.60
Manila	5400	0.50
Kolkata	3500	0.51
Karanchi	4500	0.50
Jakarta	6741	0.60
Delhi	4500	0.40

Source : UNEP/WRI (1988); UNEP(1989); NEERI(1996); Hindustan Times (March 2, 1996); India Today (Oct. 31, 1994); Sivaramakrishnan and Green (1986)

A. Sewage and sludge treatment processes

(a) Sewage Treatment

The sequential treatment of sewage water can be done by the following steps: screening to remove gross solids - maceration by commuter to break up the solids into finer particles - sedimentation to remove settleable solids so as to avoid the formation of putrefying sludges - chlorination of the settled sewage - aerobic and biological treatment - electrolytic treatment of sewage to reduce the BOD by 70-80% (Fig. 1)

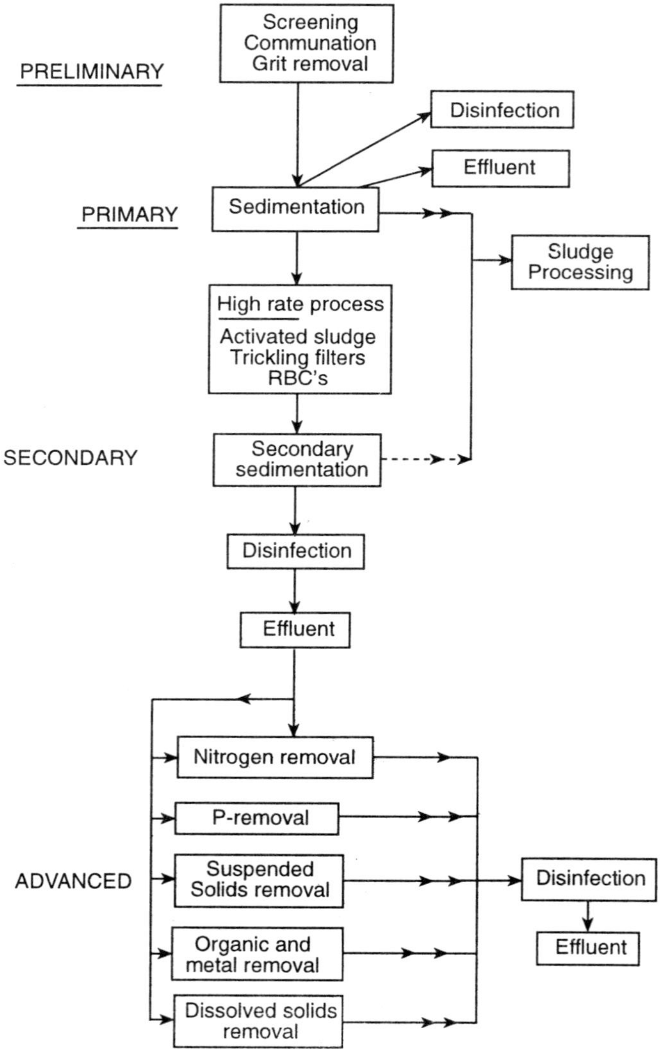

Fig. 1 : General Scheme of sewage treatment process

Treatment of sewage wastewater removes the undesirable components and makes it safe from health and environment points of view. The process removes the pathogenic organisms as well as noxious substances and improves the aesthetic value of the end product. The type of treatment process to be adopted depends on the physical, chemical and biological nature of the pollutants present in the wastewater, as well as on the purpose for which the treated wastewater is to be used. The three main types or levels of treatment are primary, secondary and tertiary, which are preceded by a preliminary treatment.

Preliminary Treatment of wastewater aims at physical removal of suspended and floating matter. Suspended coarse materials like sand, ash, etc. are removed by the process of screening. Light material like fats, greases etc., float as scum in the stagnant wastewater, and are removed by the process of skimming, preliminary treatment is a physical treatment process in which fine suspended impurities, not removable by screening and skimming of the preliminary treatment, are removed by the process of sedimentation in the sedimentation tanks. These tanks are provided with skinning device to remove the floating scum. During primary treatment, between 40 to 55% of the suspended solid matter and 15 to 18% of the organic matter (BOD) are removed.

Secondary treatment is a biological process in which soluble and colloidal organic matters, unaffected by the preliminary treatment, are removed. Most commonly used process is called the activated sludge process. In this, aerobic micro-organisms are mixed with primary wastewater to form "mixed liquor" and oxygen is passed through the chamber. This quickens the growth of micro-organisms feeding upon the organic matter of the wastewater. The micro-organisms gather as organic sludge at the bottom of the tank, even as the wastewater is purified of organic impurities. Most of this sludge is again mixed with primary wastewater and the process continues. Other lesser used methods of secondary treatment are stabilization ponds, rotating biological contractors and trickling filters amongst others. Biological treatments including secondary sedimentation typically reduces the total BOD to 15 to 30 mg L^{-1}, COD to 40 to 70 mg L^{-1} and TOC to 15 to 25 mg L^{-1}. Very little of dissolved minerals are removed during the conventional secondary treatment.

Tertiary or advanced treatment of wastewater is performed when even better quality of wastewater is needed e.g., to irrigate food crops consumed without being cooked. Tertiary treatment may include several different processes, each of which aims to remove a specific pollutant. The process of filtration removes suspended solid matter. Nitrification-denitrification removes nitrogen, while carbon adsorption process is used to remove soluble, biodegradable organic matter with the help of carbon. The latter process also removes a number of metal ions. The most common tertiary treatment process of sewage wastewater is chemical addition for phosphorus removal, which can be accomplished in the primary treatment tank or the aeration chamber of the secondary treatment.

(b) Sewage Sludge Treatment Process

The sewage sludge is obtained during the treatment of sewage wastewater. This sludge contains much organic matter, referred to as biosolids, which has potential nutritive value for raising the field crops. The primary treatment of wastewater removes the solids through the process of sedimentation. This solid part or primary sludge, is stabilised through the process of anaerobic digestion. However, most of the soluble organic matter still remains elusive and dissolved in the wastewater. Secondary treatment of wastewater uses bacterial population to breakdown the soluble organic matter of the wastewater into food, and to produce bio-solids, which are rich in organic matter. The biosolids have potential nutritive value for the soil.

Tertiary treatment of wastewater is performed to further improve the quality of treated wastewater. It may however, result in further generation of sludge. The primary, secondary or tertiary sludge needs to be processed in order to stabilize the sludge and to reduce its pathogen content. The processing also reduces the volume of the sludge. Anaerobic or aerobic digestion and chemical stabilization are the chief stabilization processes which help reduce the odour, pathogens, and volume of the sludge. To remove the parasitic cysts and ova, viral and bacterial pathogens, various disinfections processes like pasteurization, high energy irradiation with γ and β rays and chlorination are employed. Composting aerobically for 21 days also decomposes the organic wastes, and provides good soil conditioner, though poor fertilizer, for land application. The compost is low in nitrogen due to mineralization and volatilization of organic nitrogen during the process of composting. Sewage sludge has evolved almost its own exclusive, cheap and efficient composting techniques, which are different from the less controlled processing and composting of solid wastes. Reduction in the volume of sewage sludge can be achieved through the processes of thickening, dewatering or conditioning. This enables easy handling and cheap transport of the sludge.

B. Composting and Processing of Garbage

The urban solid waste stream consists of a substantial amount of organic wastes, especially, in the developing countries. This organic waste has, here, been referred to as garbage. The garbage may be composed of household organic wastes, dairy cattle manure, market green wastes, food wastes, poultry farm manure, slaughter house residues, and food processing industry wastes. From ancient times, farmers have known that decaying organic wastes improve the fertility of the soil. The Mayan civilization declined because it did not know how to fertilize its croplands. On the other hand, the Chinese have, for fifty centuries, used animal, human and vegetable wastes, in order to sustain the fertility of their soils (Hughes, 1980).

Composting is the microbial decomposition of piled organic wastes into partially decomposed organic matter, referred to as compost or humus. Composting is not a usual process in nature because either piles of organic matter are unavailable, or where they do occur, conditions for composting are not optimum. Composting as a systematic process was first developed in 1925 in India by Sir Albert Howard. The procedure developed by him came to be called the Indore process, and involved anaerobic microbial digestion of leaves garbage, animal manure and sewage in the pits. Another variant of the anaerobic digestion is known as Bangalore process and still used in India. Solid organic wastes and sewage are placed in alternate layers for several months. For successful anaerobic digestion, maintenance of high temperature, moisture and sufficient microbial nutrients is required. Though a low cost process, anaerobic composting requires a large area as it requires a long incubation period. It may also produce phytotoxic organic acids, ethylene gas, and bad odour.

Aerobic composting, on the other hand, is characterised by rapid decomposition, high temperatures and lack of bad odours. It is a short duration process, completed between 1 to 10 weeks. High temperatures generated during the process kill the pathogens and the insect eggs. Aerobic digestion also helps avoid generation of bad odours because the compostable mixture is continuously turned around for ensuring O_2

supply. The conditions of moisture and nutrient supply for aerobic digestion are the same as in the anaerobic composting. Several kinds of organisms take part in the digestion-bacteria dominate throughout the process, fungi appear only after a week while actinomycetes come into the scene during the last stages of the process. During the initial phase, mesophilic bacteria oxidise carbon compounds to raise the temperature upto 45^0 C, At this temperature, only thermophilic bacteria can remain active and these work in temperature range of 55 to 70^0 C. This thermophilic stage lasts for about two weeks. Current composting is mostly of aerobic type, and is based on high technology, low space requirement, fermentation, rapid generation of compost and higher costs.

Wastewater use in Agriculture

Wastewater is the water that contains materials, which pollute natural waters. Sewage wastewater is the waste water that emanates from the households, commercial centres and institution. Domestic sewage contains a variety of constituents ranging from solids, readily decomposable organic materials, nutrients (mainly nitrogen and phosphorus), detergents and pathogenic organisms like bacteria viruses and parasites. With the advent of sewage system in the nineteenth century "sewage farms" came to be established, which are used for disposal of sewage wastewater. Use of this wastewater for farming purposes was an exception than the rule. However, since the beginning of the last century treated wastewater has been used for toilets, gardens cooling water and boiler fed water, as a dual water supply system. In the arid and semi-arid regions, reclamation and reuse of wastewater is becoming a strong necessity with increasing population pressure. However, due to increasing environmental awareness wastewater reclamation is being done in the humid regions too. Such water is being reused for non-potable purposes like irrigation of crops, parks and golf courses or for groundwater recharge (Tchobanoglous and Burton, 1996; Mara and Cairncross, 1989).

In water scarce areas like Singapore, reclaimed sewage wastewater is being used indirectly to enhance potable water supplies. This reclaimed wastewater is fed into water reservoirs, which is further treated before being supplied for potable use.

Potential of wastewater reuse

Disposal of raw sewage wastewater can be highly pollutive for ground or surface water resources. Dumping of treated sewage wastewater in the lakes and rivers can also choke these water sources due to the process of eutrophication. This happens because treated wastewater still has significant amount of N and P, which encourage excessive growth of algae and, ultimately lead to the death of lakes through their filling up with dead algal matter. Hence, treated sewage wastewater can better be reused by applying its nutritional properties to the agricultural crops and forests. This is because the treatment requirements of wastewater for agricultural use are less strict than when it is dumped into the lakes or rivers.

Infrastructure for wastewater collection and treatment is very limited in the urban India. Only a part of the wastewater generated in the cities and towns is collected and treated (Table 3). Treatment of wastewater is generally of the primary level, though secondary level treatment is also available to a limited extent. The partially treated wastewater is disposed of in either/both of the open grounds and water bodies. Wastewater collection and treatment infrastructure is inequitably distributed, with a heavy bias towards metropolitan and big cities. These facilities are practically non-existent in class III and other smaller towns.

Table 3 : Waste water generation, collection and treatment in urban India.

City/Town type	Number	Waste water generated (Million cm^3 $annum^{-1}$)	Waste water collected (%)	Waste water treated (%)
Metropolitan Cities	12	2358	26	20 - 25
Class I cities (Population : 100000 and more)	212	4433	22	20 - 25
Class II Towns (Population : 50000 - 99999)	242	467	5	2

Source : Kaul *et al.* (2002)

If all the wastewater generated in the urban India is collected and treated appropriately, between 0.50 to 0.55 million ha of additional land can be brought under irrigation. Utilization of domestic wastewater for irrigating agricultural land is an old tradition in India. The first wastewater irrigation farm was established in 1895 at Ahmedabad. By the end of 1960s, 216 wastewater irrigated farms, with an area of 10693 hectares, utilized more than 40% of the available wastewater. Before the start of 1980s, wastewater irrigated area had already reached 59,679 ha. However, 75% of the wastewater used to irrigate farms in India is of raw type. The remaining 25% of the utilized wastewater is treated at primary and /or secondary level (Kaul *et al.*, 2002). The raw or untreated wastewater has excessive amount of nutrients and other pollutants and is, thus, unsuitable for direct use on several accounts.

Quality of treated wastewater and sewage sludge

(a) Treated wastewater

The characteristics and quality of the treated wastewater are of paramount significance because there is a dynamic balance between the irrigation water and the soil. A poor quality wastewater can bring about undesirable changes in the soil attributes which are, then reflected in the crops grown in that soil. Humans are affected directly by coming into touch with the wastewater or, indirectly, by consuming the edible crops grown therein. The quality parameters of wastewater are:

(i) Salinity

Salinity of treated wastewater is the single most important criterion used for deciding its appropriateness for irrigation purposes. It is determined by measuring the electrical conductivity of the water. The electrical conductivity (EC) itself is used as a substitute measure for finding the total dissolved salts (TDS) concentration. For the purposes of irrigation, EC and TDS values are directly related, and convertible within an accuracy of about 10 percent.

High levels of salinity is harmful to the plants because dissolved salts increase the osmotic pressure of the soil water. Continuous irrigation of soil with sewage wastewater has been found to increase the EC value of the soil (El - Motaium and Badway, 2000).

(ii) Specific Ion Toxicity

If the treated wastewater contains ions at levels greater than threshold values, it can cause toxicity to the plants. The most common causes of toxicity are sodium (Na), chloride (Cl^-) and boron (B).

Amongst these, the toxicity originating from boron is predominant. The source of boron is the detergent used in cleansing clothes at home.

The effects of toxicity become visible in blocking plant growth, decline in productivity and changes in plant morphology leading ultimately to its death. The extent of damage due to toxicity will depend on the nature of crop, its stage of growth, concentration of ions, and climate especially the high rate of evapo-transpiration due to hot and dry conditions. For some crops, the problem of toxicity can not be alleviated without improving the wastewater quality.

(iii) Sodicity or Permeability Problems

High levels of sodium (sodicity) in the irrigation water can bring about indirect changes in the soil structure. These changes are in the form of reduced soil permeability, crust formation and water logging. The crust formation has following effects: it makes the soil difficult to cultivate. At the same time, it does not allow the plant to germinate. Secondly, it acts as a barrier, so that sufficient irrigation water does not reach the root zone.

The potential problem of soil permeability arising from sodicity can be predicted by using the sodium adsorption ratio (SAR) :

$$\text{SAR} = \frac{\text{Na}}{\sqrt{(\text{Ca}^{2+} + \text{Mg}^{2+})/2}}$$

The concentration of cations is expressed in meqL^{-1} when the solubility of calcium is high due to carbon dioxide (CO_2), bicarbonate (HCO_3) or salinity (EC), adj. SAR is used. The SAR or adj. SAR should be used in tandem with electrical conductivity (EC) of irrigation in order to evaluate the potential problem of permeability. This is because at a given

SAR, the rate of permeability increases or decreases with increase or decrease in salinity.

(iv) Nutrients

Sewage wastewater contains a large quantity of plant nutrients. But, excessive concentration of nutrients can rather be problematic. The highest amount of nutrient in the wastewater is that of N. Application of large volumes of wastewater rich in N can cause NO_3 toxicity in the crops. Nitrate can also be leached down and thus, pollute the groundwater. Toxicity hazard due to P is rare because its concentration is usually low in wastewater. The weight of a particular nutrient applied to the soil can be found with the following equation (EPP, 1989):

$$\text{Nutrient weight (kg ha}^{-1}) = \frac{\text{Conc. of nutrient (mg l}^{-1})}{10} \times \text{wastewater applied (cm)}$$

The nitrogen in the treated wastewater can substitute an equal amount of nitrogen in the chemical fertilizers during early and middle crop growing period. However, excessive use of N rich wastewater in the latter growing period can cause excessive vegetative growth, delayed maturation of crop or deterioration in its quality (Tchobanoglous and Burton, 1996).

(v) Trace elements and Heavy metals

Several inorganic chemical contaminants may be present in abnormal amounts in the treated wastewater, especially when industrial wastewater is suspected to fall into it. These inorganic chemicals may be classified into trace elements and heavy metals. The former are present in normal irrigation waters in trace quantities, but their higher concentrations may be hazardous (Table 4). Heavy metals are one of trace elements which pose a definite heath hazard when taken up by the plants. Heavy metals are called so because in their metallic form, their densities are greater than 4 gm cm^{-3}.

Table 4 : Maximum recommended concentration of trace elements in irrigation waters and phytotoxic levels

Element	Recommended maximum concentration (mg L^{-1})	Phytotoxic levels (mg kg^{-1} dry foliage)
As	0.10	3 - 10
Cd	0.01	5 - 700
Co	0.05	25 - 100
Cu	0.20	25 - 40
Fe	5.00	-
Mn	0.20	400 - 2000
Mo	0.01	-
Ni	0.20	50 - 100
Pb	5.00	-
Se	0.02	100
Zn	2.00	500 - 1500

Source : Tchobanoglous and Burton (1996); EPP (1989)

The trace elements are classed as posing 'little hazard'. Such elements include aluminum, fluoride, iron, lithium, maganese, selenium, chronium, arsenic, antimony, mercury and lead. Iron, aluminium, manganese and chromium have little soil solubility. Lead is zootoxic but not easily transferable from the roots of the plants. Arsenic, mercury, selenium and tin are hazardous, but their presence in the sewage sludge is nominal. The elements which pose "Significant potential hazard" are copper (Cu), Nickel (Ni), Zinc (Zn), cadmium (Cd) and molybdenum (Mo). Of these, Ni, Cu, and Zn are phytotoxic. Nickel is phytotoxic at nearly 50 mg kg^{-1} in plant tissues. Decline in crop yields results when Cu and Zn rich wastewater and sludge are applied heavily. Uptake of Mo, Zn and Ni is greatly enhanced when soil is acidic (pH<6.5). Generally, transfer of Cu from roots to other parts of plant is negligible. Molybdenum is particularly harmful to cattle when concentrations are high. The greatest potential risk to animal, plant and, especially human health can occur due to Cd toxicity, which is related to various health disorders. To prevent toxicity hazards to men and animals, concentration of heavy metals should be strictly monitored and controlled. In a study in Cairo, heavy metals like Fe, Mn, Cu, Zn, Cd, Co, Ni and Pb were found to increase in the soil with the number of increase in irrigation with sewage water (El - Motaium and Badawy, 2000). In another comparative study of fields irrigated with treated wastewater and well-water, it was found that amounts of Zn, Mg, Cu, and Fe in soils irrigated with wastewater were higher but the differences were not significant. Singh *et al* (1998), analysed sewage water samples of different locations of Bikaner city for heavy metals like Pb, Ni and Cd contents and data are presented in Table 5. The concentration of total Pb, Ni and Cd varied from 1.2 to 3.0, 0.12 to 0.42 and 0.62 to 1.67 mgL^{-1}, respectively. The maximum Pb, Cd and Ni concentration were observed in sewerage water of industrial area. The soluble Pb, Cd and Ni ranged from 0.98 to 1.50, 0.08 to 0.12 and 0.30 to 0.65 mgL^{-1} respectively. The higher concentration of toxic/heavy metals in industrial area sewage water may be due to industrial discharge into the sewage. The higher concentration of these toxic metals in the sewage water may also be ascribed due to the discharge from automobile, utensil, iron & steel, oil, dye and paint industries. Thus, erratic use of untreated sewage water lead to metal accumulation in soils to such an extent that may hamper plant growth. None of these sewage waste is fit for irrigation use.

Table 5 : Total and soluble micronutrient concentration (mgL^{-1}) in sewage waters at different locations

S.No.	Location	Total			Soluble		
		Pb	Cd	Ni	Pb	Cd	Ni
1.	Sursagar	1.2	0.21	0.98	0.98	0.08	0.33
2.	Railway Station	1.2	0.12	0.62	0.98	0.08	0.30
3.	Industrial area	3.0	0.42	1.67	1.50	0.12	0.65
4.	Ballabh garden pond water	2.5	0.30	1.23	1.20	0.10	0.50

Source : Singh *et al.* (1998)

(vi) Pathogenic organisms

The greatest health related risk, arises, perhaps, from the pathogenic organisms in the raw sewage wastewater (Table 6). There is little evidence to suggest that inflections can spread from treated sewage wastewater. Main sources of pathogens are humans inflected with enteric diseases. Other sources include effluents from slaughter-houses, dairies and animal faeces. Sewage wastewater treatment greatly reduces the number of pathogens but negligible amounts may usually persist even after treatment.

Table 6 : Pathogens in raw sewage and sewage solids

Pathogens	Diseases caused	Health risk	Survival period in soils
BACTERIA			
Shgella spp	Bacillary dysentery	Medium	-
Salmonella typi	Typhoid	Medium	1 - 20 days
Vibrio Cholera	Chalera	Medium	-

Contd.

VIRUSES			
Hepatitis A virus	Infections hepatitis	-	-
Polio Viruses	Poliomyelitis	-	-
Norwalk & Rota Viruses	Acute gastroenteritis	Low	8 days
PROTOZOA			
Entamoeba hystolytica	Amebiasis	-	6 - 8 days
Giardia lamblia	Giardiasis	-	-
HELMINTHS			
Ascaris sp. (Roundworm)	Ascariasis	High	upto 7 years (ova)
Taenia sp. (Tapeworm)	Taeniasis	High	
Trichuris trichuria (Whipworm)	Trichuriasis	High	

Source : Sabey (1980); Kaul *et al.* (2002)

Pathogenic organisms can be classified into bacteria, protozoa and helminths. The most common bacterial pathogens found are those belonging to *Salmonella*. There are more than 1700 *Salmonella* sp. pathogenic to man and animals. In fact, this is most widely spread pathogenic bacterium, which causes a number of diseases ranging from typhoid, gestraonteritis, enteric fever. *Salmonelle shigella* is another bacterium causing shigellosis, an acute diarrheal disease. *Escherichia coli*, causing gastroenteritis and urinary infections and *Mycobacterium* causing TB and leprosy, have differing responses to disinfection. While *E. coli* is easily amenable to disinfection and gets inactivated in the environment, mycobacteria are just opposite. However, evidence suggesting increased infection rates of mycobacteria due to land application of wastewater is almost negligible (EPP, 1989).

Viruses are small pathogens which may percolate into soil and may persist for months therein. Groundwater at a depth of even 27.5 m below the wastewater application sites showed traces of animal virus (Sree Ramulu, 2001). Enteroviruses like poliovirus, multiply in the intestine and cause various diseases like paralysis, meningitis and fever, viruses are associated with solids, and usually concentrate in primary and secondary sludges. Viruses do not create health-related risks when secondary treated and disinfected wastewater is used for irrigation. Protozoa like *Entomoeba histolytica* and *Giardia lambia* cause amoebiases and giardiasis respectively. Cysts of protozoa are found in the sewage, which are resistant to disinfectants and environmental stresses. Protozoan cysts found in the treated wastewater applied to land do not have direct human health danger. However, animals grasing on the land, soon after wastewater irrigation or sludge application, have some risk of ingesting cysts. Helminths are parasitic intestinal worms falling into two clear groups : nematodes (roundworms) and cestodes (tapeworms). Nematodes are a large group of organisms which are transmitted to man or animal without intermediaries. *Ascaris lumbricoides* which infect the small intestine of human, are very resistant - their eggs can survive in the soil for upto seven years. Exposure to the environment greatly reduces the number of eggs. Cestodes like *Taenia saginata* (beef tapeworm) and *T. solium* (pork tapeworm) are among the most serious health risks for humans, and are transmitted via intermediary animals. Traditional sewage wastewater treatment does not remove the animal's health risk from tapeworm - egg ingestion. Hot and dry weather shortens the survival period of cestodes' eggs on the land.

(vii) Organic Chemicals

Many of the synthetic organic chemicals used at home or released from industries, can be very stable and resistant to biodegradation. These chemicals in wastewater can be hazardous to man and animals because they have low water solubility and do not easily move in soil. They tend to accumulate in the tissue and are fat soluble. The mammals are particularly susceptible to them. Besides, these chemicals are carcinogenic and mutagenic too. Various compounds included in this category are pesticides, chlorinated phenolics, polybrominated biphenyles (PBBs), polychlorinated biphenyls (PCBs), phthalates, polynuclear aromatic hydrocarbons, etc. (EPP, 1989). There has been little knowledge about the consequences of land application of wastewater contaminated with such chemicals. This study is much needed because of high toxicity and health implications for the man and animals.

(b) Quality of sewage sludge

Treatment of sewage wastewater removes solids, metals, soluble organics and to a limited extent, nutrients and pathogens, most of which get concentrated into the sludge. Land application of sewage sludge can have various potentially beneficial and harmful consequences, which will depend upon the quality and characteristics of the sludge itself. Hence, various constituents as well as qualitative aspects of the sewage sludge that is applied need to be closely monitored.

(i) Nutrients

Sewage sludge is an important source of nutrients. Ayade *et al*. (1999), found that application of sludge upto 15 tonnes ha^{-1} increased the level of soil O.M. by 66%, the contents of total N and available P by 26%, the content of exchangeable

Ca by 40% and that of exchangeable K by 31%. Maize height, stem girth and grain yield were also found to significantly increase by sludge application.

High amount of nitrogen and phosphorus in the sludge can lead to algal blooms in the streams and eutrophication of lakes. Sludge containated water can cause methenoglobinemia (Blue baby disease) in the small babies when there is high concentration of nitrate nitrogen in it. Application of sewage sludge can considerably enhance the decomposition rates of native soil organic matter. This can release extra nitrogen for plant growth than what one normally expects from the soil organic matter. Parkpian *et al.* (2003) reported that when nitrogen was applied at a rate greater than 75 kg ha^{-1}, there was an increase in the biomass of rice with reduced grain yield. As compared to sewage sludge alone, nitrogen mineralization from urea combined with sewage sludge was higher.

Extent of mineralization of sludge born organic nitrogen varies from a small proportion to 100% per year. The nitrogen not mineralized in the first cropping year is mineralized in the latter years, though at a declining rate. The level of phosphorus in the sewage sludge is, normally, sufficient to supply the needs of the crop. Sometimes, when the sewage sludge contains animal manure the excessive concentration of phosphorus can cause the risk of surface water pollution.

(ii) Pathogens

Sewage sludge can have all the pathogens that are usually found in the sewage wastewater. However chances of groundwater contamination due to bacteria and viruses in the sludge are lesser than that in the wastewater. Almost pathogen free sludge can be obtained by various treatment procedures like pasteurization and use of lime (Table 7). Due to their high level of concentration, parasitic ova and cysts pose the biggest challenge to land application of sludge. No negative health impacts of the use of treated sewage sludge on agriculture farms has been reported even when sewage sludge has been used for about 100 years in Europe (Sree Ramulu, 2001).

Table 7 : Effectiveness of sewage sludge stabilization processes

Processes	Effectiveness		
	Pathogen deactivation	**Putrefaction Potential**	**Odour**
Aerobic digestion	Fair	Good	Good
Anaerobic digestion (60 days, 20 ^{0}C)	Fair	Good	Good
Composting (21 days, 60 ^{0}C)	Good	Good	Good
Heat Treatment (195 ^{0}C)	Excellent	Poor	Poor
Ionization	Excellent	Poor	Poor
Lime Treatment (In moisture, 3 hours)	Good	Fair	Good
Pasteurization (30 minutes, 70 ^{0}C)	Excellent	Poor	Poor

Source : EPP (1989) and Miller and Donahue (1992)

(iii) Heavy metals

Application of very high amounts of sewage sludge can raise the level of heavy metals in the soil. A decline in the pH value of the soil increases the solubility and plant uptake of the heavy metals. Heavy metals have generally been found to concentrate in the upper layers of the soil. Copper, zinc and lead, for example, tend to concentrate at the surface of the soil. Copper and ferrous show tendency to leach down the soil horizons (Samaras *et al.*, 1999). High level of heavy metals in the sewage sludge tends to inhibit the enzymatic activities in the soil through its toxic effects. Leafy and root vegetables exhibit increased concentrations of heavy metals like copper and zinc, when increased amount of sewage sludge is applied to the soil. It has been observed that heavy metals tend to persist in the soil for a long duration. In a field, which had been receiving sewage sludge for over 41 years, cadmium which is considered to be the most toxic of the heavy metals, showed a negligible loss, even after four decades, from the soil profile. About 92% of the applied cadmium was recovered in the top soil and 7% in the upper 17 cm of the sub-soil (Bergkvist and Jarvis, 2003).

Use of Treated Sewage Wastewater Sludge and Garbage in Agriculture

(a) Treated Sewage Wastewater

Formulation of proper strategy for using treated sewage wastewater is made by taking into consideration the quality and quantity of available wastewater so that selection of the crops to be grown may be made and efficient irrigation methods may be employed.

(i) Crop Selection

Crops should be selected according to the salinity, toxicity and health hazards present in the irrigation wastewater. Different plants respond variously to changing salinity levels of the wastewater. Some plants are able to give better yields at higher salinity levels than others (Table 8). These are able to make the required osmotic adjustments, unabling them to extract more water from a saline soil.

Table 8 : Salt tolerance of some crops

(A) Tolerant Crops

High : Barley, cotton, sugarbeet, datepalm, dhaincha (*Sesbania* sp.)

Moderate : Wheat, oats, soyabean, tobacco, rapeseed.

(B) Semi - tolerant

High : Oats, rice, jowar (sorghum), maize, bajra(pearlmillet), tomato, cabbage

Moderate : Wheat, arhar, castor, jute, soybean, rye, gram, berseem, cowpea

(C) Sensitive crops

High : Sesame, carrot, onion, beans, green gram, guar (*Cyamopsis* sp.)

Moderate : Maize, groundnut, rice, sugarcane

Source : FAO (1985)

Phytotoxicity normally results when certain ions in the soil water are taken up by the plants and accumulate in 'the leaves in harmful quantities. During dry summer, toxic ions of sodium and chloride can directly be absorbed by leaves moistened during sprinkling irrigation (Pescod, 1994). Though some plants are more tolerant, high levels of toxic ions can be damaging.

In case of vegetables, fruits and forage crops eaten raw, the microbiological quality of the wastewater has to be of the highest quality. In case of other non-food crops and trees, lower quality wastewater may be used, especially where there is no risk of exposure for the common man.

(ii) Wastewater irrigation methods

Irrigation with wastewater is unlike usual irrigation, Firstly, the quantity of treated wastewater available for irrigation may generally be limited. Secondly, high levels of chemical and biological contaminants in this wastewater raise the issues of contaminants of crop plants and unhygienic situations to farm workers and environment, besides the hazards of salinity and toxicity. Selection of suitable irrigation method can considerable reduce the above mentioned risks. Different irrigation methods of irrigation with respect to treated wastewater are given in Table 9. Drip irrigation method have several advantages for wastewater irrigation, however, this option requires high capital investment.

Table 9 : Evaluation of irrigation methods in relation to treated wastewater

Parameter	Furrow Irrigation	Flood Irrigation	Sprinkler Irrigation	Drip Irrigation
Foliar wetting and leaf damage causing poor yield	No	Negligible	Severe	No
Salt accumulation in root zone with repeated application	Yes	No	No	Yes (b/w drip points)
Maintaining high soil water potential	Stress b/w irrigation	Stress b/w irrigation	Not possible throughout	Possible throughout growing season
Suitability to handle brackish water (without significant yield loss)	Fair to Medium	Fair to Medium	Poor to Fair	Good to excellent
Wind drift and public exposure	Variable	High	High	Very low
Usable with small flows	No	No	Yes	Best Option
Control and measurement of applied water	Difficult	Difficult	Possible	Possible

Source : Pescod (1994) and EPP (1989)

If the farmer has access to conventional sources of water, wastewater can be blended with other water supplies, or it can be used alternatively with irrigation water. This water management practice conserves good quality water resources, and reduces the toxic hazards arising from poor quality wastewater (or water, if the treated wastewater is of better quality). Land development can also minimize potential hazards resulting from wastewater use for irrigation. It includes leveling of land to control salinity effects, establishing adequate drainage, deep ploughing, and leaching to reduce soil salinity (Pescod, 1994).

(b) Sewage Sludge

Sewage sludge is the residual product of sewage wastewater treatment. It is a concentrated suspension of solids composed of soluble organic matter, laden, more or less, with nutrients. It also contains various pathogens and other pollutants removed from the wastewater. The consistency of sewage sludge can vary from slurry to dry solids, depending upon the type of sludge treatment (Sree Ramulu, 2001).

Sewage sludge is rich in human and animal faecal matter; dairy and poultry house wastes and effluents from food processing industries. Nutrient composition of sludge is considered to be similar to other organic wastes based soil amendments, such as animal manure, that are usually applied to agricultural land, though it varies from place to place, sewage sludges contain about 4.0% nitrogen, 2.0% phosphorus and 0.4% potassium on a dry weight basis (Miller and Donahue, 1992). Agricultural use of sewage sludge not only provides nutrients for plant growth, but also organic matter for soil conditioning.

Environmentally, safe disposal of wastewater and sludge presents the biggest technological and economic challenges to our society. Cities often dump these polluting wastes into the rivers and oceans. Several western cities burn the sewage sludge. However, combusting is pollutive of the atmosphere and consumes a heavy amount of energy. Burying sludge in landfills, along with other solids wastes, is common practice, but scarcity of land and increasing costs of conveyance are making it more and more non-feasible. The main remaining alternative is application of composted/treated sludge to the crop land. Using sludge without treatment can prove pollutive to environment, and toxic for the organisms. Land application of sludge, thus, avoids pollution of air, groundwater and oceanic water. It is also the most economic means of sludge disposal.

(c) Garbage

Municipalities are traditionally focused on land filling or combustion of solid wastes. The sheer volume of urban wastes, their ecological and health hazards, the rising transportation and other costs, associated with urban waste management, require more environment-friendly and cost effective strategies. Composting of organic, urban wastes can be one of them. Organic urban wastes including sewage sludge and garbage, can be used to feed depleted soils. However, direct land application of sewage sludge and garbage is not desirable as these may contain several pathogens. These should first be decomposed before they can be used. Such decomposed organic matter is called compost. The compost has about 1.5% N, 0.50% P and 1.0% K. Besides micro-nutrients sewage sludge is comparatively richer in the nutrients like P and N, along with trace elements of zinc (Zn) and copper (Cu) (Table 10).

Table 10 : Chemical composition of some organic manures and crop residues (dry weight basis)

Source	Primary Nutrients %			Micronutrients (mg kg^{-1})					
	N	P	K	Fe	Zn	Mn	Cu	B	Mo
Azolla	4.03	0.29	1.70	-	-	-	-	-	-
City compost	1.50	0.50	1.00	-	400	400	560	15	9
Green manure (Sesbania or Dhaincha)	2.25	0.37	-	140	17	17	80	20	0.2
Goat/Sheep manure	0.65	0.50	0.03	-	2570	2570	150	4600	-
Human waste	1.60	0.50	0.46	-	-	-	-	-	-
Pig manure	1.88	2.13	0.67	1200	50	50	70	-	-
Poultry manure	1.85	1.81	-	1075	50	50	196	7	-
Sewage Sludge	2.40	1.20	0.002	-	2459	2459	262	9	6

Source : Yojana, August, 1997

The compost has greater value as a soil conditioner that as a fertilizer. When applied, the compost turns the poor soil into a high quality loam, which is free from the defects of both heavy clay soil as well as light sandy soil. Very minute particles of the clay soil get stuck together while the large particles of the sandy soil allow moisture to drain away. The humus of the compost not only improves the structure of the soil, but also increases retention of water and nutrients around the roots of the plants. As nutrients are retained where they are needed, less fertilizers will be needed. When used together with chemical fertilizers, the compost makes phosphorus more easily available and also prolongs the availability period of nitrogen. This improves the uptake of nutrients by the plants. The use of compost may increase the crop yield upto 30%, while the dose of fertilizers reduces to one half (Hughes, 1980). Rao and Shantaram (1995), found that crop yields increased due to use of garbage as a manure, but at higher doses the yields declined.

The composting of organic matter for land application does not always improves its nutrient value. Fresh and nutritious organic matter like vegetable and fruit remains, manures and young legume plants should be directly applied to the land without composting because they rapidly decompose and release nutrients, which plants can use. Organic matter with low level of nutrients, i.e. high C:N ratio e.g. straw, woody plants or sawdust can better be used after composting (Miller and Donahue, 1992).

The composted urban wastes increase the soil aggregation, available water, and soil hydraulic conductivity which may even reduce the erosion of the soil. Application of compost is also found to decease the C:N ratio of the soil (Roman and Fortun, 2003). The initial C:N ratio decides the speed of decomposition of the organic matter into compost. The ideal initial ratio is between 30:1 and 35:1. As the organic matter decomposes, the organic carbon declines due to its oxidation as CO_2 while the nitrogen remains within the system. As the composting proceeds, the C:N ratio declines. The C:N ratio of the compost is of utmost importance, and decides its usefulness, or otherwise, as soil complement when this ratio is greater than 20:1, microbial activity in the soil will rob the available nitrogen in the compost, causing a nitrogen deficiency therein. Use of municipal compost can increase the content of heavy metals in the soil, yet the plant uptake of these metals is inhibited by high levels of soil pH and humus. Accumulation of heavy metals, salts and sodium may cause phytotoxicity in the long-term. Rao and Shantaram (1995), reported that uptake of micronutrients and heavy metals by the crops varied according to the plant species and plant parts. Some of the heavy metals were found to remain in the roots and were not translocated to the parts of plants.

Management and Restoration of Soil Fertility

(i) Inorganic or organic fertilizers

Broadly, two main types of fertilizers are used for raising crops viz., inorganic and organic. Excessive use of some inorganic fertilizers may limit the ability of soil bacteria, fungi and micro-organisms to decompose the wastes and, thus, to release the nutrients that enhance the growth of the plants. Such inhibition of the activity of the soil micro-organisms may gradually harden the soil. A hardened soil loses much of its ability to absorb rainwater and becomes easily eroded. Erosion of the soil treated with fertilizers results in higher concentration of nutrients in the lakes and streams through overflow from land. Greater availability of nutrients in the lakes and streams encourages fast growth of algae, which generate a large amount of algal waste after death. Decaying of the algal waste consumes the oxygen supply of the water, killing fish and other aquatic life. Moreover, excessive use of fertilizers may pollute the water of the lakes, streams and even underground water (Science Net Q.No. 18093).

Use of mineral phosphoric fertilizers always means unwitting addition of significant amounts of toxic elements like Cd to the soil. Citrus gardens for example, treated with triple super phosphate @ 400 kg ha^{-1} yr^{-1} showed an average Cd build up of 1.0 μgg^{-1} of soil over 36 years, as compared to only 0.07 μg Cd ha^{-1} for the normal field which was treated with 30 kg $ha^{-1}gm^{-1}$ of triple super phosphate (Sree Ramula, 2001). Thus, balanced use of fertilizers along with manures is utmost need to attain the goal of sustainable soil fertility management.

(ii) Urban wastes

The consumption of goods and services and generation of wastes, per unit area is much higher in the urban areas because of high population inhabiting these areas. Thus, urban areas generate a large quantity of sewage wastewater and garbage. These urban wastes are dumped raw in the open grounds, landfills, incinerators, rivers or oceans. The disposal of these wastes poses a serious challenge as it requires sufficient open and cheap space, resources and waste management infrastructure, all of which are not adequately available in the cities of developing world. Due to inadequate disposal of wastes, pollution of air and water and prevalence of related diseases is widespread in the cities. About 5.2 million people, including 4 million children, fall prey to diseases caused by improper disposal of sewage wastewater and garbage every year (Sanio, 1998; Baud and Schenk, 1994).

On the other hand, the chief concern of rural areas and agricultural sector is maintaining or raising the land productivity so that growing population can be properly fed. The rural sector imports fertilizers, pesticides and herbicides for fulfilling this purpose. In this way, the urban and rural sectors tackle their respective problems of waste disposal and soil fertility management in an isolated manner. However, there is a possibility of linking the management of these problems in a mutually beneficial way (UNDP, 1996; Smit and Nasr, 1992).

The urban wastes generated in the cities contain a large proportion of organic matter. The proportion is between one-half and two-thirds in the cities of the developing world. The organic portion of the waste stream can be recycled to obtain compost, which can be reused for increasing crop yield. The sewage sludge can also be recycled and reused for soil application, while the purified sewage wastewater can be used for irrigation. In this process, the rural hinterland gains by enrichment of degraded/depleted soils, by increased supply of irrigation water, and by overall growth of food production.

(iii) Wastewater

Reuse of wastewater helps in the conservation and optimum use of water resources. This is especially important in the arid and semi-arid regions. It provides irrigation water for crops, orchards, forests, grasslands, parks and golf-courses. Sewage wastewater carries a lot of organic matter and dissolved nutrients which can partially or fully replace the chemical fertilizers (Kandiah, 1990). According to Miller and Donahue (1992) the irrigation with sewage water lead to recharging of groundwater. An increase in the yield, biomass production, plant height and leaf width in maize was higher when irrigated with treated wastewater. However, the infiltration capacity of the soil in wastewater treatment showed a decline of 15.6% (Alizadeh, 2001).

(iv) Sewage Sludge

Sewage sludge is an excellent soil conditioner as it contains about 50% organic matter. It has several beneficial impacts on the physico-chemical properties of the soil. Application of the sewage sludge increases the porosity of the soil, when it is applied at 180 $m^3 ha^{-1}$. Sludge application has been reported to improve the soil aggregation, or the ability of soil to resist the stress coming from rainfall impact and agricultural machinery use. The increased release of metabolites by the microbes was noticed when sewage sludge was added to the soil. The variation in soil pH due to sewage sludge use generally tends towards neutrality. The concomitant decline in pH can occur due to the release of organic acids. On the other hand, rise in pH occurs when treated sludge rich in calcium is applied to the soil (Sree Ramulu, 2001). The addition of sewage sludge to soil increases the soluble salt concentration in the surface soil leading to higher EC of the soil (Tsadilas *et al.*, 1999). The contaminated sewage sludge may be best used in the fiber crops and forests etc.

Conclusions

The world's population is growing with a rapid pace. The cities are swelling too. The growing population does not have sufficient food rather nutritions food. The areable land have limitations for further expansion. The productivity of soil can only be increased with increased utilization of irrigation water and fertilizers. On the other hand, expanding cities are logged down with ever increasing quantity of wastewater and garbage, causing serious environmental pollution hazards. The urban wastes can be used to restore soil fertility and enhance food production. Agricultural use of sewage wastewater, sludge and garbage can reduce ecological economic and health burden of the urban areas. These urban wastes should be used only after proper treatment in order to keep them free from contaminants.

Recycling and reuse of urban wastes for agricultural land on a large scale would require formulation of an appropriate policy and plan as well as its efficient management. Implementation of this strategy will require engineering, organizational, legal as well as public attitudinal aspects.

References

Alizadeh, A., Bazari, M.E., Velayati, S. (Eds.) [2001] Using reclaimed municipal wastewater for irrigation of corn, 52nd IEC Meeting of the International commission on Irrigation and Drainage International Workshop on Wastewater Reuse & Management, Seoul, 19-20 September, 147-154.

Ayade, B.B. Eneji, A.E., Olukayode, B. (1999) The use of sewage sludge for soil fertility restoration in the Tropics. Japanese J. Tropical Agriculture, 43(3) : 145 - 148.

Baud, I. and Schenk, H.(Eds.) (1994) Solid waste management : Modes Assessments, Appraisals and Linkages in Bangalore, Manohar Publishers, New Delhi.

Bergkvist, P. and Jarvis, N. (2003) Long-term effects of sewage sludge applications on soil properties, cadmium availability and distribution in arable soil. Agriculture Ecosystems and Environment, 97 (1-3) : 167 - 179.

Carter, H. (1982) *The Study of Urban Geography*, 3rd edn. Arnold - Heinemann, New Delhi.

Chandna, R.C. (2003) *Geography of Population : Concepts, Determinants and Patterns.* Kalyani Publishers, Ludhiana, pp., 529-530

Clarke, John I. (1972) *Population Geography*, Pergamon Press, Oxford.

El-Motaium, R.A. and Badawy, S.H. (2000) Effect of irrigation using sewage water on the distribution of some heavy metals in bulk and rhizosphere soils and different, plant species : *Brassica oleracca* and *Citrus sinensis*. Egyption J. Soil Sci., 40 (1-2) : 285-303

ENV (1997) Singapore : *A Sustainable City*. Ministry of Environment, Singapore.

EPP (1989) *Manual for Land Application of Wastewater and Sludge.* Environmental Protection Programs Canada, Geo-Environ Academia, Jodhpur, pp., 206

FAO (1985) *Water Quality for Agriculture.* Irrigation and Drainage, Paper 29, FAO, Rome, pp., 174.

Feizi, M., Ragab, R., and Pearce , G. (2001) Effect of treated wastewater on accumulation of heavy metals in plants and soil. 52nd IEC Meeting of the International commission on Irrigation and Drainage Seoul, 19-20 September. International workshop on wastewater reuse management, Seoul., pp., 137 - 146.

Ghosh, A. (1997) Organic Manure and Natural Farming Yojna, August, 1997.

Hughes, E.G. (1980) The composting of Municipal wastes *In : Handbook of Organic Waste Conversion* (Ed. Michael, W.M. Bewick) Van Nostrand Reinhold Co., New York, pp., 108-134.

India Today (1994) "Can we clean up the Mess?", October, 31, 1994, pp., 63-79.

Kandiah, A. (1990) Water quality management for sustainable agricultural development. Natural Resources Forum, 14(1) : 22-32.

Kanwar, J.S. (1997) Fertilizer Policy Issues (2000-2025). National Academy of Agricultural Science, India, 3rd Agricultural Science Congress, March 12-15, 1997.

Kaul, S.N. *et al.* (2002) *Utilization of Wastewater in Agriculture and Aquaculture*. Scientific Publishers, Jodhpur, pp. 675.

Leeper, G.W. (1978) Managing the heavy metals on the land. Dekker, Newyork.

Mara, D.D. and Cairncross, S. (1989) Guidelines for the safe use of wastewater and Excreta in Agriculture and Aquaculture, WHO, Geneva.

Miller, Raymond D. and Donahue, Roy L. (1992) *Soils : An Introduction to Soils and Plant Growth,* 6th edn., Prentice Hall of India Pvt, Ltd,. New Delhi, pp., 768.

Mukhopadhay, K. Ranjan, B. and Roy, R. (2005) Modern Agriculture and Environmental Pollution. Everyman's Science, 10(3) : 186-192.

NEERI (1996) Solid waste management in MDC Area. National Environmental Engineering Research Institute, June 21, Unpublished Report.

Parkpian, P., Ranamukhaarchchi, S.L., Hansen, G.K. (2003) Benefits and risks of using a combination of sewage sludge and chemical fertilizer on rice in acid sulphate soil. Nutrient cycling in Agroecosystems, 65(2) : 173-182.

Pescod, M.B. (1994) Wastewater treatment and use in Agriculture. FAO Irrigation and Drainage Paper 47, Reprint, Scientific Publishers, pp., 125.

Rao, K.J. and Shantaram, M.V. (1985) Effect of the application of garbage on the soil-plant system - A review. Agricultural Reviews, 16(3) : 105-116.

Sabey, B.R. (1980) The use of sewage sludge as a fertilizer, *In : Handbook of Organic Waste Conversion* (Eds. Michael, W.M., Bewick), Vas Nostrand Reinhold Co., New York, pp. 72-107.

Samaras, V., Tsadilas, C.D. and Robert, P.C. (Eds.) (1999) Proc, 4th Int. Conf. Precision Agriculture, St. Paul, USA, 19-22 July, 1998, pp., 1733-1744.

Sanio, M. (1998) Waste Not, Want Not. Urban Age, Summer, pp., 18-20.

Science Net (*n.d.*) Singapore Science centre, Q.No. 18093.

Singh, K.K., Rao, A.K., Kumar, R. and Basit, A. (1998) Pollution potential of some sewage waters of Bikaner city. J. Nature conservation, 10(1) : 15-21.

Sivaramakrishnan, K.C. and Green, L. (1986) *Metropolitan Management : The Asian Experience.* Oxford University Press, NewYork, pp., 100-197.

Smit, J. And Nasr, J. (1992) Urban Agriculture for sustainable cities : Using wastes and idle land and water bodies as resources. Environment and Urbanization, 4(2) : 141-151.

Sree Ramulu, U.S. (2001) *Reuse of Municipal Sewage and Sludge in Agriculture*. Scientific Publishers (India), Jodhpur, pp., 342.

Tchobanoglous, G. and Burton, Franklin, L(1996) *Wastewater Engineering : Treatment, Disposal, Reuse*, Tata McGraw Hill Publishing Co. Ltd., NewDelhi, pp. 1334.

The Hindustan Times (1996), March 2, 1996, New Delhi.

Tsadilas, C.D., Dimoyiannis, D.G. and Samaras, V. (1999) Sewage sludge usage in cotton crop : Influence on soil properties. Pedosphere, 9(2):147-152.

UNDP (1996) Urban Agriculture : Food, Jobs and Sustainable Cities. UNDP Publication Series for Habitat II, Vol.1, UNDP, New York.

UNEP(1989) *Environmental Data Report*, with World Resource . Institute, Washington, Blackwell Reference, Oxford.

UNEP/WRI (1988) World Resource 1988-89. A Report by World Resource Institute and IIED in collaboration with UNEP. Basic Books, New York.

CHAPTER 7

MUNICIPAL SOLID WASTES AND THEIR SAFE DISPOSAL

U.Sivakumar, K.Ramasamy, G.Kalaichelvan and N.Ramalingam

Fermentation Laboratory, Tamil Nadu Agricultural University, Coimbatore-641 003, (T.N.), India.

ABSTRACT

Municipal Solid waste (MSW) management constitutes a serious problem in many developing countries. Most cities do not collect the totality of wastes generated and of the wastes collected, only a fraction receives proper disposal. The insufficient collection and inappropriate disposal of solid wastes represent a source of water, land and air pollution and pose risks to human health and the environment. Over the next several decades, globalization, rapid urbanization and economic growth in the developing world tend to further deteriorate this situation. Cities spend increasing resources attempting to improve their MSW management. This chapter examines the various approaches to MSW management used by development agencies in general, and by bilateral and multilateral development organizations in particular. The socioeconomic conditions in the developing countries are so different from the developed world, that a different approach is needed. Whatever may be the approach, it should help solve the problem of solid wastes in a socially desirable, economically viable and environmentally sound manner. Depending on the type of waste generated from urban population, wastes can be segregated and bio-processed for energy and nutrient recovery. Various waste management options including composting and its applications in large scale industries were also reviewed. Compost derived from such processes should be tested for quality and plant reaction. Judicial activism and environmental controls directing for Municipal Solid Waste composting should be taken in the positive side to provide quality compost to plant nutrients and to support organic agriculture.

Key Words : Waste management, municipal solid wastes and composting

Introduction

Human kind has been generating waste since from the beginning, be it the bones and other parts of animals they slaughter for their food or the wood they cut to make their carts. With the progress of civilization, the waste generated became of a more complex nature. At the end of the 19th century, the industrial revolution saw the rise of the world consumers. Not only did the air get more and more polluted, but the earth itself became more polluted with the generation of non-biodegradable solid wastes. The increase in population and urbanization also contributed to the increase in solid wastes. Each household generates garbage or waste day in and day out. Items that we no longer need or do not have any further use fall in the category of waste, and we tend to throw them away.

Municipal solid waste (MSW) refers to the materials discarded in the urban areas for which municipalities are usually held responsible for collection, transport and final disposal. MSW encompasses household refuse, institutional wastes, street sweepings, commercial wastes, as well as construction and demolition debris. In developing countries,

MSW also contains varying amounts of industrial wastes from small industries, as well as dead animals, and fecal matter. Municipal solid waste, also called trash, garbage, refuse and rubbish, is the stuff we throw away everyday. In our trash, there are everyday items such as product packaging, grass clippings, furniture, clothing, bottles, food scraps, newspaper, appliances, and batteries that we don't need any more. MSW is generated by people and by businesses. Not counted as MSW are other discarded materials such as construction and demolition debris, municipal wastewater treatment sludge, and non-hazardous industrial wastes. Although, these materials often end up in MSW landfills, they can also be sent to non-MSW landfills for disposal.

The growth in MSW (municipal solid waste) generation in India has outpaced the growth in population in the recent years. The daily per capita generation of municipal solid waste in India ranges from about 100 g in small towns to 500 g in large towns. MSW resulting out of rapid urbanization has become a serious concern for government departments, pollution control agencies, regulatory bodies and also public in most of the developing countries. MSW management in the developing countries is unsatisfactory. The improper management of solid wastes represents a source of air, land and water pollution and poses risks to human health and the environment. Despite considerable expenses, the situation tends to further deteriorate due to the rapid growth of cities likely to occur over the next few decades. Globalization is likely to boost economic growth in the developing world, which would increase the amount of wastes that need to be collected, transported and disposed of, further straining Third World cities. Inefficient management and disposal of solid waste is an obvious cause for degradation of environment in most cities of the developing world. Improper disposal of this waste leads to spread of communicable diseases, causes obnoxious conditions and spoils biosphere as a whole. Our society must find new ways to reuse and recycle our waste materials, and to detoxify toxic component present in these wastes. The solution to this problem lies with the widespread use of micro-organisms to convert these waste materials into nutrient rich manure. Moreover, compost environments are excellent habitats for many micro-organisms, since they contain all organic substrates necessary for microbial growth and development.

Growing concerns relating to land degradation, threat to eco-systems from over and inappropriate use of inorganic fertilizers, atmospheric pollution, soil health, soil biodiversity and sanitation have rekindled the global interest in organic recycling practices like composting. Among the various options that are available for MSW management, composting is most commonly followed and cheapest method of solid waste disposal. In this review, more emphasis is given on the areas like composting; its methods, enrichment and acceleration of composting process, quality analysis and maturity indices of compost and their plant reaction.

Classification and Composition of solid wastes

Solid waste can be classified into different types depending on their source: Household waste is generally classified as municipal waste, Industrial waste as hazardous waste, and Biomedical waste or hospital waste as infectious waste.

Municipal solid waste

Municipal solid waste consists of household waste, construction and demolition debris, sanitation residue, and waste from streets. This garbage is generated mainly from residential and commercial complexes. With rising urbanization and change in lifestyle and food habits, the amount of municipal solid waste has been increasing rapidly and its composition changing (Fig 1.). The growth in MSW (municipal solid waste) generation in India has outpaced the growth in population in the recent years. The daily per capita generation of municipal solid waste in India ranges from about 100 g in small towns to 500 g in large towns. In 1947, cities and towns in India generated an estimated 6 million tonnes of solid waste, in 1997 it was about 48 million tonnes. The recyclable content of waste ranges from 13% to 20%. More than 25% of the municipal solid waste is not collected at all; 70% of the Indian cities lack adequate capacity to transport it and there are no sanitary landfills to dispose of the waste. The existing landfills are neither well equipped nor well managed and are not lined properly to protect against contamination of soil and groundwater.

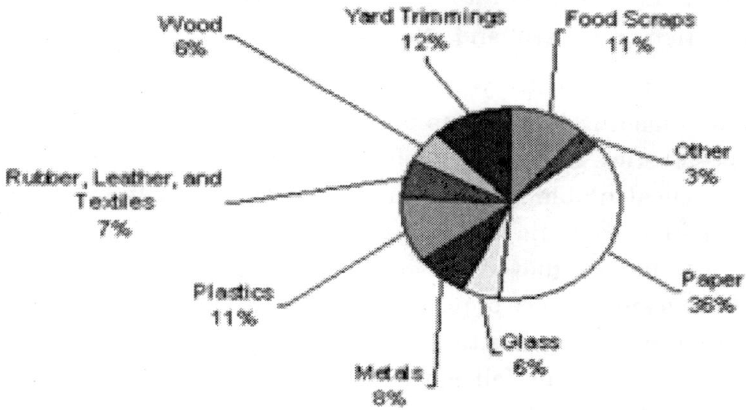

Fig. 1 : Proportions of materials generated in municipal solid waste

The TERI 'Green India 2047' study made the following observations on the situation of municipal solid waste management in the country :

- Increasing urbanization and changing lifestyles has led to, the solid waste generated in Indian cities having increased from 6 million tonnes in 1947 to 47.8 million tonnes in 1997.

- The production and consumption of plastic increased over 70 times between 1960 and 1995.
- The collection of municipal solid waste is inefficient (more than 25% of the total is not collected at all), its transport is inadequate, and its disposal is unscientific.
- More than one-fourth of the municipal solid waste is not collected at all, and the landfills to dispose of the waste are neither well equipped nor managed efficiently.

The organic fraction of MSW (less plastic, rubber and leather) is converted into an earthy, humus-like, material by the action of bacteria and other microbes.

Over the last few years, the consumer market has grown rapidly leading to products being packed in cans, aluminium foils, plastics, and other such non-biodegradable items that cause incalculable harm to the environment. In India, some municipal areas have banned the use of plastics and they seem to have achieved success. For example, today one will not see a single piece of plastic in the entire district of Ladakh where the local authorities imposed a ban on plastics in 1998. Other states should follow the example of this region and ban the use of items that cause harm to the environment. One positive note is that in many large cities, shops have begun packing items in reusable or biodegradable bags. Certain biodegradable items can also be composted and reused. In fact proper handling of the biodegradable waste will considerably lessen the burden of solid waste that each city has to tackle. There are different categories of waste generated, each take their own time to decompose (Table 1).

Table 1 : Type of litter generated and the approximate time it takes to degenerate

Type of litter	**Approximate time it takes to degenerate the litter**
Organic waste such as vegetable and fruit peels, leftover foodstuff, etc.	a week or two
Paper	10–30 days
Cotton cloth	2–5 months
Wood	10–15 years
Woolen items	1 year
Tin, aluminum and other metal items such as cans	100–500 years
Plastic bags	One million years?
Glass bottles	Undetermined

Garbage: There are four broad categories of garbage .i.e.,

Organic waste: kitchen waste, vegetables, flowers, leaves, fruits.

Toxic waste: old medicines, paints, chemicals, Tube lights and bulbs, spray cans, fertilizer and pesticide containers, batteries, shoe polish.

Recyclable: paper, glass, metals, plastics.

Soiled: hospital waste such as cloth soiled with blood and other body fluids.

Hazardous waste

Industrial and hospital waste is considered hazardous as they may contain toxic substances and pathogens. Certain types of household waste are also hazardous. Hazardous wastes could be highly toxic to humans, animals, and plants;

are corrosive, highly inflammable, or explosive; and react when exposed to certain things e.g. gases. India generates around 7 million tonnes of hazardous wastes every year, most of which is concentrated in four states: Andhra Pradesh, Bihar, Uttar Pradesh, and Tamil Nadu. Household waste that can be categorized as hazardous waste include old batteries, shoe polish, paint tins, old medicines and ,medicine bottles. Hospital waste contaminated by chemicals used in hospitals is also considered hazardous. These chemicals include formaldehyde and phenols, which are used as disinfectants, and mercury, which is used in thermometers or equipment that measure blood pressure. Most hospitals in India do not have proper disposal facilities for these hazardous wastes. In the industrial sector, the major generators of hazardous waste are the industries involved in the production of metals, chemical, paper, pesticide, dye, refining, and rubber. Direct exposure to chemicals in hazardous waste such as mercury and cyanide can be fatal.

Hospital waste

Hospital wastes are generated during the diagnosis, treatment or immunization of human beings or animals or in research activities in these fields or in the production or testing of biologicals. It may include wastes like sharps, soiled waste, disposables, anatomical waste, cultures, discarded medicines, chemical wastes, etc. These are in the form of disposable syringes, swabs, bandages, body fluids, human excreta, etc. This waste is highly infectious and can be a serious threat to human health if not managed in a scientific and discriminate manner. It has been roughly estimated that of the 4 kg of waste generated in a hospital at least 1 kg would be infected. Surveys carried out by various agencies show that the health care establishments in India are not giving due attention to their waste management. After the notification of the bio-medical waste (Handling and Management) Rules, 1998, these establishments are slowly streamlining the process of waste segregation, collection, treatment, and disposal. Many of the larger hospitals have either installed the treatment facilities or are in the process of doing so.

The principal classification of MSW based on physical and chemical properties is given in Table 2.

Table 2 : Classification of municipal solid waste

Types of solid wastes	Description	Sources
Food waste (Garbage)	Waste from preparation, cooking and serving of food. Market refuse, waste from the handling, storage, and sale of produce and meats and vegetables	
Rubbish	Combustible: (Primary organic) paper, card board, cartons, wood, boxes, plastics, rags, cloth, bedding, leather, rubber, grass, leaves, yard trimmings Noncombustible: (Primary inorganic) metals, tin cans, metal foils, dirt, stones, bricks, ceramics, crockery, glass bottles, other mineral refuse	House holds, institutions and commercial such as hotels, stores, restaurants, markets, etc.
Ashes and residues	Residue from fires used for cooking and for heating buildings, cinders, clinkers, thermal power plants	

Contd.

Bulky waste	Large autoparts, tyres, stoves refrigerators, other large appliances, furniture, large crates, trees, branches, palm fronts, stumps, flotage	
Street waste	Street sweepings, dirt, leaves, catch basin dirt, animal droppings, contents of litter receptacles, dead animals	Streets, sidewalks, alleys, vacant lots, etc.
Dead animals	Small animals: cats, dogs, poultry, etc. Large animals: horses, cows, etc.	
Construction and demolition waste	Lumber, roofing and sheathing scraps, crop residues, rubble, broken concrete, plaster, conduit, pipe, wire, insulation, etc.	Construction and demolition waste sites, remodeling, repairing sites
Industrial waste and sludge	Solid waste resulting from industry processes and manufacturing operations, such as food processing wastes boiler house cinders, wood, plastic and metal scrap and shavings, etc. Effluent treatment plant sludge of industries and sewage treatment plant sludges, coarse screening, grit & septic tank	Factories, power plants, treatment plants, etc.
Hazardous waste	Pathological waste, explosives, radioactive material, toxic waste, etc.	House holds, hospitals, institution, stores, industry, etc.
Horticultural waste	Tree-trimmings, leaves, waste from parks and gardens, etc.	Parks, gardens, residue trees, etc.

Source : Bhide and Sundereran (1983)

MSW is heterogeneous in nature and consists of a number of different materials derived from various types of activities. Waste compositions also vary with socio economic status within a particular community (Table 3). Typical municipal solid waste components generated from Indian cities are enlisted in Table 4.

Table 3 : Patterns of composition, characteristics and quantities of MSW

Wastes	Low income countries[1]	Middle income countries[2]	High income countries[3]
Metal	02-0.5	1-5	3-13
Glass, ceramics	0.5-3.5	1-10	4-10
Food and garden waste	40-65	20-60	20-50
Paper	1-10	15-40	15-40
Textiles	1-5	2-10	2-10
Plastics/Rubber	1-5	2-6	2-10
Miscellaneous combustible	1-8	-	-
Miscellaneous incombustible	-	-	-
Inert	20-50	1-30	1-20
Density (kg m^{-3})	250-500	170-330	100-170
Moisture content (% by wt.)	40-80	40-60	20-30
Waste generation (kg $Cap^{-1} day^{-1}$)	04-0.6	0.5-0.9	0.7-1.8

[1] Countries having a per capita income less than US$ 360

[2] Countries having a per capita income between US$ 360-3500

[3] Countries having a per capita income higher than US$ 3500

Source : (Holmes, J: Managing Solid waste in developing countries)

Table 4 : Typical municipal solid waste (MSW) components from Indian cities

Waste components	Percentage
Vegetable, fruit and animal matter	27.0
Dry grass and leaves	5.6
Paper and paper products	10.9
Plastic materials	5.4
Leather, foam and human hair	3.7
Cotton, jute and burlap	6.1
Rubber including cycle and auto tyres	2.9
Metals (tins, iron and aluminum)	2.0
Concrete, pebbles, earth, sands and dust	25.0
Ash and coal	9.0
Wood	0.4
Glass and ceramics	2.0
Total	**100.0**

Source : Sinha and Sinha, (2000)

Characteristics of MSW in Indian urban centers

National Environmental Engineering Research Institute (NEERI) carried out extensive studies on characterization of solid waste from 43 cities during 1970 -1994 and the average physical, chemical and biological characteristics are presented in tables 5, 6 and 7, respectively.

Table 5 : Physical Characteristics of Municipal Solid Waste

Population (million)	No. of cities	Paper	Rubber, Leather, and Synthetics	Glass	Metals	Total compostable matter	Inert
0.1 to 0.5	12	2.91	0.78	0.56	0.33	44.57	43.59
0.5 to 1.0	15	2.95	0.73	0.35	0.32	40.04	48.38
1.0 to 2.0	9	4.71	0.71	0.46	0.49	38.67	44.73
2.0 to 5.0	3	3.18	0.48	0.48	0.59	56.67	49.07
> 5.0	4	6.43	0.28	0.94	0.80	30.84	53.90

Table 6 : Chemical characteristics of Municipal Solid Waste

Population (million)	No. of cities	Moisture (%)	Organic matter (%)	Total Nitrogen (%)	Phosphorous as P_2O_5 (%)	Potassium as K_2O (%)	C:N ratio	Calori-fic value Kcal kg^{-1}
0.1 to 0.5	12	25.81	37.09	0.71	0.63	0.82	30.94	1009.89
0.5 to 1.0	15	19.52	25.14	0.66	0.56	0.69	21.13	900.61
1.0 to 2.0	9	26.98	26.89	0.64	0.82	0.72	23.68	980.05
2.0 to 5.0	3	21.03	25.60	0.56	0.69	0.78	22.45	907.18
> 5.0	4	38.72	39.07	0.56	0.52	0.52	30.11	800.70

Table 7 : Biological properties of Municipal Solid Waste

Biological properties	**Total bacteria count 10^{10}**
Actinomycetes/gm	10^4
Fungi/gm	10^6
Azotobacter/gm	10^6
Root nodule bacteria (*Rhizobium*)	
Phosphate solubilizers	10^6
Nitrobacter/gm	10^2
Chemical properties	
pH	7–8.2
Organic carbon	16.0%
Nitrogen	1.50%
Available phosphorus	1.25%
Potassium	1.05–1.20%
Calcium	1–2%
Magnesium	0.7%
Sulphates	0.5%
Iron	0.6%
Zinc	300–700 ppm
Manganese	250–740 ppm
Copper	200–375 ppm

The characteristics of MSW collected from any area depends on a number of factors such as food habits, cultural traditions of inhabitants, lifestyles, climate, etc. Table 8 below presents the changes in the characteristics of waste in past two decades. The changes in the relative shares of different constituents of waste in the past several decades, as shown by the data, can be attributed largely to changing lifestyles and increasing consumerism.

Table 8 : Physico-chemical characteristics of Municipal Solid Waste

Component	% of wet weight	
	1971-73(40 cities)	1995(23 cities)
Paper	4.14	5.78
Plastics	0.69	3.90
Metals	0.50	1.90
Glass	0.40	2.10
Rags	3.83	3.50
Ash and fine earth	49.20	40.30
Total compostable matter	41.24	41.80
Calorific value (kcal/kg)	800-1100	<1500
Carbon-nitrogen ratio	20-30	25-40

Disposal of waste is a major issue of concern in India. Respective municipalities collect MSW in cities and transport to the designated disposal sites, which is normally a low-lying area on the outskirts of a city. The choice of a disposal site is more a matter of what is available than what is suitable. Only a few cities follow good practices such as organized dumping of wastes, using mechanized equipment for leveling and compacting the wastes, and covering the top layer with earth before compacting it further. Of late, some cities have also started to practice composting the organic fraction of waste.

Impacts of solid waste on health

Modernization and progress has had its share of disadvantages and one of the main aspects of concern is the pollution, it is causing to the earth – be it land, air and water. With increase in the global population and the rising demand for food and other essentials, there has been a rise in the amount of waste being generated daily by each household. This waste is ultimately thrown into municipal waste collection centres from where it is collected by the area municipalities to be further thrown into the landfills and dumps. However, either due to resource crunch or inefficient infrastructure, not all of this waste gets collected and transported to the final dumpsites. If at this stage the management and disposal is improperly done, it can cause serious impacts on health and environmental quality.

Wastes that are not properly managed, especially excreta and other liquid and solid wastes from households and the community, are a serious health hazard and lead to the spread of infectious diseases. Unattended waste lying around attracts flies, rats and other creatures that in turn spread disease. Normally, it is the wet waste that decomposes and releases a bad odour. This leads to unhygienic conditions and thereby to a rise in the health problems. The plague outbreak in Surat is a good example of a city suffering due to the callous attitude of the local body in maintaining cleanliness in the city. Plastic waste is another cause for ill-health. Thus, excessive solid waste that is generated should be controlled by taking certain preventive measures.

The group at risk from the unscientific disposal of solid waste include – the population in areas where there is no proper waste disposal method, especially the pre-school children; waste workers; and workers in facilities producing toxic and infectious material. Other high-risk groups include population living close to a waste dump and those, whose water supply has become contaminated either due to waste dumping or leakage from landfill sites. Uncollected solid waste also increases risk of injury and infection.

In particular, *organic domestic waste* poses a serious threat, since they ferment, creating conditions favorable to the survival and growth of microbial pathogens. Direct handling of solid waste can result in various types of infectious and chronic diseases to the waste workers and the rag pickers being the most vulnerable.

Exposure to hazardous waste can affect human health, children being more vulnerable to these pollutants. In fact, direct exposure can lead to diseases through chemical exposure as the release of chemical waste into the environment leads to chemical poisoning. Many studies have been carried out in various parts of the world to establish a connection between health and hazardous waste.

Waste from agriculture and industries can also cause serious health risks. Other than this, co-disposal of industrial hazardous waste with municipal waste can expose people to chemical and radioactive hazards. Uncollected solid waste can also obstruct storm water runoff, resulting in the forming of stagnant water bodies that become the breeding ground of disease. Waste dumped near a water source also causes contamination of the water body or the ground water source. Direct dumping of untreated waste in rivers, seas, and lakes results in the accumulation of toxic substances in the food chain through the plants and animals that feed on it (Anonymous, 2005a)

Disposal of hospital and other medical waste requires special attention since this can create major health hazards. This waste generated from the hospitals, health care centers, medical laboratories, and research centres such as discarded syringe needles, bandages, swabs, plasters, and other types of infectious waste are often disposed with the regular non-infectious waste.

Waste treatment and disposal sites can also create health hazards for the neighbourhood. Improperly operated incineration plants cause air pollution and improperly managed and designed landfills attract all types of insects and rodents that spread disease. Ideally, these sites should be located at a safe distance from all human settlement. Landfill sites should be well lined and walled to ensure that there is no leakage into the nearby ground water sources.

Recycling too carries health risks if proper precautions are not taken. Workers working with waste containing chemical and metals may experience toxic exposure. Disposal of health-care wastes require special attention since it can create major health hazards, such as Hepatitis B and C, through wounds caused by discarded syringes. Rag pickers and others who are involved in scavenging in the waste dumps for items that can be recycled, may sustain injuries and come into direct contact with these infectious items.

Diseases

Certain chemicals if released untreated, e.g. cyanides, mercury, and polychlorinated biphenyls are highly toxic and exposure can lead to disease or death. Some studies have detected excesses of cancer in residents exposed to hazardous waste. Many studies have been carried out in various parts of the world to establish a connection between health and hazardous waste.

Role of plastics

The unhygienic use and disposal of plastics and its effects on human health has become a matter of concern. Coloured plastics are harmful as their pigment contains heavy metals that are highly toxic. Some of the harmful metals found in plastics are copper, lead, chromium, cobalt, selenium, and cadmium. In most industrialized countries, coloured plastics have been legally banned. In India, the Government of Himachal Pradesh has banned the use of plastics and so has Ladakh district. Other states should emulate their example.

Proper methods of waste disposal have to be undertaken to ensure that it does not affect the environment around the area or cause health hazards to the people living there. Plastic with its exclusive qualities of being light yet strong and economical, has invaded every aspect of our day-to-day life. It has many advantages: it is durable, light, easy to mould, and can be adapted to different user requirements. Once hailed as a 'wonder material', plastic is now a serious worldwide environmental and health concern, essentially due to its non biodegradable nature. In India, the plastic industry is growing phenomenally. Plastics are used in all sectors of the economy – infrastructure, construction, agriculture, consumer goods, telecommunications, and packaging. But the good news is that along with a growth in the use, a country-wide network for collection of plastic waste through rag pickers, waste collectors and waste dealers and recycling enterprises has sprung all over the country over the last decade or so. More than 50% of the plastic waste generated in the country is recycled and used in the manufacture of various plastic products.

Conventional plastics have been associated with reproductive problems in both wildlife and humans. Studies have shown a decline in human sperm count and quality, genital abnormalities and a rise in the incidence of breast cancer. Dioxin a highly carcinogenic and toxic by-product of the manufacturing process of plastics, is one of the chemicals believed to be passed on through breast milk to the nursing infant. Burning of plastics, especially PVC releases this dioxin and also furan into the atmosphere. Thus, conventional plastics, right from their manufacture to their disposal are a major problem to the environment.

Plastics are so versatile in use that their impacts on the environment are extremely wide ranging. Careless disposal of plastic bags chokes drains, blocks the porosity of the soil and causes problems for groundwater recharge. Plastic disturbs the soil microbe activity, and once ingested, can kill animals. Plastic bags can also contaminate foodstuffs due to leaching of toxic dyes and transfer of pathogens. In fact, a major portion of the plastic bags i.e. approximately 60-80% of the plastic waste generated in India is collected and segregated to be recycled. The rest remains strewn on the ground, littered around in open drains, or in unmanaged garbage dumps. Though, only a small percentage lies strewn, it is this portion that is of concern as it causes extensive damage to the environment.

The plastic industry in the developed world has realized the need of environmentally acceptable modes for recycling plastics wastes and has set out targets and missions. Prominent among such missions are the Plastic Waste Management Institute in Japan, the European Centre for Plastics in Environment, the Plastic Waste Management Task Force in Malaysia. Manufacturers, civic authorities, environmentalists and the public have begun to acknowledge the need for plastics to conform to certain guidelines/standards and code of conduct for its use.

Designing eco-friendly, biodegradable plastics is the need of the hour. Though, partially biodegradable plastics have been developed and used, completely biodegradable plastics based on renewable starch rather than petrochemicals have only recently been developed and are in the early stages of commercialization (Anonymous, 2005b).

Functional elements of MSW

The activities associated with the management of MSW from the point of generation to final disposal can be grouped into six functional elements;

Waste generation
↓
Waste handling, Sorting, Storage and processing at the source
↓
Collection
↓
Sorting, Processing and Transformation of solid waste
↓
Transfer and transport
↓
Disposal

Source of generation of waste plastics

Household

Carry bags
Bottles
Containers
Trash bags

Health and Medicare

Disposable syringes
Glucose bottles
Blood and uro bags
Intravenous tubes
Catheters
Surgical gloves

Hotel and catering

Packaging items
Mineral water bottles
Plastic plates, glasses, spoons

Air / rail travel

Mineral water bottles
Plastic plates, glasses, spoons

Waste management options

The current options available for management of solid wastes are as follows :

Waste management options	Option components
Source reduction / reuse	The collection and disposal / recovery of many packaging materials such as boxes, wrappings, pellets, and other dunn age may be avoided through source reduction and reuse activities
Recycling	Some paper, glass, metal, plastic, and other materials, (including textiles, batteries, motor oil, appliances, and tires) may be collected and recovered at appropriate residential and commercial recycling facilities
Composting	Leaves, grass, brush, wood waste, and even food waste may be collected and composted at appropriate facilities. Many of these materials may be home composted as well.
Incineration	Disposing of solid waste through an appropriate incineration facility with possible energy recovery. Ash residue would be disposed of at an appropriate land fill within or outside the community.
Land filling	Disposing of solid waste at an appropriate landfill within or outside the community.

Among the options, waste minimization or reduction at source is of prime importance followed by material recycling, waste processing, waste transformation and land filling. There is a growing concern on the value addition of waste both by waste recycling and transformation to energy rich commodities.

Recycling and reuse

Recycling involves the collection of used and discarded materials; processing these materials; and making them into new products. It reduces the amount of waste that is thrown into the community dustbins thereby making the environment cleaner and the air more fresh to breathe. Surveys carried out by Government and non-government agencies in the country have all recognized the importance of recycling wastes. However, the methodology for safe recycling of waste has not been standardized. Studies have revealed that 7-15% of the waste is recycled. If recycling is done in a proper manner, it will solve the problems of waste or garbage. At the community level, a large number of NGOs (Non Governmental Organizations) and private sector enterprises have taken an initiative in segregation and recycling of waste (EXNORA International in Chennai recycles a large part of the waste that is collected). It is being used for composting, making pellets to be used in gasifiers, etc. Plastics are sold to the factories that reuse them.

The steps involved in the process prior to recycling include :

(*a*) Collection of waste from doorsteps, commercial places, etc.

(*b*) Collection of waste from community dumps.

(*c*) Collection/picking up of waste from final disposal sites.

Most of the garbage generated in the household can be recycled and reused. Organic kitchen waste such as leftover foodstuff, vegetable peels, and spoilt or dried fruits and vegetables can be recycled by putting them in the compost pits that have been dug in the garden. Old newspapers, magazines and bottles can be sold to the *kabadiwala*, the man who buys these items from homes.

In your own homes you can contribute to waste reduction and the recycling and reuse of certain items. To cover you books you can use old calendars; old greeting cards can also be reused. Paper can also be made at home through a very simple process and you can paint on them.

The schematic diagram (Fig. 2) below depicts recycling of wastes.

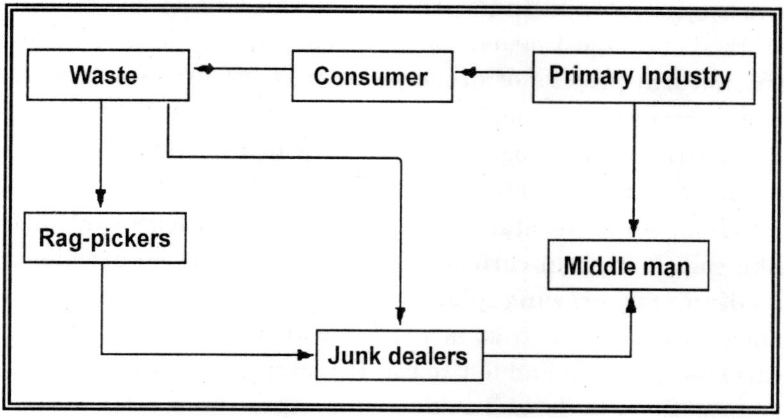

Fig. 2 : Recycling of Wastes

Waste recycling has some significant advantages. It

- leads to reduced usage of raw materials,
- reduces environmental impacts arising from waste treatment and disposal,

- makes the surroundings cleaner and healthier,
- saves on landfill space,
- saves money, and
- reduces the amount of energy required to manufacture new products.

In fact, recycling can prevent the creation of waste at the source (Anonymous. 2005c)

Composting

Composting is a biological conversion of heterogeneous organic substrate under controlled conditions into hygienic humus-rich and relatively biostable product that conditions soils and nourishes plants.

Organic matter constitutes 35–40% of the municipal solid waste generated in India. This waste can be recycled by the method of composting, one of the oldest forms of disposal. It is the natural process of decomposition of organic waste that yields manure or compost, which is very rich in nutrients. Composting is a biological process in which micro-organisms, mainly fungi and bacteria, convert degradable organic waste into humus like substance. This finished product, which looks like soil, is high in carbon and nitrogen and is an excellent medium for growing plants. The process of composting ensures the waste that is produced in the kitchens is not carelessly thrown and left to rot. It recycles the nutrients and returns them to the soil as nutrients. Apart from being clean, cheap, and safe, composting can significantly reduce the amount of disposable garbage. The organic fertilizer can be used instead of chemical fertilizers and is better specially when used for vegetables. It increases the soil's ability to hold water and makes the soil easier to cultivate. It helps the soil retain more of the plant nutrients.

The organic fraction of MSW (less plastic, rubber and leather) is converted into an earthy, humus-like, material by the action of bacteria and other microbes.

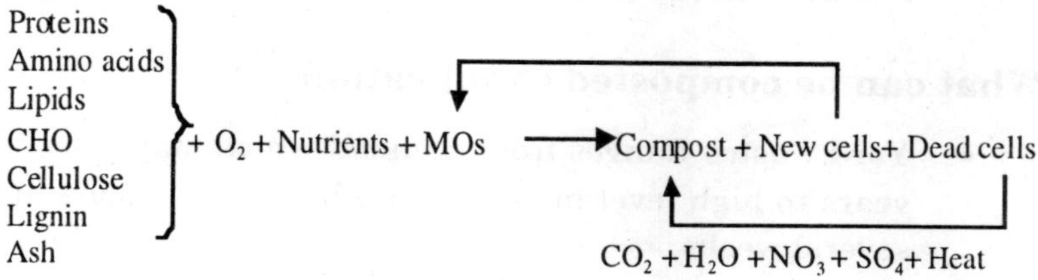

Some benefits of composting are :

- Compost allows the soil to retain more plant nutrients over a longer period.
- It supplies part of the 16 essential elements needed by the plants.
- It helps reduce the adverse effects of excessive alkalinity, acidity, or the excessive use of chemical fertilizer.
- It makes soil easier to cultivate.
- It helps keep the soil cool in summer and warm in winter.
- It aids in preventing soil erosion by keeping the soil covered.
- It helps in controlling the growth of weeds in the garden (Anonymous, 2005a).

Objectives of composting

- Convert the MSW into a biologically stable material which is reduced in volume.
- Destroy unwanted biologicals: pathogens, weeds, insect eggs.

- Retain the maximum nutrient (N, P, K).
- To produce a valuable, soil amendment product. Not a fertilizer. Lousy C : N ratio.

What can be composted (Applications) ?

- Yard wastes Ranges from minimal which may take 3 years to high level in container which can be done in several weeks.
- MSW (organic fraction) : Metals or household hazardous waste can easily contaminate the compost. If a high quality product is desired, source separation is a must.
- MSW (commingled, partially processed) : Not suitable as a gardener's compost; use as an intermediate cover if allowed.
- MSW (with sewer sludge) : May avoid sludge dewatering. Increases the nutrient and moisture contents of the mix; may also contain heavy metals, MSW: sludge is recommended as a starting point.

There are a variety of parameters used to assess both compostable feedstock's and to classify finished compost product. These include criteria such as pH, electrical conductivity (to measure salt content), heavy metal concentrations, pathogen levels, presence of physical contaminants, toxin levels, nutrient concentrations (such as C:N ratio) and particle size. Processing methods used to produce compost will largely be determined by the nature of the feedstock's used and are ideally selected to minimize as many potential problems as possible.

The choice of preprocessing techniques such as manual or mechanical sorting, screening, separation and grinding depends upon the need to remove contaminants from feedstock's and to reduce or homogenize particle size. Complex feedstock's containing high levels of contamination require a greater degree of preprocessing before they can be composted. C:N ratio can be manipulated by mixing feedstock's of different ratios. pH may be adjusted by adding acidic materials (such as fruit residue) to alkaline feedstock's or by adding basic amendments (such as lime) to acidic feedstock's. Feedstock's containing large pieces of organic matter need to be ground before they can be processed. Collection methods of some feedstock material (especially MSW) affect their nature and composition and should be considered.

Selection of feedstock's and processing methods are also determined, in part, by the intended end-use of the compost product. For example, compost destined for use in food production must be free from unwanted components than compost used for non-agricultural purposes such as landfill cover or the reclamation of disturbed soils. Given the wide range of compostable materials available, testing of both feedstock's and finished materials by environmental or soil laboratories are recommended on a regular basis to ensure product quality. Reference to the applicable sections of this resource guide will assist managers of composting operations in optimizing the composting process to produce a product suitable for the markets they have developed.

Where did the Composting Tradition Begin?

Most traditional societies recognized the wisdom and practical benefits of composting. References have been found pertaining to compost dating to ancient Mesopotamian, Israelite, Greek and Roman civilizations. Arab scholars and Christian monks helped keep ancient appreciation for composting alive during the Middle Ages in Europe. The

Chinese have been returning their organic wastes (including human fecal material) to soil for millennia. This fact has been used to help explain how they have been able to keep their farmlands productive for thousands of years. In more primitive societies, compost heaps may have provided the additional benefit of being the "first source of beneficial fire for mankind" given their ability to generate heat and, occasionally, fire.

More recently, many of the founding fathers of the United States were advocates of composting. George Washington and Thomas Jefferson were both farmers who conducted composting experiments. Washington constructed a special building at Mount Vernon, called a "stercorary", used for the collection and composting of manures. Jefferson developed the practice of mixing manures with muck (natural organic residues taken from waterlogged environments). James Madison eloquently summed up the idea of the "Law of Return" (i.e. the returning of nutrient-rich organic wastes to the soil) when he said:

> "Nothing is more certain that continual cropping without manure deprives the soil of its fertility. It is equally certain that fertility may be preserved or restored by giving to the earth animal or vegetable manure equivalent to the matter taken from it. That restoration to the earth of all that naturally grows on it prevents its impoverishment is sufficiently seen in our forests where the annual exuviae of the trees and plants replace the fertility of which they deprived the earth." [Minnich *et al.*, 1979]

The term "manure" is used above in the widest sense, referring not only to human and animal excrement, but also to other organic materials (such as crop residues that have fertilizing capabilities).

How did Composting become an Industrial Process?

Many of the traditional examples of composting mentioned above were probably more akin to “natural decomposition” of wastes collected and randomly piled together than to modern “controlled composting”. One of the first people to develop a systematic methodology for large-scale composting was Sir Albert Howard, a British scientist trained in mycology and interested in the relationship between soil health and plant disease. Sir Howard had traveled widely to study traditional farming systems, and while in India between the years 1924 and 1931, developed a composting process inspired by his research. It involved the placement of organic materials (mostly crop residues and manures) in long, shallow pits or in six feet high piles (Howard,1947). Since the residues were turned infrequently, composting by his method was largely anaerobic. The process was later modified to an aerobic process. Sir Howard noticed the need to aerate (or turn) compost piles to keep their interiors from developing anaerobic conditions. He (along with others of his time) began to recognize the potential of composting for disinfecting urban wastes and transforming them into an amendment capable of replenishing soil humus.

The rapid expansion of urban areas in the early twentieth century necessitated more rapid processing of wastes. Mechanized systems were developed to aid in refuse handling and in the acceleration of the composting process (especially by pre-processing techniques such as shredding and mixing). Giovanni Beccari, of Italy, was the first to patent a mechanical process.

The composting of municipal wastes grew most rapidly in Europe where arable land was scarcer and where several governments provided financial support for state-run operations. The first full-scale composting facility was opened in the Netherlands in 1932 . This facility employed a low-technology process using overhead cranes to arrange and turn under ground wastes. Several other European composting plants were successfully operating before World War II, and by 1950s composting was widely recognized in Europe as a viable solution to the growing waste problem.

The composting industry developed later in the United States. Research had been conducted as early as the 1880's [Epstein, 1997], and early twentieth century conservationists and proponents of sustainable agriculture issued solemn warnings about the perils of organic matter depletion in soils (especially after the Dust Bowl problems of the 1930's). However, composting did not receive widespread public support until much later. The growing complexity of early modern American cities made the retrieval of organic wastes difficult. Large distances between urban and agricultural areas (and the enormous size of some farms themselves) presented obstacles to both the transportation of wastes and the application of finished product. Emphasis of the agricultural industry on the chemical strength of synthetic fertilizers (and neglect of the physical and biological benefits of compost) acted as a further disincentive to the establishment of large-scale composting enterprises. Nuisance concerns and public fears of potential problems arising from the inappropriate application of compost also dissuaded authorities from encouraging composting on a large scale.

During 1980's onwards, the circumstances became more favorable to the growth of the compost industry as a whole. Greater environmental awareness and a desire to divert organic wastes from increasingly strained waste management systems led policy makers to encourage and support the composting alternative. Economic changes (such as increased costs involved in land filling wastes) have made composting more competitive and viable solution. Air pollution controls now seriously limit incineration as an option in many regions. Today, many municipalities are separating organic materials out of MSW (municipal solid wastes) in an effort to reduce their disposal costs and extend the life of their landfills.

The combined efforts of many other industry, scientific and governmental agencies and professionals have helped to improve the engineering of processing facilities and to understand the factors involved in composting such as microbial processes, pathogen control and heavy metal uptake by plants. Continued research and development will ensure the future success of composting operations.

Is large-scale composting always practical and profitable?

As the compost industry has expanded, so have the possibilities to profit from composting enterprises. Waste generators and municipalities are finding they can save money by decreasing their disposal costs, and they are finding ready markets for the compost they are generating. Gardeners, landscapers and farmers alike, are all rediscovering the potential compost has in improving their soils, and they are willing to pay for it. As a result, compost markets are blossoming and opening up new opportunities for composters. Revenues from the sale of compost are helping operators to become more self-supporting. Even where composting is not a profit-generating venture, it is a valuable service to the community and can obviate the disposal costs involved in other waste management schemes.

Composting has yet to be fully utilized in the reclamation of all of the organic byproducts generated by modern societies. Some potential suppliers to the composting industry are not currently converting unwanted organic materials into compost. Where they are not already being composted, more efficient use can be made of a wide range of organic materials including (but not limited to) agricultural and horticultural wastes, animal carcasses, manure from livestock operations, slaughterhouse wastes, fishery and aquaculture wastes, food processing residues, viticulture pomace, papermill sludge, non-salvageable paper and cardboard, unusable fabrics, cotton gin trash, wool and leather processing residuals, municipal wastes and biosolids.

Composting is a form of recycling. Recycling is encouraged by both state and federal waste management authorities. It is second in preference only to "source reduction" in waste management hierarchies. Reclamation of wastes is usually considered more desirable than disposal of wastes (as by land filling or incineration). Composting is now widely accepted as a viable alternative to the disposal of organic material and has become a key component in "integrated" waste management strategies. In an effort to promote the composting of organic materials, many local governments are offering incentive programs and grants to composters and potential suppliers of organic material.

Within the composting industry, better engineered systems and an expanded industry infrastructure are helping to make composting on a large scale more economically viable. Research on the composting process over the past few decades has clarified many of the factors involved in compost production, thus improving operational efficiency. Better understanding of the nature of compost has also helped to validate the benefits and inherent safety of agricultural and horticultural applications of compost. Educational programs promoting the values of composting and a growing environmental awareness in general are both increasing public acceptance of this ancient art form. Finally, the need for quality organic amendments by a diverse group of potential compost users is helping to ensure a market for the compost produced. Compost is of proven value on farms, in nurseries, in landscaping and forestry operations, to golf and turf managers, in parks and public grounds operated by municipalities and to homeowners. Compost not suitable for cultivation of crops may still be of use in erosion control, bioremediation, and land reclamation and even as an alternate daily cover (ADC) in landfill operations.

Increased governmental promotion, industry support, scientific validation, economic viability, public acceptance and demonstrated need in sustainable soil management all bode well for the future of the composting industry. Nevertheless, there are many concerns which potential composters must take into consideration before starting an operation. Plans to initiate a composting enterprise must be well thought out in advance and include overall goals, financing methods, design criteria, siting requirements, management techniques, availability of feedstock's and market potentials. Large scale composting is a business and requires time and money. Equipment, labor and management needs must be addressed before any composting operation can become successful. Local and regional considerations (such as proximity to residential or business districts and weather patterns) can affect the placement and management of a composting facility and must be accounted for. Before a product is generated, strategies must be in place for its marketing and distribution. Potential sources of competition should be analyzed (especially in areas where disposal alternatives for organic materials are relatively inexpensive). A composter must also be able to handle public concerns, which can arise in spite of growing acceptance for the composting industry as a whole. Nuisance and environmental concerns such as odor, noise, dust, vectors, runoff, litter and visual aesthetics need to be dealt with effectively, particularly when a composting facility is located near where people live and/or work.

In composting ventures, as in any business, special concerns unique to the individual enterprise will arise and require appropriate handling. With wise planning and good management practices, many potential obstacles to a successful operation can be avoided. This resource guide is intended to provide potential and existing composters with the tools needed to maintain a profitable, efficient and safe operation in this vital and growing industry.

Methods of composting

The Indore Method

The Indore method was developed by Howard and Wad (1931), at Indore. This method requires a heap of trapezoidal cross section. The heap is about 4 m to 5 m in length, 1 m in breadth and 1 m in height. The heap is alternatively layered with carbonaceous and nitrogenous wastes, starting with 20 cm of carbon rich and 10 cm of nitrogen rich material. Finally it is covered with soil or hay as thermal insulator. Under these conditions, the rate of decomposition is very rapid and high temperature develops quickly. The process is accelerated by periodically turning the materials. In this method, losses of organic matter and nitrogen are very high, amounting to 50 to 60% of the initial levels.

The Bangalore Method

Acharya (1939), developed the Bangalore Method to produce compost from city refuse and night soil in pits. Pits of about 1 m depth, breadth and length are used. In this process, at first the refuse is dumped into the trench and spread out with rakes to make a layer of 15 cm. Night soil is then discharged and spread over the refuse in a layer of about 5 cm. This is then covered with 15 cm layer of refuse. The night soil and the refuse thus follow in alternate layers until the pit is filled to 15 cm above ground level, with a final layer of refuse on the top. This may be dome-shaped and covered with a thin layer of soil. The decomposition of dumped materials in the pit takes place large in the absence of air except in the surface layer. This anaerobic decomposition is comparatively slow but markedly less wasteful.

High temperature compost

High temperature compost is prepared from night soil, urine, sewage and animal dung and chopped plant residues at a ratio of 1:4. The materials are heaped in alternate layers starting with chopped plants stalks and followed by human and animal wastes. Water is added to optimum amount.

At the time of making the heap, a number of bamboo poles are inserted for aeration purposes. After the heap formation, it is sealed with 3 cm of mud plaster. The bamboo poles are withdrawn after one day of composting, leaving the holes for aeration of the heap. Within four to five days, the temperature rises to 60 to 70 °C and the holes are then sealed. The first sealing is usually done after 2 weeks and the moisture is made up with water or animal or human excreta; the turned heap is again sealed with mud. The compost is ready for use within two months and is considered free from pathogens.

Windrow composting

The windrow composting is a traditional and widely practiced method of composting in USA (Kychenrither *et al.*, 1984). In this process, the waste materials are piled in long rows of 2 to 4 m width and 1 to 2 m height on a hard surface and usually in the open area. Aeration of the windrow is by periodic turning using equipment such as front-end loader or by specially designed machinery. Occasionally, forced aeration in conjunction with turning has been applied to the windrow process.

Static pile composting

In static pile method of composting a mixture of solid wastes is stockpiled in the open air and turned occasionally for aeration. This technology is considered to waste both ammonia and energy. But these disadvantages have been substantially mitigated by mechanical forcing of air through perforated pipes at the bottom of the static pile by (a) Continuous air suction, or (b) continuous air blowing or (c) alternate air blowing or (d) alternate blowing and sucking or (e) intermittent air blowing to keep the temperature below 60°C. There are two kinds of static pile composting system. One, the Beltsville process in which piles are aerated by time controlled system (Willson *et al*., 1980). Another, the Rutgers process, involves blowing air through the compost mass in response to a thermistor and fan both controlled by a microcomputer to maintain temperatures below 60°C (Finstein *et al*., 1980). In the enclosed mechanical composting system, the process takes place in a vessel or bio-reactor. Advantages of these systems are that external environmental factors do not affect the process, less land is required and that better odour and operational control are possible. Disadvantages are that these systems require high equipment, maintenance and energy costs.

Synthetic compost

In the preparation of synthetic compost, the organic nitrogen in the form of dung required by micro-organisms can be completely substituted with inorganic nitrogen compounds like ammonium sulphate or urea which are utilized with equal effectiveness for decomposition of carbonaceous materials into compost. This facilitates utilization of large quantities of various organic waste materials where supplies of dung are limited or not available at all as in mechanized farms. The manure becomes ready for application in about 4 to 6 months (Gaur and Sadasivam, 1993).

Accelerated composting and enrichment

The conventional method of composting takes a long time to produce quality compost. In order to hasten the process and to improve the quality of the end product, the material to be composted is inoculated with microbes such as celluloytic, ligninolytic, and nitrogen fixing and phosphate solubilizing micro-organisms. Addition of sources of nitrogen and phosphorus may also be desirable when the materials to be composted lack much of these elements. The best additive for a compost mix is to add mature compost that will produce a suitable starting population throughout the composting mass and furnish bioavailable minor elements essential to life.

The development and implementation of both types of composting (aerobic and vermicomposting) is well documented in India, and the use of composting has attracted a great deal of attention from those outside the South Asian region. Reliance on composting is perhaps a case of necessity being the mother of invention. Indian cities, particularly megacities, are fraught with the challenge of dealing with increasing reams of garbage. Kitchen waste, as well as organic waste from industry (food service, hotels, and slaughterhouses) is being composted in schemes of various scales throughout the country though there is certainly potential to further the practice, given India's vast amounts of organic waste. The nutrient rich compost is then used to grow fruits and vegetables – much of it being sold to farmers in rural areas and peri-urban areas. It is unknown to what extent compost is being purchased by urban householders for their own gardens, but it is clear that many city farmers, such as Dr. R.T. Doshi, are producing compost for their own use. Composting can therefore potentially be a significant livelihood activity for urbanites. Currently, all types of composting appear to be well developed in *rural* India.

Examples from Mumbai, Pune and Bangalore are the most prominent places for various types of composting activities. A special issue of the *Worm Digest* published in Oregon, details many vermicomposting initiatives in a short, accessible and easy to read format.

Government Agencies

There is one arm of government that needs to be profiled here. The very existence of the Karnataka Compost Development Corporation is a testimony to the importance of vermiculture within the state. The KCDC manufactures compost from city wastes. They supply compost in the city for kitchen gardens through a mobile unit and they also have dealers in the city and other nurseries that sell their compost.

In a recent publication by Inge Lardinois and Rogier Marchand (Bidlingmaier and Scheelhaase, 1999), it was found that KCDC's plant on the outskirts of Bangalore was producing 27 tonnes of compost per day. Despite this remarkable figure, the KCDC's output only accounts for 1.5% of organic waste composted in and around Bangalore.

Civil Society Organisations

There are a number of prominent civil society organisations that have advanced the cause of promoting worm composting in urban areas. In Mumbai the work of Prakruti and the Institute for Natural and Organic Agriculture has drawn widespread attention, as have the relentless efforts of Shantu Shenai of the Green Cross Society and SOS (Save Our Selves).

In Bangalore, the work of Waste Wise, led by Anselm Rosario and Agriculture Man Ecology (in consort with ETC Netherlands) are examples of civil society organisations active in waste management in general and composting in particular. Swabhimana and Civic are other prominent examples of community-based organisations working to promote urban sustainability through effective waste-management.

Exnora (an acronym of Excellent, Novel and Radical Ideas) was founded in 1989. The organisation has been extensively involved in promoting effective solid waste management at the community level. All their schemes revolve around extensive public participation in community-ownership. There are now more than 3000 community-based Exnora "chapters", known as Civic Exnoras, which promote integrated SWM involving rag pickers (scavengers), separation at source and extensive composting of organic waste.

According to Exnora:

> The households in this street have formed a Civic Exnora. Every house segregates their waste at source. The Civic Exnoras has distributed a green colour basket to every household, into which the residents store organic wastes. The street beautifier collects these wastes in one compartment of his tricycle, and the other inorganic recyclable waste in another. The organic wastes are converted to manure through aerobic composting, which is used in their own gardens. The street beautifier separates inorganic waste, sells it to waste buyers and earns an additional income. A small quantity of waste that cannot be recovered is transported to secondary collection points for collection by the Municipal authorities.

Exnora is also involved in a program in Cochin (Kotchi) the largest city in the State of Kerala. This Solid Waste Management program is a joint project of the Corporation of Cochin, Greater Cochin Development Authority (GCDA), Institutions of Engineers, Rotary and Exnora with the support of Indian Express and Mathru Bhumi. The scheme involves separation at source (i.e. the household level), the development of a municipal composting facility resulting in the construction of a three-chambered compost shed.

The composting process in the shed takes about 20 days and involves "inoculation of organic waste by a bacterium called 'garbactum' by spraying, or by mixing with bio-dung. The process does not generate foul orders and the resulting soil conditioner is given to local farmers, gardeners and other agriculturists.

With respect to all of the civil society initiatives described above, there is a need for further research to quantify production, processing, and marketing. Also, the effectiveness of the above schemes needs to be fully evaluated.

In composting ventures, as in any business, special concerns unique to the individual enterprise will arise and require appropriate handling. With wise planning and good management practices, many potential obstacles to a successful operation can be avoided. This resource guide is intended to provide potential and existing composters with the tools needed to maintain a profitable, efficient and safe operation in this vital and growing industry. There are several approaches for the testing of compost quality of which few are more important.

Qualitative tests for composts

i. Humification

ii. Respirometer

iii. Spectroscopic and

iv. Plant growth tests

(i) Humification parameters

It is based on the fact that during composting low molecular components are converted into heavy molecular humus like product. Hence, increase in humic substances is associated with stabilisation of organic matter. The following parameters are applied to evaluate the humification of organic matter in compost.

Humic acid per cent = C_{ha} / C_{ex} x100

Where, C_{ha} - Carbon content in humic acid fraction

C_{ex} - Carbon content in alkali extract

Humificaion index (HI) = NH/HA + FA

Where NH – organic carbon content in the non humified fraction

HA and FA - Organic carbon content in the humified (Humic acid and fulvic acid) fractions

Degree of humification (DH)

DH % = HA + FA / TEC X 100

Where, TEC – organic carbon content in the alkali extract

Humification ratio = Cex / C_o X 100

Where, C ex - Carbon content in alkali extract

C_o - Oxidizable carbon content

Humification rate (HR)

HR % = HA + FA / TOC X 100

Where TOC, Total organic carbon content in the solids

Polymerization ratio = $\frac{\text{Carbon in fulvic acid}}{\text{Carbon in humic acid}}$

(ii) Respirometery

Changes in compost stability or degree to which composts have been decomposed can be predicted with oxygen respirometry. In this method, maturity is predicted based on the rate of oxygen uptake per kg of volatile solids per hour. The oxygen uptake rate is determined with dissolved oxygen respirometery.

$$\text{Mean oxygen uptake} = \frac{\text{-C .V.S. 60. D}}{\text{K. Wt. V.S}}$$

Where C – Oxygen content by volume in the air, usually 0.2%

V – Volume of air in the flask (ml)

S – Slope of relative oxygen uptake rate (% saturation min)

D – The density of the oxygen (gL^{-1}) at experimental conditions is converted from STP.

60 – Factor change from minutes to hours.

K – Compost dry matter weight in flask (g)

V_s – The fraction of volatile solids (from 0 to 1)

The respiration bioassay is to determine the stability of municipal solid waste composts. The oxygen uptake rate has been found to decrease with age of the composts indicating the depletion of biodegradable organic material which is essential for microbial growth.

(iii) Spectroscopic Analysis

Compost maturity discussed above is related to the degree to which fresh organic matter has been transformed into a stable end product. Recently, tests have been developed to determine the amount of stable organic end products which are lignin and humic substances. These procedures do not distinguish residual biodegradable carbon from that resistant to biological decomposition. Hence, it is essential to analyze the bulk organic matter. The quantitative procedures developed to study the bulk organic matter are solid state Cross Polarization Magic Angle Spinning ^{13}C-Nuclear Magnetic Resonance (CPMAS ^{13}C – NMR) and Infra Red (IR) spectroscopy (Inbar *et al.*, 1990). A $^{13}CNMR$ spectrum can provide carbon "finger prints" of various solid samples such as peats, whole soils and humic substances *etc*. IR spectroscopy indicates the transformation of organic matter during composting. Therefore, with these spectroscopic procedures, it is possible to develop direct correlations between maturity and

i) The rate of decomposition of biodegradable components during the composting process,

ii) The potential for re-growth in compost of pathogens,

iii) Biocontrol of plant diseases,

iv) Plant growth response and

v) Heavy metals and complexes.

Unfortunately, these studies require sophisticated and expensive equipment.

(iv) Plant growth response test

Blanco and Almendros (1995), assessed the factors potentially connected with the positive or depressive effect of composts in soil by involving mineral fertilization and successive harvesting of rye grass. Based on the results obtained, they have concluded that the most classical maturity indices (germination index, water soluble organic fraction, spectroscopic analysis of water extracts) applied to straw composts have limited diagnostic value as regards forecasting plant yield. These parameters may have applicability in differentiating raw materials from those subjected to composting, but they do not correlate with the crop yield when different composts are simultaneously evaluated.

Compost

Physical	**Chemical**	**Biological**
1 Particle size *	1 pH * ■	1 Microbes *
2 Colour*	2 EC *■	2 Annelids
3 Moisture *	3 C/N ratio *■	3 Worms
4 Porosity	4 Nitrogen test *	4 Collembola
5 Bulk density	5 Sulphur test *	5 Aerobes
6 Water holding capacity	6 Starch – Iodine test *	6 Anaerobes
7 Temperature	7 Heavy metals	7 Thermophiles
8 Total solids	8 Pesticide residues	8 Pathogenic microbes ■
9 Volatile solids	9 Plant nutrient content *■	9 Verticillium test *
10 Total ash content	10 Cellulose	10 Amoena
	11 Lignin	11 Plant growth response test *
	12 Protein	
	13 CEC *■	
	14 Humification index	
	15 Organic acids content	
	16 Solid state ^{13}C NMR Spectroscopy □	
	17 Infra Red Spectroscopy □	
	18 Analyses of water extract □	

Regular tests * Quality control tests ■ Quick screening □

Methods to evaluate maturity of compost

- Mature compost should have a tea brown colour, no noxious smell and a good stability which would no longer produce high temperatures.
- The maximum diameter should not exceed 10 mm, with 5 mm as the optimum and the water holding capacity should be below 30%.
- The most common pH values range between 6.5 and 8.0. Compatibility with plant growth is within the range of 5.5 to 8.0. If pH values are higher or lower than the above mentioned range, the reason for that should be specified.
- Total salinity should not exceed 2 g salt L^{-1} (expressed as NaCl) and the concentration of sodium and chloride ions should be specified in mature composts.
- Irrespective of the sources of composting mass, C/N ratio of the mature compost should be less than 20 and cation exchange capacity should be more than 70 meq $100g^{-1}$ of ash free material.
- Absence of transitory or permanent bioinhibiting factors such as ammonium, water soluble aliphatic acids, amino acids, proteins and polysaccharides in the water extract of compost indicates the maturity of compost.
- Decomposition of the organic matter involves both mineralization and humification. Hence, formation of water insoluble humus is a characteristic of complete decomposition of organic matter. At least 10 per cent of the total organic carbon present in the original material should be humified at the end of the composting.

- A good quality compost should contain minimum levels of toxic components and non-biodegradable materials.
- Composting process should give complete inactivation of *Salmonella sp* in infected eggs of parasites (*Ascaris* as indicator organism), a reduction of four logs of paravirus and fecal *Streptococci* (indicator micro-organism for bacteria) and five logs of Enterobacteria.

A marketed compost should posses the following specifications on the label.

- Origin
- Composition
- Moisture content
- pH
- Electrical conductivity
- C:N ratio
- Cation exchange capacity
- Organic matter content
- Mineral nutrients content
- Heavy metals concentration, and
- Inert materials.

Issues with composting facilities

- Odours. Usually caused by : Wide C:N ratio- Poor temperature control- Excessive moisture.
- Poor mixing : Can be controlled with various towers and facilities and odor-masking agents and enzymes.
- Pathogens : Usually destroyed by normal composting parameters of 55°C for 15-20 days.

- Heavy metals : Particles are created when the waste is shredded and these particles may become attached to the lighter fractions.
- Definition of acceptable compost.

Management of biomedical waste is another issue of concern for municipalities. This waste produced in hospitals generally has high contamination of pathogens, making it hazardous. It also includes scalpels, needles, bandages and other wastes from operating theatres and laboratories as well as infectious items, e.g. amputated body-parts, body fluids, cultures of contagious viruses, excreta from patients with highly contagious diseases, etc. Though waste from hospitals and nursing homes are required to be collected and treated separately, in most cities and towns such waste continues to form a part of the MSW in absence of any dedicated disposal facilities for hospital waste. The MoEF, Government of India has issued the Municipal Solid Wastes (management and handling) Rules in the year 2000, which identify the CPCB (Central Pollution Control Board) as the agency to monitor the implementation of these rules. For the management of bio-medical waste, the MoEF has notified Bio-Medical Waste (management and handling) Rules in 1998 under sections 6, 8 and 25 of the Environment (Protection) Act of 1986.

Compost (final produce) exceeding the concentration limits stated as below, shall not be used for food crops. However, it may be utilized for purposes other than growing food crops. Ministry of Environment & Forests – Municipal Solid Waste (Management & Handling) Rules under the Environment Protection Act of 1986 has made it mandatory for all municipalities to set up waste process and disposal facilities by 01.12.2003, and has also laid down standards for composition and concentration limits of MSW compost, which can be used for food crops.

Ministry of Environment & Forests vide gazette notification S.O.908 (E) dated 03.10.2000 has set guidelines and maximum permissible limits of heavy metals and impurities as per following table, which need to be followed for selling urban compost for production of food

Parameter	Maximum permitted concentration (mg kg^{-1} dry basis)
Arsenic	10.00
Cadmium	5.00
Chromium	50.00
Copper	300.00
Lead	100.00
Mercury	0.15
Nickel	50.00
Zinc	1000.00
C:N ratio	20:40
pH	5.5-8.5

MSW after segregation by the local community along with the recovery of a valuable resource in the form of compost. The non-biodegradable materials in the un-segregated wastes which do not decompose are usually separated mechanically and from them some recyclable components are retrieved. The balance residue in the form of inert materials is safely disposed in an adjacent landfill site (Coad, 1997). The technology was developed by Ms. Excel Industries, Mumbai, India. The Mumbai Municipal Corporation (MMC) is participating in the project by providing a part of a dump yard on lease and required delivery of garbage onto this waste dump site. The MMC takes 25% royalty on the sale of the compost which is marketed in the trade.

Land fill

The basis of a good solid waste management system is the municipal solid waste (MSW) landfill. MSW landfills provide for the environmentally sound disposal of waste that cannot be reduced, recycled, composted, combusted, or processed in some other manner. A landfill is needed for disposing of residues from recycling, composting, combustion or other processing facilities and can be used if the alternative facilities break down.

The central government sets minimum national standards applicable to municipal solid waste landfills and these central regulations are implemented by the states. A properly designed MSW landfill includes provisions for leachate management and the possible collection of landfill gas and its potential use as an energy source. Innovative planning will also facilitate productive use of the landfill property after closure. Good design and operation will also limit the effort and cost necessary for maintaining the landfill after final site closure.

Modern MSW landfills differ greatly from simple land disposal. Today's MSW landfills which have evolved in design and operating procedures over the last 20 years, are very different from landfills of even 5 or 10 years ago. Design improvements have reduced environmental impacts and improved the efficient use of resources. Note that in the completed landfill, the waste is enclosed by cover material at the top and by a liner system at the bottom. Appropriate systems are in place to control contaminated water and gas emissions and reduce adverse impacts on the environment.

The goal of MSW land filling is to place residuals in the land according to a coordinated plan designed to minimize environmental impacts, maximize benefits, and keep the resource and financial cost as low as possible. To achieve these ends, the solid waste manager and the landfill owner and operator must carefully plan the development of new facilities and optimize the performance of existing facilities.

Soil-Plant Interactions

Trace elements in compost form various compounds or associations when applied to soil, which can affect their uptake by plants and their mobility through soils. They can be complexed by organic compounds, co-precipitated in meal oxides, in a water soluble state, or in an exchangeable form on soil or organic matter colloids. Measuring the total trace element content does not predict the soil-plant interactions.

Several investigators have attempted to fractionate trace elements in compost in order to identify in what form the element exists. This knowledge could possibly predict their potential uptake and bioavailability as well as mobility through soils. The more common extraction procedures are the water soluble, KNO_3 for exchangeable, $Na_2P_2O_7$ for organic matter bound, EDTA for carbonate and sulfide precipitates, and HNO_3 for residual form of the trace element.

In compost, the water-soluble fraction that is readily available to plants is small. Leita and De Nobili (1991), observed that during the early stages of composting, the water-soluble fraction of Cd initially increased; however, towards the later stages of composting the water-extractable Cd fraction decreased to non-detectable levels.

Oconnor *et al*. (1991), indicated that the concentrations of extractable heavy metal are lower at the end of the composting period is the process which is carried out properly. Humic and fulvic acids have strong affinities to divalent cations with reactions being strongly pH dependant. Humic substances are some of the most powerful metal-binding agents among organic substances (Buffle, 1988).

Understanding the soil-plant relationship is extremely important in managing our soils so as to reduce uptake of trace elements or their movement to water resources. One of the most important aspects of beneficial use of compost an other organic materials is the ability to mange and control their application in order to reduce or eliminate potential harmful effects. The use of organic residues in themselves reduces potential uptake by the plants of heavy metals. Other factors such as pH and phosphorus also influence plant uptake. Management involves such aspects as crop selection to reduce potential uptake and accumulation of trace elements, soil pH control and organic matter maintenance.

When compost is applied to soil, there are many potential pathways for the movement of trace elements: uptake by plants, movement with water to ground or surface water sources, volatilization from surface-applied compost, and immobilization in the soil matrix. Immobilization refers to exchange on the soil colloidal system and fixation in forms unavailable to plants. Figure 3 below shows these potential pathways.

The particular pathway depends on the soil-plant-water relationships of the trace element in question as well as on the amount of the trace element, and interactions among soil-plant-water factors. Trace elements applied to soil may pass through the soil unchanged, react with organic and inorganic compounds to form soluble or insoluble compounds, be adsorbed on the soil colloids, and volatilize from the soil or taken up by the plants (Epstein and Chaney, 1978).

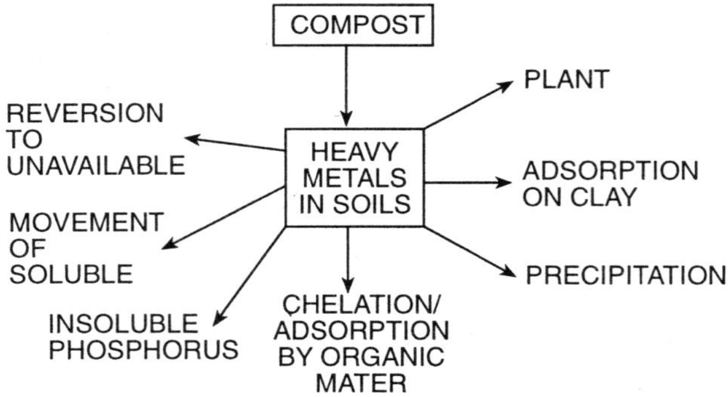

Fig. 3 : Major pathways of heavy metals in compost applied to soil.

Various factors influence the potential pathways. These include:

- type if trace element and chemical state,
- soil acidity,
- organic matter,
- cation exchange capacity, and
- reversion to unavailable forms.

MSW to energy

There are various options available to convert solid waste to energy. Mainly, the following types of technologies are available: (1). sanitary landfill, (2) incineration, (3) gasification, (4) anaerobic digestion, and (5) other types. Sanitary landfill is the scientific dumping of municipal solid waste due to which the maturity of the waste material is achieved faster and hence gas collection starts even during the landfill procedure. Incineration technology is the controlled combustion of waste with the recovery of heat, to produce steam that in turn produces power through steam turbines. About 75% of weight reduction and 90% of volume reduction is achieved through burning. A gasification technology involves pyrolysis under limited air in the first stage, followed by higher temperature reactions of the pyrolysis products to generate low molecular weight gases with calorific value of 1000–1200 kcal nm^{-3}. These gases could be used in internal combustion engines for direct power generation or in boilers for steam generation to produce power. In biomethanation, the putrescible fraction of waste is digested an aerobically (in absence of air), in specially designed digesters. Under this active bacterial activity, the digested pulp produces the combustible gas methane and inert gas carbon dioxide. The remaining digestate is a good quality soil conditioner. Other technologies available are pelletization, pyro-plasma, and flash pyrolysis. All these technologies have merits and demerits. The choice of technology has to be made based on the waste, quality, and local conditions. The best compromise would be to choose the technology, which (1) has lowest life cycle cost, (2) needs least land area, (3) causes practically no air and land pollution, (4) produces more power with less waste, and (5) causes maximum volume reduction.

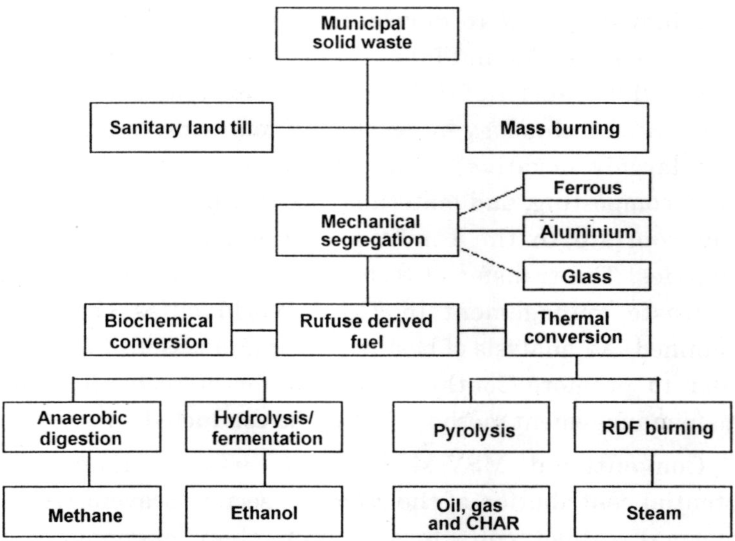

Fig. 4 : Options for energy production from MSW

As described in Fig. 4, MSW without segregation could be used either in sanitary landfill or mass burning to produce power. However, after mechanical segregation, an energy-rich fuel called RDF (refuse derived fuel) is obtained, which can be used to produce power either through biochemical or thermal rout. In biochemical rout, only anaerobic digestion has been used commercially while in the case of thermal rout, both pyrolysis and RDF burning have been used successfully for commercial purposes.

Conclusions

Conventional solutions to municipal solid waste management in the developing countries often rely in high-tech, high-cost, bureaucratic, and centralized alternatives. Conventional solutions usually do not consider the profound differences between First and Third World conditions, resulting in less than optimum outcomes. Conventional solutions frequently involve the transfer of MSWM technology from industrialized to developing countries. International development banks and bilateral development agencies tend to favor this transfer of technology. The experience on the use of advanced technology in developing countries, however, has been largely negative. Compactor trucks, incinerators, in vessel composting, and materials recovery facilities tend to be inappropriate to the conditions prevalent in developing countries. The transfer of technology and successful models for waste management in Third World cities should be examined. An analysis of best practices and lessons learned in order to promote South-South transfer of technology and waste management methods should be conducted.

Conventional MSWM solutions usually ignore the potential contribution of the informal sector. Scavengers and informal refuse collectors render clear economic and environmental benefits to society, and their activities should be improved and supported. Given the failures of conventional solutions, that a different approach is necessary. Low-tech, low-cost, labor-intensive and decentralized options are available today. A decentralized system would be more appropriate to the conditions prevalent in the developing world, while encouraging self-reliance and private investment in the communities. A great potential exists for the formation of Public- Private Partnerships between scavenger coops / micro-enterprises and public agencies for the provision of MSWM services at a low cost. Successful use of low-tech approaches and incorporation of informal refuse collectors and scavengers exist in various cities. A decentralized MSWM system could help solve the seemingly intractable problem of MSWM in Third World cities in an economically viable, socially desirable and environmentally sound manner.

Recognition is necessary that what is taken out from the soil as nutrients as food has to go back from the waste into the soil, instead of being dumped into rivers and land fills uselessly. This means that the cities will feed the rural farms with nutrient inputs. This will also be less energy intensive than chemical fertilizers, toxic pesticides being applied currently. This calls for integration with our agricultural practices, where we should use more and more of organic manures, instead of chemical fertilizers.

Depending on the type of waste generated from urban population, wastes can be segregated and bioprocessed for energy and nutrient recovery. If the segregation is properly executed with suitable microbial inoculants, the derived product is free from heavy metals or toxic materials. However, admixture of sewage sludge or any other sludge biosolid wastes results in enhanced heavy metal concentration in compost. Compost derived from such admixtures should be tested for quality and plant reaction. Otherwise most of the plants will mobilize heavy metal through the rhizosphere activity resulting in increased bioavailability and accumulation in plant parts. Judicial activism and environmental controls directing for MSW composting should be taken in the positive side to provide quality compost to plant nutrients and to support organic agriculture. Any deviation will result in dilution of pollutants in the ecosystem with an ultimate reaction for a biomagnifications.

References

Acharya, C.N. (1939) Comparison of different methods of composting waste materials. Ind. J. Agric. Sci., 9: 817-833.

Affairs, London. http://www.defra.gov.uk/animalh/by-prods/cater/compost.htm

Albert Howard, A. and Wad, Y.D. (1931) *The Waste Products of Agriculture. Their Utilization as Humus.* Humphrey Milford Oxford University Press, London.

Anonymous (2005a) Health impacts of solid waste, http://edugreen.teri.res.in/explore/explore.htm.

Anonymous (2005b) Plastics, http://www.plasticsresources.com/plastics_101/index.html.

Anonymous (2005c) Recycling and reuse http://edugreen.teri.res.in/explore/explore.htm

Batchelder, A. R. (1982) Chlorotetracycline and oxytetracycline effect on plant growth and development in soil systems, 11 : 675-678.

Bhide A.D. and Sunderesan, B.B. (1983) Processing method for the future solid waste management in developing countries. pp., 124–134 New Delhi: Indian National Science Documentation Centre.

Bidlingermaier W. and Scheelhaase, T. (1999) Characterization of solid waste and determination of the emission potential, Proceedings Sardinia 99, Seventh International landfill symposium.

Bjeldanes M.N. and Beardm, G. V. Z. (1996) Resource recovery *In : Power Plant Engineering,* Chapman and Hall, New York pp., 710–732.

Blanco, M. J. and Almendros, G. (1995) Forecasting agrobiological properties of wheat straw with different additives-multiple regression models including chemical parameters. Communications in Soil Science and Plant Analysis, 26(15-16): 2473-2484.

Bollen, G. J. (1985). The fate of plant pathogens during composting of crop residues. *In*: *Composting of Agricultural and Other Wastes* (Ed. J.K. R. Gasser), Elsevier Applied Science Publishers, London, pp. 282-290.

Brinton, W. F. and Evans E, (2001) How compost maturity affects container grown plants. Bio Cycle, 42 : 56-60.

Brinton, W. F., Evans E. and Davies, W (2001) Maturity testing for compost end-product quality classification. *In: Orbit,* pp., 65-70.

Brinton, W.F., Tränkner A. and Droffner, M. (1996). Investigations into liquid compost extracts. Biocycle, 37 : 68-70.

BSI (2002) PAS 100 Specification for composted materials. British Standards Institution, London.

Buffle, J. (1988) Complexation Reaction in Aquatic Systems: An Analytical Approach. Ellis Horwood Limited, Chichester, England.

Burden, J. (2001) Composting - the mushroom way. Composting News, 5 : 6-7.

Chaney, R.L. (1978) Land disposal of toxic substances and water-related problems. J. Water Pollut. Control Fed., 50: 2037-2042.

Coad, A. (1997) Lessons from India in Solid Waste Management. Loughborough: Water, Environment and Development Centre.

DEFRA (2002b). Briefing note on composting. Department for Environment, Food and Rural .

Deportes, I., Benoit-Guyod J.L. and Zmirou, D. (1995) Hazard to man and the environment posed by the use of urban waste compost: a review. Sci. Total Environ., 172 : 197-222.

Diver, S. (2001) Controlled Microbial Composting and Humus Management: Luebke Compost. Appropriate Technology Transfer for Rural Areas, Fayetteville, Arkansas, USA.

DTI (2001) Industrial Solid Waste Treatment. A Review of Composting Technology. BIO-WISE, Department of Trade and Industry.

EA (2001) Technical guidance on composting operations. Environment Agency, UK.

EPA530-F00-024. (2000) US Environmental Protection Agency. Greenhouse Gas Emissions from Management of Selected Materials in Municipal Solid Waste. EPA530-R-98-013. September,1998.

Epstein, E. (1997) *The Science of Composting*. Technomic Publishing Company Inc., Lancaster, Pennsylvania, USA.

Finstein, M. S., and Morris, M. L., (1975). Microbiology of municipal solid waste composting. Advances in Applied Microbiology, 19 : 113-151.

Finstein, M.S., Cirello, J. MacGregor, S.T., Miller F.C. Suler, D.J. and Strom, P.F. (1980) Discussion of paper by R. T. Haug . J. Water Pollut. Control Fed. 52: 2037-2042.

Finstein, M.S., Cirello, J., MacGregor, S.T., Miller, F.C. Psarianos, K.M. (1980) Sludge composting and utilization:rational approach to process control. (Final Report to USEPA, NJDEP, CCMUA.) U.S. Dept. Commerce, NTIS, Springfield, VA., No. PB82 136243.

Gaur, A. C. and Sadasivam. K. V. (1993) Theory and practical consideration of composting organic waste. Peekay Tree Crops Development Foundation, Kerala, India

Gonzales-Vila, F. J., Saiz-Jimenez, C. and Martin. F. (1982) Identification of free organic chemicals in composted municipal refuse. J. Environ. Qual., 11 : 251-254.

Health Impacts of Solid Waste (2004). http://edugreen.teri.res.in/explore/explore.htm

Hellmann, B., Zelles, L., Palojarvi, A. and Bai, Q. (1997) Emissions of climate-relevant trace gases and succession of microbial communities during open-windrow composting. Applied and Environmental Microbiology, 63 : 1011-1018.

Herrmann, R. F. and Shann, J. R. (1993) Enzyme activities as indicators of municipal solid waste compost maturity. Compost Science and Utilization, 1 : 54-63.

Hirsch, R., Ternes, T. Haberer, K. and Kratz, K. L. (1999) Occurrence of antibiotics in the aquatic environment. Sci. Total Environ., 225 : 109-118.

Hoitink, H.A.J., Stone, A.G. and Han, D.Y. (1997) Suppression of plant disease by composts. Hort Science, 32 : 184-187.

Howard, A. (1947) The Soil and Health: a Study of Organic Agriculture. New York: Devin Adair Company, pp., 307.

IEA (International Energy Agency). (1997) System and market overview of anaerobic digester, [Anaerobic Digestion Activity] Paris, IEA, pp., 1– 21

Inbar, Y, Chen, Y. and Hader, Y. (1990) Humic substances formed during the composting of organic matter. Soil Sci. Soc. Am. J., 54:1316-1323.

Ingham, E.R. (1999) Making a high quality compost tea, Part II, Biocycle, 40 : 94.

Itävaara, M., Venelampi, O. Samsøe-Petersen, L. Lystad, H. Bjarnadottir, H. and Öberg, L. (1998) Assessment of compost maturity and ecotoxicity, Nordtest, Espoo Finland, NT Techn Report 404. 84 pages. NT Project No. 1363-97.

Itavaari, M., Vikman, M. and Venelampi, O. (1997) Windrow composting of biodegradable packaging materials. Compost Science and Utilization, 5 : 84-92.

Kalaiselvi, T and Rramasamy, K. (1996) Compost maturity: can it be evaluated? Madras Agric. J., 83(10):609-618.

Kychenrither *et al.* (1985) Desigen and operation of an aerated window composting facility. J. Water Pollut. Control Fed., 57: 213

Leita, L. and De Nobili. M. (1991) Water-soluble fractions of heavy metals during composting of municipal solid waste. J. Environ. Qual., 20:73-78.

Minnich *et al.* (1979) The Rodale Guide to Composting. Emmaus, PA: Rodale Press.

O'Connor, G.A., Chaney, R.L. and Ryan, J. A. (1991) Bioavailability to plants of sludge-borne toxic organics. Review of Environmental Contaminants and Toxicology, 121 : 129-155.

O'Leary, P and Walsh P., (1991a) Introduction to solid waste landfills. Waste Age, 22(1): 42–50.

O'Leary, P and Walsh, P., (1991b) Landfilling principles Waste Age, 22(1): 109–114.

Parker, C and Roberts, T. (Eds.) (1985) *Energy from waste – an evaluation of conversion technologies* Elsevier Applied Science Publishers, London. pp., 217.

Ramasamy, K. (2001) Industrial biosolid composting from distilleries. In: Biocycle Conference September 2-5, Atlanda, USA. pp. 12

Ramasamy, K., Kalaiselvi, T. and Devagi, P. (1999) ICAR Adhoc Sheme Report on Biological and chemical indices for maturity and quality of composts, pp., 244.

Riggle, D., (1996) Compost teas in agriculture. BioCycle, 37 : 65-57.

Scheuerell, S., and W.Mahafee. (2002) Compost tea: principles and prospects for plant disease control. Compost Science and Utilization, 10 : 313-338.

Slater, R. A., Frederickson, J. and Gilbert, E. J. (2001) *The State of Composting,* The Composting Association, Wellingborough.

Smith, A., Brown, K. Ogilvie, S. Rushton, K. and Bates, J. (2001a) Waste Management Options and Climate Change.Final report to the European Commission, DG Environment. AEA Technology, Culham, Abingdon.

Solar Energy Research Institute., (1979) A Survey of Biomass Gasification. Vol. I and Vol. II. (Ed. Golden Colorado, USA: Solar Energy Research Institute [SERI / TR-SERI]

Strom, P. F. (1985) Effect of temperature on bacterial species diversity in thermophilic waste composting. Applied and Environmental Microbiology, 50 : 899-905.

Thorneloe, S A. (1992) Landfill gas recovery / utilisation - options and economics Paper presented at the 16th Annual Types of solid wastes http://edugreen.teri.res.in/explore/explore.htm

UKROFS. (2001) UKROFS Standards. UKROFS.

US Environmental Protection Agency (1998) Environmental Fact Sheet: Municipal Solid Waste Generation, Recycling and Disposal in the United States: Facts and Figures for 1998.

US EPA Municipal Solid Waste http://www.epa.gov/epaoswer/ non-hw/muncpl/index.htm U.S. Environmental Protection Agency, Office of Solid Waste http://www.epa.gov/osw U.S.

Environmental Protection Agency: "Greenhouse Gas Emissions from Management of Selected Materials in Municipal Solid Waste".

Webley, D. M. (1947) The microbiology of composting. 1. The behavior of the aerobic mesophilic bacterial flora of composts and its relation to other changes taking place during composting. Proc. Soc. Applied Bacteriology, 2 : 83-89.

Weltzein, H. C., 1991. Biocontrol of foliar fungal disease with compost extracts. *In: Microbial Ecology of Leaves* (Ed. J.H.A.A. SS. Hirano) Springer-Verlag, New York, pp. 430-450.

Willson, G.B., Parr, J.F. Epstein, E. Marsh, P.B. Chaney, R.C. Colacicco, D. Burge, W.D. Sikora, L.J. Teste, C.E. Hornick, S. (1980) Manual for composting sewage sludge by the Beltsville aerated-pile method. Report, EPA-600/8-80-022, MERL/ORD Cincinnati.

Yuen, G. Y., and Raabe, R. D. (1979) Eradication of fungal plant pathogens by aerobic composting. Phytopathology 69, 922.

Zibilske, L. M. (1998). Composting of organic wastes. *In: Principles and Applications of Soil Microbiology*. (Eds. D.M. Sylvia, J.F. Fuhrmann, P.G. Hartel and D.A. Zuberer) Prentice-Hall, Inc., Upper Saddle River, NJ, USA., pp., 482-497.

Zibilske, L.M. (1998) Composting of organic wastes, In : *Principles and Applications of Soil Microbiology* (Eds. Sybria, D.M., Fuhrmann, J.F., Hartel P.G.), and Zuberer, D.A.), Prentice Hall, Inc., Upper Saddle River, JH, USA, pp,. 482-497.

CHAPTER 8

RADIOACTIVE WASTES—THEIR STORAGE AND DISPOSAL

Suman Phogat[1], V. Phogat[2] and K.K. Singh[3]

[1] C.R. College of Education, Hisar, Haryana.

[2] Department of Soil Science, CCS Haryana Agricultural University, Hisar, Haryana.

[3] Project Directorate (Res.), Agriculture & Soil Survey, Krishi Bhavan, Bikaner- 334002, (Raj.), India.

ABSTRACT

Waste, by definition, is any material that has been or will be discarded as being of no further use. Radioactivity can be termed 'natural' or 'artificial' depending on whether it occurs in nature or is made by artificial transmutation in the laboratory. Radioactive elements decay at different rates and is measured as half-life. Essentially all substances contain radioactive elements of natural origin to some extent or the other. The source of radioactive waste is a part of industrial mining activity; civilian nuclear programmes, including nuclear power production, medical and industrial applications of radioactive nuclides for peaceful purposes; and the military nuclear programme, including atmospheric and underground nuclear-weapon testing and weapon production. Potential biological effects depend on how much and how fast a radiation dose is received. Radioactive nuclides of elements like ^{137}Cs or ^{90}Sr or ^{131}I are the most hazardous on the scale of a human beings' lifetime. Other long-life nuclides like

^{239}Pu, ^{241}Am, ^{237}Np pose a long-term hazard to future generations.

The nuclear-waste management encompasses operations from the waste's production until its final disposal, including the various regulatory, sociopolitical and economic issues. The main objective in managing and disposing of radioactive (or other) waste is to protect people and the environment. The management of radioactive waste is not a static process. Annual reviews of on-site and centralized programmes should be conducted. The identified goal of radioactive waste management can be met with reasonable cost and resource use by implementing a carefully planned waste management strategy using appropriate technologies. Safe methods for the final disposal of high-level waste are technically proven; the international consensus is that this should be deep geological disposal. When developing a waste management strategy, consideration should be given to the entire sequence of waste management operations from the waste's production to its final disposal, and all related issues, including the various regulatory, sociopolitical and economic issues. The interaction of all these aspects must be analysed and understood before the entire waste management system can be properly built up and safely managed.

Key Words : Radioactive wastes, storage, disposal.

Introduction

Many activities dealing with radioactive materials produce nuclear wastes, including civilian nuclear power programs (nuclear power plant operations and nuclear fuel-cycle activities), defence nuclear programs (nuclear weapons production, naval nuclear reactor programs, and related R&D), and industrial and institutional activities (scientific research, medical operations, and other industrial uses of radioisotopic sources or radiochemicals). During the production and use of these materials, radioactive waste inevitably arise; this must be managed with particular care owing to its inherent radiological, biological, chemical and physical hazards. High-level radioactive waste is potentially toxic for tens of thousands to millions of years. It is also the most difficult to be disposed safely because of its heat and radiation output. Secondly, one may also note that a 1000 MW electric coal-fired power plant releases into the environment nearly 6 million tonnes of greenhouse gases, 500,000 tons of mixtures of sulphur and nitrogen oxides and about 320,000 tonnes of ashes. These ashes containing Naturally Occurring Radioactive Materials (NORMs) are potentially capable of subjecting humanity to a collective dose of radiation higher than that attributable to wastes discharged into the environment by nuclear power plants generating the same amount of electricity. In spite of this ground reality, public perception about nuclear wastes is rather skewed against nuclear power in several countries.

The scope of nuclear-waste management encompasses generation, processing (treatment and packaging), storage, transport, and disposal. A well developed waste management strategy should consider the entire sequence of waste management operations, from the waste's production until its final disposal, including the various regulatory, sociopolitical and economic issues. The overall goal of radioactive waste management is to deal with radioactive waste in a manner that protects both human health and the environment now and in the future, without imposing an undue burden on future generations. This can be met with reasonable cost and resource use by implementing a carefully planned waste management strategy using appropriate technologies. Waste containing long lived radionuclides must be stored and disposed of at a repository specifically designed for this purpose. Ample storage capacity is needed for the decay of short lived radionuclides and for storing long lived waste prior to, and after, the treatment and conditioning steps.

Decay is the only natural way of reducing radioactivity. Since, radionuclides have decay rates ranging from days to thousands of years, proper segregation of wastes depending on their half-lives, and separate treatment and conditioning of these wastes, is an important factor in the overall scheme of radioactive waste management. This chapter provides information on basic concept of radioactivity, type of waste generation, storage, disposal and decay of waste arising from the various activities associated with the production and application of radioisotopes in medical, industrial, educational and research facilities.

Radioactivity

The phenomenon of radioactivity was discovered by Henri Becquerel in 1896. Certain elements that compose matter emit particles and radiations spontaneously. This phenomenon is referred to as 'radioactivity'. It cannot be altered by application of heat, electricity or any other force and remains unchangeable. Radioactivity can be termed 'natural' or 'artificial' depending on whether it occurs in nature or is made by artificial transmutation in the laboratory. Three different kinds of rays, known as alpha, beta and gamma are associated with radioactivity. The alpha rays consist of particles (nuclei of helium atoms) carrying a positive charge, beta rays particles have negative charge (streams of electrons) and gamma rays are chargeless electromagnetic radiation with shorter wavelengths than any X-rays. Every element can be made to emit such rays artificially. If such radioactive elements are placed in the body through food or by other methods, the rays can be traced through the body. But because they can disrupt chemical bonds in the molecules of important chemicals within the cells, they help in treating cancers and other diseases. Thus, use of tracer elements is extremely helpful in monitoring life processes. Geologists use radioactivity to determine the age of rocks. As atoms lose particles as heavy as nuclei of helium, they become atoms of some other element. That is, the elements change or 'transmute' into other elements until the series ends with a stable element. Radioactive elements decay at different rates. Rates are measured as half-lives – that is, the time it takes for one half of any given quantity of a radioactive element to disintegrate. The longest half-life is that of the 'isotope' ^{238}U of uranium. It is 4.5 billion years. Some isotopes have half-lives of years, months, days, minutes, seconds, or even less than millionths of a second. Measurement units and permissible dosages of Radioactivity is measured in Becquerel (Bq) units. 1 Bq = 1 decay or disintegration per second. Curie (Ci) was used earlier and 1 Ci = 37 billion Bq ($3.7x10^{10}$ disintegrations per second) or 37 Bq = 1 nano-Ci. To measure the health risk through ionization, in the US the most commonly used unit is rem or mrem (milli-rem). In Europe, the most commonly used measuring unit for this purpose is Sv (Sievert) or mSv (milli-Sv). Conversion of rem to Sieverts: 1 rem = 0.01 Sv = 10 mSv.

Natural radioactivity

It is somewhat surprising that nature has been a large producer of radioactive waste. The surface of the Earth and the terrestrial crust happens to be an enormous reservoir of primordial radioactivity. Small amounts of radioactive materials are contained in mineral springs, sand mounds and volcanic eruptions. Essentially, all substances contain radioactive elements of natural origin to some extent or the other. The second source of radioactive waste is a part of industrial mining activity where, during mineral exploration and exploitation, one excavates the primordial material from the earth that contains radioactivity, uses part of it and rejects the radioactive residues as waste. These are referred to as Naturally Occurring Radioactive Materials (NORMs) and are ubiquitous as residual wastes in processing industries that cover fertilizers, iron and steel, fossil fuel, cement, mineral sands, titanium, thorium and uranium mining as well as emanations and waste from coal and gas-fired power plants. One should note that in many industries, radiation exposure to the workers and the general public would be at least as high as those from nuclear installations and in some cases it is even higher. It is also known that certain mineral springs contain fairly large amounts of ^{222}radon. Monazite sand deposits in coastal areas may result in radiation exposure to humans around an order of magnitude in excess of the currently set international exposure limits to radioactive waste disposal (one mSv yr^{-1}) and volcanic deposits result in similar exposure. There is no place on earth that is free from natural radioactive background; it may vary from place to place all the way from the low to the high. The content of radioactivity in the seas is estimated to be nearly 10,000 exa-becquerel (Ebq = 10^{18} Bq). The residual waste tailings from past mining and milling operations are estimated to be around several million tons at many places and the radioactivity contained may be nearly 0.001

EBq. Thousands of such sites are scattered all around the world.

Artificial radioactivity

Following the Second World War and discovery of the fission process, human activity added radioactivity artificially to the natural one. Two main sources have been: (a) the civilian nuclear programmes, including nuclear power production, medical and industrial applications of radioactive nuclides for peaceful purposes, and (b) the military nuclear programme, including atmospheric and underground nuclear-weapon testing and weapon production.

The activities comprising mining, processing, fuel fabrication and ultimately use of fuel in nuclear reactors result in power generation. Reprocessing spent fuel helps in recycling plutonium for fuel fabrication. The byproducts in this activity are enriched fissile material useful for fuel as well as for weapons, depleted uranium used for DU shells, the actinides and radioactive waste. The ore that is mined in uranium mines is sent to a uranium mill, where a small uranium-containing fraction is separated from the ore, leaving behind virtually almost the entire ore in the tailings. The uranium fraction is processed to recover pure uranium in metallic form. Uranium metal consists of the isotope ^{235}U to the extent of 0.7%, the remaining 99.3% being ^{238}U. The ^{235}U fissions on absorption of thermal neutrons, while ^{238}U does not. Hence, this small fraction of ^{235}U is 'enriched' for use in light-water reactors for deriving power. Highly enriched ^{235}U is used for nuclear weapons also. Fresh fuel made of uranium (sometimes containing plutonium, in addition) is weak radioactive. The fuel, after sufficient use in reactors, is referred as 'spent fuel'; the 'ash' after 'burning' the fuel contains fission-fragment debris from spontaneous or neutron-induced fission of uranium and actinides, actinide elements and unutilized uranium. This irradiated fuel is highly radioactive. Transuranic actinides (principally neptunium, plutonium, americium and curium) are created by absorption of neutrons in non-fissioned uranium and by sequential absorption of neutrons in the consequently formed daughter elements. Although nearly 200 radionuclides are produced during the burn-up of the fuel, most of them are relatively short-lived and decay to low levels within a few decades (Table 1). The short-lived radionuclides therefore do not pose a big problem for long-term disposal. The spent fuel, when subjected to chemical processing, yields uranium and plutonium fractions apart from the rest of the 'ash'. Normally, the irradiated uranium is dissolved in an acid medium and treated with organic solvents to recover plutonium and remnants of uranium. The byproduct is a highly acidic liquid, a high-level radioactive waste containing fission fragments and transuranic elements. The transuranic elements can be separated further, as they constitute rare, precious and often fissile materials themselves. This is the 'wealth' from the waste.

Table 1 : Common radioactive isotopes produced during nuclear reactions

Isotope	**Half-life***	**Isotope**	**Half-life ***
Relatively short half-life			
Strontium-89	54 days	Zirconium-95	65 days
Niobium-95	39 days	Ruthenium-103	40 days
Rhodium-103	57 minutes	Rhodium-106	30 seconds
Iodine-131	8 days	Xenon-133	8 days
Tellurium-134	42 minutes	Barium-140	13 days
Lanthanum-140	40 h	Cerium-141	32 days

Contd.

Year to century-scale half-life*			
Hydrogen-3	12 years	Krypton-85	10 years
Strontium-90	29 years	Ruthenium-106	1 year
Cesium-137	30 years	Cerium-144	1.3 years
Promethium-147	2.3 years	Plutonium-238	85.3 years
Americium-241	440 years	Curium-224	17.4 years
Longer half-life			
Technecium-99	2×10^6 years	Iodine-129	1.7×10^7 years
Plutonium-239	24000 years	Plutonium-240	6500 years
Americium-243	7300 years		

Source: Rao (2001)

*Half-lives of the order of years to decades of isotopes of elements that can seek tissues or organs biologically (being akin to other elements chemically) are the most hazardous from point of view of radiation. For example, ^{90}Sr, being chemically akin to Ca, can seek the bone and lodge itself there for years causing radioactive dam-age to surrounding tissues.

Radiation effects

Every inhabitant on this planet is constantly exposed to naturally occurring ionizing radiation called back-ground radiation. Sources of background radiation include cosmic rays from the Sun and stars, naturally occurring radioactive materials in rocks and soil, radionuclides normally incorporated into our body's tissues, and radon and its products, which we inhale. We are also exposed to ionizing radiation from man-made sources, mostly through medical procedures like X-ray diagnostics. Radiation therapy is usually targeted only to the affected tissues. Much of the data on the effects of large doses of radiation comes from survivors of the atomic bombs dropped on Hiroshima and Nagasaki in 1945, Chernobyl in 1986 and from other people who received large doses of radiation, usually for treatment. Only about 12% of all the cancers that have developed among those survivors are estimated to be related to radiation.

Ionizing radiation can cause important changes in our cells by breaking the electron bonds that hold molecules together. For example, radiation can damage our genetic material (DNA). But the cells also have several mechanisms to repair the damage done to DNA by radiation. Potential biological effects depend on how much and how fast a radiation dose is received. An acute radiation dose (a large dose delivered during a short period of time) may result in effects which are observable within a period of hours to weeks. A chronic dose is a relatively small amount of radiation received over a long period of time. The body is better equipped to tolerate a chronic dose than an acute dose as the cells need time to repair themselves. Radiation effects are also classified in two other ways, namely somatic and genetic effects. Somatic effects appear in the exposed person. The delayed somatic effects have a potential for the development of cancer and cataracts. Acute somatic effects of radiation include skin burns, vomiting, hair loss, temporary sterility or sub-fertility in men and blood changes. Chronic somatic effects include the development of eye cataracts and cancers. The second class of effects, namely genetic or heritable effects appears in the future generations of the exposed person as a result of radiation damage to the reproductive cells, but risks from genetic effects in humans are seen to be considerably smaller than the risks for somatic effects.

The quantum of exposure (dose duration of exposure) decides the deleterious effects that may result. Exposure may occur to particular organs locally or to the whole body. The radiotoxicity of a particular radionuclide is quantified in terms of what is referred to as 'potential hazard index' that is defined in terms of the nuclide availability, its activity, maximum permissible intake annually and its half-life. This depends on a variety of factors like physical half-life, biological half-life, sensitivity of the organ or tissue where the nuclide is likely to concentrate, ionizing power of the radiation from the nuclide that depends on the energy of the radiation emitted from the radionuclide, etc. It is from such considerations that one concludes that radioactive nuclides of elements like ^{137}Cs or ^{90}Sr or ^{131}I are the most hazardous on the scale of a human beings' lifetime. Other long-life nuclides like ^{239}Pu, ^{241}Am, ^{237}Np pose a long-term hazard, on the other hand, to future generations.

Radioactive waste

Waste, by definition, is any material (solid materials such as process residues as well as liquid and gaseous effluents) that has been or will be discarded as being of no further use. Note that, what may be considered as one's waste may turn out to be another's wealth. Reusable plastics and other components in day-to-day household waste are good examples in this context. This concept holds good for radioactive waste also, in some sense. Waste that emits nuclear radiation is radioactive waste. The preliminary estimate of the nuclear waste generation in India is given in Table 2. The amount of radioactive waste produced in different countries varies widely, depending on the scale of the applications and the range of activity associated with particular nuclear materials.

The level of radioactive waste is quoted in terms of volume (in cubic metres) or in tonnage. Another way is to quote the radioactivity contained in such waste in bequerels (Bq). Both the units are useful because one needs to know the volume or weight of the waste to be handled for disposal purposes and also the radioactivity contained therein. The nuclear waste from natural sources, including mining and related operations, could have resulted in production of radioactive waste of a few EBq and the sea is repository of several thousand EBq of radioactivity. Compared to this it is estimated that in the military nuclear operations, the cold-war era resulted in release of more than 1000 EBq of nuclear debris in the atmosphere. Production of weapon-grade material resulted in about 1000 EBq of residual waste and 'accidents and losses' of nuclear submarines and nuclear powered satellites might have resulted in waste of a few EBq. In the civilian regime, it is estimated that the nuclear waste, as a result of nuclear power production around the world over the past 50 years, is of the order of 1000 EBq and is growing at the rate of approximately 100 EBq yr^{-1}. Typically, a large nuclear power plant of generating capacity of 1000 MW electricity produces around 27 tonnes of high level radioactive waste, 310 tonnes of intermediate level and 460 tonnes of low level radioactive waste.

Table 2: Total nuclear waste generation in India

Step in nuclear fuel cycle	**Waste estimate**
Uranium mining and milling	4.1 million tonnes
Fuel fabrication	2000 m^3
Reactor operations (low-level waste)	22000 m^3
Reactor operations (intermediate-level waste)	280 m^3
Spent fuel storage (not to be reprocessed)	400 tonnes
Reprocessing (high-level waste)	5000 m^3
Reprocessing (intermediate-level waste)	35000 m^3
Reprocessing (low-level waste)	210000 m^3

Ramanna *et al.* (2001)

Radioactive waste is generated in all stages of nuclear research reactor operations and in operations involving the production of radioisotopes and their application in medicine, industry and research. The types and volumes of waste produced depend upon the particular operation being conducted, and can vary extensively in radio-chemical, chemical and physical content. The principal types of waste generated during the production and application of radioisotopes are listed in Table 3.

Table 3 : Types of radioactive waste generated during the production and application of radioisotopes

Waste category	**Waste type**
Liquids, aqueous	Laboratory effluents, hot cell (isotope production) effluents, fuel storage pool (research reactor) purges, decontamination effluents, sump and rinsing waters, mining and milling raffinates with uranium and thorium from laboratory and pilot plant scale extraction.
Liquids, organic	Oil from pumps, etc., scintillation liquids. extraction solvents (tributylphosphate (TBP)/kerosene, amine, etc.)
Solids, compactible	Tissues, swabs, paper, cardboard, plastics (polyvinylchloride, polyethylene), rubber gloves, protective clothes, filters and glassware.
Solids, non-compactible	Metallic scrap, brickwork, sealed sources, radium needles, ion exchange resins, animal carcasses and excreta.

Source: IAEA (1994a)

Sources of Waste

(i) Nuclear research centres

In small nuclear research centres radioisotopes are produced in research reactors or in particle accelerators. The desired radioisotopes are subsequently extracted or processed in nearby hot cells or laboratories. Most of the radioactive waste generated during these operations contains a mixture of long and short lived radioisotopes and should be managed to provide for decay, dilution and subsequent discharge, or for conditioning into a form suitable for long term storage and/or disposal. Waste containing long lived fission products and/or transuranic radio-nuclides is not usually generated in the laboratories of small nuclear research centres in developing countries. Only a small part of radioactive waste from these centres will be contaminated with long lived radioisotopes, for example ^{14}C and ^{3}H from limited laboratory experiments or uranium and thorium from processing investigations in laboratory and pilot plant scale operations.

(ii) Hospitals

The application of radioactive materials in medical diagnosis and therapy is extremely important and continuously expanding. In many instances alternative methods are not available. The main areas of applications are in radioimmunoassay, radiopharmaceuticals, diagnostic procedures, radiotherapy and research. These represent the use not only of small quantities of unsealed sources and liquid solutions, but also of highly concentrated sealed sources housed in shielded assemblies (Table 4). Most of the radioisotopes used in hospitals for medical diagnostic procedures and treatments are very short lived, and in most cases the only treatment performed on the waste is storage for decay before further treatment to eliminate biological hazards and/or release to the environment.

(iii) Industry

Certain industrial establishments use particular forms of radioactive materials and techniques, such as radioactive tracers, sealed sources and luminous displays, and specialized devices for non-destructive testing, quality control, evaluation of plant performance and the development of products. The quantities of radioactive materials used depend largely on the level of the development of technology in that country. Several of these applications are shown in Table 4. One of the most valuable contributions of radioactive tracer techniques has been in the evaluation of wear and corrosion of key components in plants and machinery. In the majority of cases, waste is produced as the component containing the radionuclide slowly wears, releasing radioactivity into the product or into a designated waste stream.

(iv) Universities and Research Establishments

Users of radioactive materials in universities and research establishments are most commonly involved in monitoring the metabolic or environmental pathways associated with materials as diverse as drugs, pesticides, fertilizers and minerals. The range of useful radionuclides is normally restricted and the activity content of the labelled compounds low, but at some research establishments more exotic radionuclides may be used. The radionuclides most commonly employed in studying the toxicology of many chemical compounds and their associated metabolic pathways are ^{14}C and ^{3}H, as they can be incorporated into complex molecules with considerable uniformity. Iodine-125 has proved to be very valuable in the labeling of proteins.

Type of Wastes

(i) Aqueous waste

Aqueous (liquid) radioactive waste is generated during research reactor operations and in other operations involving the application of radioisotopes (e.g. medicine, research and education). The type of liquid waste produced depends upon the particular operation being conducted and can vary extensively in both chemical and radionuclide content. Most operations, particularly the larger ones, also produce a variety of radioactive liquid wastes from locations such as showers, laundries and analytical laboratories and from decontamination services. The specific activity of the waste generated depends upon which radioactive materials are used. Larger quantities of spent sealed sources may already be accumulated at some facilities. Each type of application of radioactive materials is likely to result in aqueous waste that has certain characteristics in terms of radioactive isotopes present and their chemical nature. The aqueous waste arisings from different types of applications are described in Table 4.

Table 4 : Aqueous waste characteristics by source and application

Source	Typical radioisotopes	Chemical characteristics	Recommended treatment/ disposal method
1. Nuclear research centres	Variable, with relatively long lived ^{59}Fe, ^{60}Co, ^{137}Cs, etc., mixed with short lived ^{24}Na, etc.	Generally, uniform batches with nearly neutral pH from regeneration of ion exchange resins by precipitation.	Storage for decay and, if necessary, treatment by precipitation.

Contd.

2. Laboratories producing radio-isotopes activity and high chemical for interim decay then removed	Wide variety, depending upon production and purity of targets.	(a) Small volumes of high specific activity and high chemical concentrations (b) Large volumes of low specific activity	Segregate (a) and (b), store (a) in hot cells for interim decay then remove for further storage and/ or treatment along with (b).
3. Radiolabelling and radiopharmaceuticals	^{14}C, ^{3}H, ^{32}P, ^{35}S, ^{125}I	Small volumes of variable but predictable chemical composition.	Decay in storage, isolate low specific activity for disposal. Treat or solidify high specific activity ^{14}C waste.
4. Medical diagnosis and treatment	$^{99}T^{m}$, ^{131}I, ^{85}Sr	(a) Large volumes of urine from patients (b) Small volumes from preparation and treatment.	(a) Direct release to sanitary waste (b) Collection, decay and release.
5. Scientific research	Variable, with much ^{14}C, ^{3}H, ^{125}I and other short and long lived radioisotopes.	Extremely variable	Segregate waste by chemical classes, specific activity and radionuclide. Decay storage prior to release. Individual waste containers taken to a central facility for treatment.
6. Industrial and pilot plants	Depends upon application.	Volumes could be large and chemical composition undefined.	Storage for decay and release. Uranium and Thorium may require processing.
7. Laundry and decontamination	Wide variety likely.	Volumes large with low specific activity but containing complexing agents	Storage for decay. If treatment is required chemical pretreatment may be necessary.

Source: IAEA (1992)

The composition of radioactive aqueous waste covers a wide range, both with regard to its activities and the presence of alpha emitting and beta/gamma emitting radionuclides. Some waste streams contain both. Many streams contain specific groups of radionuclides, others only one or two. For streams containing mainly short lived beta/gamma activity, the effluents should be kept in storage. After decay to a specific activity within prescribed limits, they can generally be safely discharged to the environment.

While specific activity and radiological safety are emphasized and are the primary reasons that these wastes are regulated, the chemical and in some cases the biological characteristics of them may influence the waste management option selection. In some laboratories or facilities of a nuclear research centre, small volumes (10 to 100 L) of liquid effluents are generated that contain higher concentrations of radioactivity with long lived radionuclides. A typical example is decontamination liquid resulting from the generally infrequent decontamination of plant piping and equipment. These effluents can include crud (corrosion products) and a wide variety of solutions containing phosphates, citrates, tartrates, detergents, acidic products and ethylenediaminetetraacetic acid (EDTA). These effluents should be carefully segregated and collected in small bottles or containers. Mixing with other radioactive effluents or concentration by evaporation and precipitation is not advisable for this type of waste. The preferred option for processing this type of waste is direct conditioning, generally with cement (IAEA, 1993). The chemical nature of the waste may require special cement formulation (because, for example, high concentrations of EDTA interfere with the hardening of ordinary Portland cement).

(ii) Liquid organic waste

Aqueous radioactive liquids are those in which the solvent and solute are both water-based. Radioactive organic liquid waste from medical, industrial and research centres forms a relatively small volume compared with other radioactive wastes.

Typically, this waste includes oils, solvents, scintillation fluids and miscellaneous biological fluids. Radioactive oil waste consists of lubricating oils, hydraulic fluids and vacuum pump oils. This type of waste generally contains only relatively small quantities of beta/gamma emitting radionuclides, but may also contain trace quantities of alpha emitting radionuclides, depending on its origin. This waste generally arises from activities in nuclear research centres; tritium contaminated oils may also arise from various medical and industrial applications. Radioactivity levels for oils may vary widely, depending on the applications they are associated with.

Scintillation liquids result from radiochemical analyses of low energy beta emitters, such as ^{3}H and ^{14}C. They typically consist of non-polar organic solvents such as toluene, xylene and hexane, but they may also include biological compounds such as steroids and lipids. Radioactivity levels are typically of the order of 350 MBq m^{-3}. Spent solvents may arise from solvent extraction processes. The most commonly used extraction solvent is TBP. TBP is diluted for the extraction process usually with a light saturated hydrocarbon, often dodecane or a mixture of paraffins. A variety of organic decontamination liquids and solvents, such as toluene, carbon tetrachloride, acetone, alcohols and trichloroethane, arise from various operations. Dry cleaning produces small quantities of perchloroethylene and Freon-112 waste. The gross alpha/beta activity of this waste is usually less than about 200 MBq m^{-3}.

(iii) Solid waste

Solid waste can be segregated into two main groups: compactible, combustible solid waste and non-compactible, non-combustible solid waste (IAEA, 1994a). Other possible groups may be processible (by compaction or incineration) and non-processible waste. The largest volume of solid waste is general rubbish, which includes protective clothing, plastic sheets and bags, rubber gloves, mats, shoe covers, paper wipes, rags, towels, metal and glass. Segregation should be preceded by an appropriate activity measurement and by distinguishing between waste that after decay storage can be disposed of with municipal refuse (i.e. waste contaminated by radionuclides with a half-life <100 days) and waste that needs treatment and conditioning. Considering the relatively small amounts of combustible waste, compaction should be the preferred volume reduction method. Incineration is technically much more complicated and should only be considered if large quantities of combustible waste can be incinerated in a continuous manner.

(iv) Spent ion exchange resins

Ion exchange media can be classified into two basic categories: inorganic ion exchangers (both natural and synthetic) and organic resins (mainly synthetic). Most commercial ion exchangers are synthetic organic resins typically consisting of polystyrene cross-linked with divinylbenzene. Spent organic and inorganic ion exchange media may require different treatment and conditioning options. Although, regeneration of spent organic resin is possible, the preferred option is direct conditioning of spent resin, as regeneration results in the production of highly acidic and caustic radioactive liquids, which may be difficult to treat (Place, 1990).

(v) Precipitation sludges

The product of treatment of liquid radioactive waste by chemical precipitation and flocculation is a sludge containing most of the radioactivity; this can vary greatly in terms of its chemical and physical characteristics, depending on the specific process used. The chemical composition of the sludge differs from the initial waste owing to the addition of the precipitating chemicals.

(vi) Evaporator concentrates

Evaporator concentrates are produced through an evaporation process by which the volatile and non-volatile components of a solution or slurry are separated to reduce both the waste volume and the amount of radioactivity in a liquid effluent. Evaporation is most effectively used for radioactive liquids with high concentrations of salts or other impurities. The concentrate or bottoms product can range from 15 % solids by weight to a virtually dry powder or cake, depending on the evaporator type and efficiency and on the chemical composition of the waste stream.

(vii) Biological waste

Biological radioactive waste arises from biological, research and teaching/training practices. This waste includes animal carcasses, contaminated body fluids and animal tissues. The inclusion of materials having a biological origin clearly distinguishes this type of waste from inorganic materials. A primary example of biological waste is the waste from research involving animals. All discharges (e.g. faeces, urine and saliva) from animals used in research involving radioactive materials must be considered to be potentially contaminated.

(viii) Medical waste

Medical radioactive waste may be defined as radioactive waste arising from diagnostic, therapeutic and research applications in medicine. In addition to, being contaminated by radioactivity, medical waste, like biological waste, can have infectious, pathological and other hazardous properties. In many instances the potential additional hazard, either from the waste's chemical, biological or physical properties, is greater than the radiological hazard. The following types of radioactive waste may occur as a result of the use of radionuclides in medicine:

— Spent radionuclide generators and spent sealed radiation sources;

— Anatomical and biological waste (e.g. body parts, tissues, organs, fluids and excreta from patients administered with radionuclides);

— Miscellaneous aqueous and organic liquids, and radioactive solutions;

— Miscellaneous solid dry waste (e.g. gloves, paper tissues and equipment parts);

— Miscellaneous waste posing a puncture hazard (e.g. needles, broken glass and nails).

Waste Classification

Classification of radioactive waste can be helpful at any stage, from the origination of the raw waste through to its collection, segregation, treatment, conditioning, storage, transportation and final disposal. Classification systems may be derived from different perspectives, for instance safety related aspects, the physical/chemical characteristics of the waste, process engineering demands or regulatory issues. Some of the important waste properties and criteria to be considered for various classification schemes are (IAEA, 1994b) :

- The origin of the waste.
- The radiological properties: half-life, heat generation, activity and concentration of the radionuclides, surface contamination, and the dose factors of the relevant radionuclides.
- The physical properties: physical state (e.g. solid, liquid or gaseous), size and weight, compactibility, dispersibility, volatility, solubility and miscibility.
- The chemical properties: potential chemical hazard, corrosion resistance/corrosiveness, organic content, combustibility, reactivity, gas generation and sorption of radionuclides.
- The biological properties: potential biological hazards (e.g. infection and putrefaction).

The radioactivity level in waste may affect its handling, treatment and interim storage options owing to its shielding requirements. To improve international communication, a simple classification system for radioactive waste based on arbitrary activity concentration levels of liquid waste and radiation dose rates on the surface of solid waste was recommended by the IAEA in 1970. In the new classification system proposed in 1994, the principal waste classes include exempt, low and intermediate level waste, which may be subdivided into short lived and long lived waste, and high level waste. Boundary levels between waste classes are presented as orders of magnitude; characteristics of waste classes are summarized in Table 5.

Table 5 : Typical characteristics of waste classes

Waste class	Typical characteristics	Disposal options
1. Exempt waste (EW)	Activity levels at or below the clearance levels, which are based on an annual dose to members of the public of less than 0.01 mSv.	No radiological restrictions.
2. Low and intermediate level waste (LILW)	Activity levels above the clearance levels and thermal power below about 2 kW m^{-1}	Near surface or geological disposal facilities.
2.1. Short lived waste (LILW–SL)	Restricted long lived radionuclide concentrations (limitation of long lived alpha emitting radionuclides to 4000 Bq g^{-1} in individual waste packages and to an overall average of 400 Bq g^{-1} per waste package).	Near surface or geological disposal facilities.
2.2. Long lived waste (LILW–LL)	Long lived radionuclide concentrations exceeding the limitations for short lived waste.	Geological disposal facilities.
3. High level waste (HLW)	Thermal power above about 2 kW m^{-1} and long lived radionuclide concentrations exceeding concentrations exceeding the limitations for short lived waste.	Geological disposal facilities.

India classifies its wastes into Low-Level Waste (LLW), Intermediate-Level Waste (ILW) and High-Level Waste (HLW). The category, potentially active waste (PAW) is also used (Table 6). In some cases, these individual categories are further divided according to radioactivity levels for operational purposes. For example, low-level solid waste is placed in four categories (Category I–IV) based on the surface beta and gamma dose and alpha activity (Rodriguez, 1996; Guha, 1997).

Table 6 : Categorization of wastes in India

Category	Activity level A (Ci m^{-3})	Remark
PAW	$< 10^{-6}$	Potentially active
LLW 1	$10^{-6} < A < 10^{-3}$	
LLW 2	$10^{-3} < A < 10^{-1}$	May require shielding
ILW	$10^{-1} < A < 10^{4}$	Shielding necessary
HLW	$>10^{4}$	Shielding and cooling necessary

Source: Rodriguez (1996)

Storage of Radioactive Waste

Spent fuel may be stored in either a wet or dry environment. In addition, it may be stored either at the reactor where it was used or away from the reactor at another site. Currently, most spent nuclear fuel is safely stored in specially designed pools at individual reactor sites. The water-pool option involves storing spent fuel in rods under at least 20 feet of water, which provides adequate shielding from the radiation for anyone near the pool. The rods are moved into the water pools from the reactor along the bottom of water canals, so that the spent fuel always is shielded to protect workers. In dry storage method, spent fuel is surrounded by inert gas inside a container called a cask. The casks can be made of metal or concrete, and some can be used for both storage and transportation. They are either placed horizontally or stand vertically on a concrete pad. Dry storage is not suitable for fuel until the fuel has been out of the reactor for a few years and the amount of heat generated by radioactive decay has been reduced. Waste storage facilities for unconditioned liquid and solid radioactive waste must provide the following:

- Operational convenience, for example allowing the accumulation of waste so as to facilitate the more cost effective use of treatment facilities, transportation and disposal routes;

- Safe and secure retention during a period long enough to permit radioactive decay prior to further radioactive waste management steps, for example storing shorter lived contamination in untreated waste prior to its disposal or discharge within exemption or clearance limits authorized by the national regulatory organization;
- Efficiency of the storage operation, with segregation of different waste categories, record keeping and easy retrieval permitting efficient further management of the waste;
- Verification and/or checking of individual packages.

Storage at radioisotope user establishments

Unconditioned waste is likely to be stored initially in the establishment where it is created. The waste must be segregated there and prepared for decay and/or further treatment or transportation in accordance with the acceptance criteria of the centralized radioactive waste management facility to which it may be subsequently transferred, or for disposal according to the selected route.

At the user establishment the storage requirements can be fulfilled in stores appropriate to the type of operation involved, normally in simple storage areas ranging from single secure cabinets or lockable wheeled bins to one or more dedicated rooms. Efficient operation of the store is essential to avoid the unnecessary accumulation of waste in work areas. This necessitates a planned system of collection and transfer of waste to the store in a well documented orderly fashion, and keeping information to be used for future management. All waste should be segregated and accumulated in containers that are suitable for further safe handling in line with future management proposals, taking into account factors such as robustness or biodegradability of containers, as required.

Storage at radioisotope production facilities

Generally, in routine radioisotope production facilities limited storage of liquid and solid waste is incorporated as part of the plant's design. Quantities of up to intermediate level waste will arise that will require local storage for decay of the predominantly short lived contaminants, before handling and transfer for treatment or disposal. Larger radioisotope producers need to install special storage facilities adjacent to the hot cells. Solid waste arising from radioisotope production may require several months of decay storage prior to release or further processing.

Storage at research reactors

In developing countries, most reactor facilities have some waste storage arrangements integrated into their original design. Cleanup of the primary circuit cooling water using normal ion exchange processing gives rise to a small amount of waste requiring treatment and conditioning. If the reactor cooling water is treated by the ion exchange process without regeneration, then the spent ion exchange media is likely to be radioactive waste approaching the intermediate activity level, which requires remote handling, shielding or in situ decay storage before manual handling. When the ion exchange media is regenerated, the small proportion of liquid waste containing the majority of the activity should be stored for subsequent treatment.

Storage of biological and medical radioactive wastes

Storage of unconditioned biological and medical waste often necessitates low temperature refrigeration, with temperatures typically –18 to –22°C. For prolonged storage at a centralized radioactive waste management facility beyond two or three years the waste should be stored at –70°C to minimize low temperature putrefaction. Specific requirements for the refrigerated storage of unconditioned biological and medical wastes include:

— Consideration of offensive odours from unconditioned waste, such as those that arise from food waste (e.g. from patients treated with therapeutic levels of radioiodine).

— Control of insects and rodents, which can present a serious threat to the containment of unconditioned packages of radioactive biological waste. The consumption of waste and dispersion through insect/rodent excretions can result in the spread of both radioactive contamination and potentially infectious materials.

— Ease of closure/sealing of the radioactive waste packages to prevent dispersion/seepage of contents.

— Ability of the packaging to withstand, without deterioration, the full range of temperature variations it is likely to encounter, such as the ability to withstand freezing without becoming brittle and liable to fracture.

— Considerations for the design of organic liquid storage facilities include chemical hazards, fire protection, and containment of spills and control of ventilation to prevent the buildup of harmful vapours.

Decay storage

When possible, and if permitted by the non-radioactive risks, advantage should be taken of the opportunity to avoid treating radioactive waste by carefully organizing the decay storage of shorter lived contaminated waste. Volatile or combustible wastes presenting a hazard through fire, biological instability or toxicity are the main risk factors to be taken into consideration. Decay storage for the common short lived radioisotopes is normally routinely applied to segregated low level waste from radionuclide users in hospitals, universities, research laboratories and other institutions. At radioactivity concentrations of 3.7 to 37.0 MBq m^{-3} (0.1 to 1 $mCim^{-3}$), decay storage of ten half-lives (giving a reduction of greater than 1000) potentially reduces the residual radioactivity content to below the limits for unconditional release/disposal. Table 6 gives the times (in years) for reduction in activity by factors of 10 to 10^6 for commonly used short lived radionuclides. Large reduction factors are achieved within short periods for very short lived radionuclides (e.g. a factor of 10^6 in five days (1.4×10^{-2} a) for $^{99}Tc^{m}$). For such short lived radionuclides there are not likely to be problems with discharge limits at the clearance level. Very short storage periods provide adequate decay, even at the lower limits for clearance. Problems arise for radionuclides with half-lives of between about six weeks to one year, but the activity reduction required is also a factor to be considered. For ^{45}Ca, of half-life 0.45 years, a period of nine years is required for a 10^6 reduction. Storage over such a long period may not be judged appropriate because of the risks associated with the long interim storage period.

The practical implementation of decay storage requires the operation of a protected, selective storage capacity with matching identification and other administrative procedures. This ensures that packages are stored for the correct length of time and the correct package is retrieved for disposal. Usual radiological protection requirements should apply regarding the handling of active or potentially active materials, even in the simplest facility.

Table 6 : Decay time for some radionuclides to specified level.

Radionuclides	Decay constant (a^{-1})	Time[a] (in years) for reduction in activity by a factor of :					
		10	10^2	10^3	10^4	10^5	10^6
^{32}P	1.8 ×10	1.3×10^{-1}	2.6×10^{-1}	3.9×10^{-1}	5.2×10^{-1}	6.5×10^{-1}	7.8×10^{-1}
^{45}Ca	1.5	1. 5	3	4. 5	6	7. 5	9.0
^{99}Mo	9.2 × 10	2.5×10^{-2}	5.0×10^{-2}	7.5×10^{-2}	1.0×10^{-1}	0.25×10^{-1}	1.5×10^{-1}
$^{99}Tc^{m}$	1.0×10^{-3}	2.3×10^{-3}	4.6×10^{-3}	6.9×10^{-3}	9.2×10^{-3}	1.2×10^{-2}	1.4×10^{-2}
^{125}I	4. 1	5.6×10^{-1}	1.1	1. 7	2.3	2. 8	3.4
^{131}I	3.2×10^{-1}	1.7×10^{-1}	3.4×10^{-1}	5.0×10^{-1}	6.7×10^{-1}	8.4×10^{-1}	1.0
^{192}Ir	3.4	6.8×10^{-1}	1.36	2.0	2.7	3.4	4.1

[a]Note: The above table is calculated from the following formula:

$T = \frac{\ln R}{\lambda}$ Where T is time in years; l is the decay constant; R is the reduction factor in 10^n ; ln is the natural logarithm.

Disposal of Radioactive Waste

Radioactive wastes of all types need to be managed responsibly in facilities under institutional control to provide public safety, protection of the environment and security from accidental or deliberate intrusion (IAEA, 1995; ICRP, 2000). There are many proposals for disposing high-level nuclear wastes. However, the most favoured solution for the disposal of these wastes is isolating radioactive waste from man and biosphere for a period of time such that any possible subsequent release of radionuclides from the waste repository will not result in undue radiation exposure. The basic idea behind this is to use stable geological environments that have retained their integrity for millions of years to provide a suitable isolation capacity for the long time-periods required. The following options have been aired sometime or the other. Each one of the options demands serious studies and technical assessments:

(i) Geologic disposal

Deep geological disposal on land is the most appropriate means for isolating and handling long-lived waste radioactive wastes permanently from man's environment (OECD, 1984). However, the full range of options also includes disposal in geological formations under the deep ocean floor, disposal on the ocean floor, disposal in glaciated areas, extraterrestrial disposal, and destruction by nuclear transmutation. In addition, extended storage, whether at production sites or in a centralised store, may, in principle, be considered an acceptable waste management strategy, provided it is not supposed to be perpetuated for longer than feasible and safe and is to be replaced by a more permanent solution at a later date. The deep geological sites provide a natural isolation system that is stable over hundreds of thousands of years to contain long-lived radioactive waste. A geological disposal system can be defined as a combination of conditioned and packaged solid wastes and other engineered barriers within an excavated or drilled repository located at a depth of some hundreds of metres in a stable geological environment. The geological formation, in which the waste is emplaced, referred to as the 'host rock', generally constitutes the most important isolation barrier. In practice, it is noted that low-level radioactive waste is generally disposed in near-surface facilities or old mines. High level radioactive waste is disposed in host rocks that are crystalline (granitic, gneiss) or argillaceous (clays) or salty or tuff. Since, in most of the countries, there is not a big backlog of high-level radioactive waste urgently awaiting disposal, interim storage facilities, which allow cooling of the wastes over a few decades, are in place.

In order to increase the safety of geological disposal, most such disposal concepts rely on a system of independent and often redundant barriers to the movement of radionuclides in an effort to provide a high degree of assurance that exposures to man will remain at acceptably low levels. These barriers generally include (OECD, 1977) the leach-resistant waste form itself, (OECD,1984) corrosion-resistant containers into which the wastes are encapsulated, (OECD, 1985) special radionuclides- and groundwater- retarding material placed around the waste containers, commonly referred to as backfill, and (OECD, 1985), the geological formation itself the principal barrier which should both retard the transport of radionuclides in circulating groundwater, and isolate the waste from man's environment. There are five important reasons why deep geological disposal on land has evolved into the disposal method of choice for virtually every country with a nuclear power programme.

1. It is an entirely passive disposal system with no requirement for continuing human involvement to ensure its safety.
2. Radioactive wastes present no hazard while they remain in a deep underground repository. Because of their depth of burial (several hundreds of metres or more), the possibility of intentional human intrusion is virtually eliminated, and, with a suitable choice of location, the likelihood of inadvertent human intrusion can be made minimal.
3. Flexibility and convenience are provided by the large variety cf geological environments suitable for disposal. Geological units under consideration are rock salt, argillaceous formations (clays), and a range of crystalline rock formations including granite, welded tuff, basalt, and various metamorphic rock types.
4. The disposal option is demonstrably practical and feasible with currently existing technology used in other mining and civil engineering practices.
5. Although, waste disposal implies the lack of intention to retrieve the waste, the repository can be designed so that the waste can be recovered, while the repository is in operation or even after closure.

(vi) Ocean-dumping

For many years the industrialized countries of the world (e.g. USA, France, Great Britain, etc.) opted for the least expensive method for disposal of the wastes by dumping them into the oceans. Before 1982, when the United States Senate declared a moratorium on the dumping of radioactive wastes, the US dumped an estimated 112,000 drums at thirty different sites in the Atlantic and Pacific oceans. Though, this practice has been banned by most of the countries with nuclear programmes, the problem still persists. Although, radioactive waste has known negative effects on humans and other animals, no substantial scientific proof of bad effects on the ocean and marine life has been found. Hence, some nations have argued that ocean-dumping should be continued. Others argue that the practice should be banned until further proof of no harm is available. Penetrator disposal is potentially both feasible and safe; its implementation would depend on international acceptance and the development of an appropriate international regulatory framework. Neither of these exists, nor are they likely to in the foreseeable future. The penetrator method has also been further constrained by a recent revision of the definition of 'dumping', by the London Dumping Convention, to include 'any deliberate disposal or storage of wastes or other matter in the seabed and the subsoil thereof'.

(iii) Sub-seabed disposal

Seabed disposal is different from sea-dumping which does not involve isolation of low-level radioactive waste within geological strata. The floor of deep oceans is a part of a large tectonic plate situated some 5 km below the sea surface, covered by hundreds of metres of thick sedimentary soft clay. These regions are desert-like, supporting virtually no life. The Seabed Burial Proposal envisages drilling these 'mud-flats' to depths of the order of hundreds of metres, such bore-holes being spaced apart several hundreds of metres. The high-level radioactive waste contained in canisters, to which we have referred to earlier, would be lowered into these holes and stacked vertically one above the other interspersed by 20 m or more of mud pumped in. The proposal to use basement rock in oceans for radioactive waste disposal is met with some problems: variability of the rock and high local permeability.

Oceanic water has a mixing time of the order of a few thousand years which does not serve as a good barrier for long lived radionuclides.

Since, experiments cannot be conducted to assure safety of seabed disposal on the basis of actual canisters deposited in the seabed over periods of interest, namely over hundreds of thousands of years, model calculations have been performed to predict the capabilities of such a disposal option. The model approach has started with selection of sites and acquisition of site-specific data using marine geological methods. These sites are away from deep-sea trenches, mid-oceanic ridges or formation zones where geological activities are high. These sites are also far away from biologically productive areas in the oceans. The sediments in chosen sites are fine-grained and are called 'abyssal red clay'. These sites are believed to have desirable barrier properties with 'continuous stable and depositional histories'. Therefore, these potential waste repositories are geologically stable over periods of the order of 10^7 years and are likely not to have human activities, as they are not resources of fishes or hydrocarbons or minerals. Core samples from most Pacific and Atlantic sites have been studied to investigate thermal, chemical and radiological effects. It is found that when sea water and sample sediment mixtures are heated at 300 C at high pressure, the solution pH changes from 8 to 3. Calculations suggest that 'less than 2 cubic metres of untreated sediment would be needed to neutralize all the acid generated in the thermally perturbed region of about 5.5 m^3. The canister material has to be compatible with this type of environment for periods of at least 500 years by which time fission fragment activity would become acceptable.

Similarly, other calculations have taken into account sediment nuclide interactions to determine ion concentration around a buried source as a function of time. Experimental work has already established that clays have the property of holding on to several radioactive elements, including plutonium; hence, seepage of these elements into saline water is minimal. Rates of migration of these elements over hundreds of thousands of years would be of the order of a few metres. Hence, during such long times, radioactivity will diminish to levels below the natural radioactivity in sea water due to natural radioactive decay. The clays also have plastic like behaviour to form natural sealing agents. Finally, the mud-flats have rather low permeability to water; hence, leaching probability is rather low. It may be noted that the method depends on standard deep-sea drilling techniques routinely practised and sealing of the bore-holes. These two aspects are well-developed, thanks to the petroleum industry and also because of an international programme called the Ocean Drilling Programme. Core samples from about half a dozen vastly separated sites in the Pacific and Atlantic oceans have 'showed an uninterrupted history of geological tranquility over the past 50–100 million years'. This method would be expensive to implement, but its cost would be an impediment to any future plutonium mining endeavour. Although, the world trend is toward the option of land-based disposal, it is doubtful whether restricting repositories to land based sites really helps prevention of sea pollution. If radionuclides from a land based repository leached out to the surface, they would be quickly transported to the sea by surface water. What is essential is to isolate radionuclides from the biosphere as reliably as possible. If sub-seabed disposal results in more reliable isolation, sub-seabed disposal is the better safeguard against sea pollution. This method takes into consideration technological feasibility, protection of marine environments and availability of international understanding.

The United Nation's Convention on the Law of the Sea delineates that a coastal state is granted sovereign rights to utilize all resources in water and under the seabed within its exclusive economic zone (EEZ), which can extend from the coast line up to 200 nautical miles (about 370 km) offshore. A repository is proposed to be constructed in bedrock 2 km beneath the seabed. To utilize sub-seabed disposal within the EEZ, it is also proposed that waste packages would be transported through a submarine tunnel connecting land with the sub-seabed repository. Sea pollution by an accident during disposal work would be improbable, because waste would never go through sea water during the work. The proposed method is a variation of geologic disposal. Long-term monitoring is also possible by maintaining the access tunnel for some time after constructing artificial barriers.

(iv) Subductive waste disposal method

Subduction is a process whereby one tectonic plate slides beneath another and is eventually reabsorbed into the mantle. The subductive waste disposal method forms a high level radioactive waste repository in a subducting plate, so that the waste will be carried beneath the earth's crust where it will be diluted and dispersed through the mantle. The rate of subduction of a plate in one of the world's slowest subduction zones is 2.1 cm annually. This is faster than the rate (1 mm annually) of diffusion of radionuclides through the turbidite sediments that would overlay a repository constructed in accordance with this method. The subducting plate is naturally predestined for consumption in the Earth's mantle. The subducting plate is constantly renewed at its originating oceanic ridge. The slow movement of the plate would seal any vertical fractures over a repository at the interface between the subducting plate and the overriding plate. It is the single viable means of disposing radioactive waste that ensures non return of the relegated material to the biosphere. At the same time, it affords inaccessibility to eliminated weapons material. It is considered that the safest, the most sensible, the most economical, the most stable long-term, the most environmentally benign, the most utterly obvious places to get rid of nuclear waste, high-level waste or low-level waste is in the deep oceans that cover 70% of the planet.

With regard to other options, disposal of high level radioactive wastes on the ocean floor in some kind of highly engineered containment would not be internationally acceptable at this stage. Disposal in glaciated areas, in Antarctica for example, would require substantial changes to international legal and political agreements. Disposal into space would provide the greatest degree of isolation from man's environment, but its practicality, cost, technological complexity, and potential risks all argue against it at the moment. Finally, nuclear transmutation, the conversion of long-lived radionuclides into shorter-lived or even stable nuclides, is not considered feasible in the near future.

Fundamental Principles of Radioactive Waste Management

Radioactive waste management committee of IAEA (1995) provided some guidelines to manage the radioactive wastes described as under:-

Protection of human health: Radioactive waste should be managed in such a way as to secure an acceptable level of protection for human health.

Protection of the environment: Radioactive waste should be managed in such a way as to provide an acceptable level of protection of the environment.

Protection beyond national borders: Radioactive waste should be managed in such a way as to assure that possible effects on human health and the environment beyond national borders will be taken into account.

Protection of future generations: Radioactive waste should be managed in such a way that predicted impacts on the health of future generations will not be greater than relevant levels of impact that are acceptable today.

Burdens on future generations: Radioactive waste should be managed in such a way that will not impose undue burdens on future generations.

National legal framework: Radioactive waste should be managed within an appropriate national legal framework including clear allocation of responsibilities and provision for independent regulatory functions.

Control of radioactive waste generation: Generation of radioactive waste should be kept to the minimum practicable.

Radioactive waste generation and management interdependencies: Interdependencies among all steps in radioactive waste generation and management should be appropriately taken into account.

Safety of facilities: The safety of facilities for radioactive waste management should be appropriately assured during their lifetime.

Conclusions

When developing a waste management strategy, consideration should be given to the entire sequence of waste management operations from the waste's production to its final disposal, and all related issues, including the various regulatory, sociopolitical and economic issues. The interaction of all these aspects must be analysed and understood before the entire waste management system can be properly built up and safely managed. While stable and simple geological environments are the obvious choice for sitting repositories for long lived radioactive wastes, it is generally recognized that there is always a scale on which natural systems can be considered complex and heterogeneous; in addition, their properties may vary over the time periods. This is particularly relevant for far field groundwater flow systems. The temporal and spatial scale dependences need to be accounted for. It could therefore be concluded that the problems of radioactive waste management will become a limiting factor for the development of nuclear power in the near and distant future. Adequate spaces are available on the earth and in the seas which have the capacity to accommodate large amounts of radioactive wastes of all levels, and our technical knowledge will guarantee that the storage and disposal conditions will be such as to prelude any hazards to man and his environment.

References

Guha, S. B. (1997) Proceedings of an International Symposium on Experience in the Planning and Operation of Low Level Waste Disposal Facilities, International Atomic Energy Agency, Vienna, pp., 329–337.

International Atomic Energy Agency (1992) Radioactive Waste Management. IAEA Bulletin No. 40, pp., 1.

International Atomic Energy Agency (1993) Improved Cement Solidification of Low and Intermediate Level Radioactive Wastes, Technical Reports Series No. 350, IAEA, Vienna.

International Atomic Energy Agency (1994a) Status of Technology for Volume Reduction and Treatment of Low and Intermediate Level Solid Radioactive Waste, Technical Reports Series No. 360, IAEA, Vienna.

International Atomic Energy Agency (1994b) Classification of Radioactive Waste, Safety Series No. 111-G-1.1, IAEA, Vienna.

International Atomic Energy Agency (1995) The Principles of Radioactive Waste Management, Safety Series No. 111-F, IAEA, Vienna.

International Commission on Radiological Protection (2000) Radiation protection recommendations as applied to the disposal of long-lived solid radioactive waste. Publication 81, Pergamon Press, Oxford and New York.

OECD (1977) Objectives, concepts and strategies for the management of radioactive waste arising from nuclear power programmes, Report by an NEA Group of Experts, , Paris.

OECD (1984) Geological disposal of radioactive waste - An overview of the current status of understanding and development, experts report sponsored by the CEC, Paris.

OECD (1985) Technical appraisal of the current situation in the field of radioactive waste management- A collective opinion by the radioactive waste management committee, Paris.

OECD (1986) System performance assessments for radioactive waste disposal, proceedings of an nea workshop, Paris.

Place, B.G. (1990) Engineering study for the treatment of spent ion exchange resins resulting from nuclear process applications, Rep. WHC-EP-0375, Westinghouse, Richmond, WA.

Ramanna, R., Thomas, D.G. and Varughese. S. (2001) Estimating nuclear waste production in India. Current Science, 81 (11) : 10.

Rao, K.R. (2001) Radioactive waste: The problem and its management. Current Science, 81 (12) : 25.

Rodriguez, P. (1996) Proceedings of the international conference on advances in chemical engineering, 11–13 December, Indian Institute of Technology, Chennai, pp., 45–58.

CHAPTER 9

ENVIRONMENT AND TOURISM : ECOLOGICAL CONSIDERATIONS

Alka Tomar[1] , Anjana Chowdhary[2] and Mahadevi Singh[3]

[1]Centre for Media Studies, Community Centre, Research House, Saket, New Delhi

[2]Dept. of Botany, Govt. Dungar College, Bikaner (Raj.)

[3]Sophia Sr. Secondary School, Bikaner (Raj.)-334002, India

ABSTRACT

This chapter deals with various kinds of tourism i.e. sustainable tourism, nature tourism and eco-tourism. New initiatives taken up by Ministry of Tourism & Ministry of Health & Welfare during 2004-2005 towards promotion of health tourism, cruise tourism, etc. are discussed. Ecological consideration in tourism and benefits of tourism are described in the chapter.

Key Words : Sustainable tourism, Tourism, Wildlife, Eco-tourism

Introduction

The scenic beauty and salubrious environment in any region attract large number of tourists putting undue strain on the fragile ecosystems with limited facilities. There has been a global tourism boom in the recent times. Tourism has already achieved the distinction of being the world's largest export industry. International and domestic tourism together is the world's greatest generator of employment opportunities.

One guess estimate, would have us believe that tourism creates a new job, worldwide, every five minutes round the clock, round the year (Hugh and Gantzer, 2000).

India had received just over 16,800 international tourists in 1951. The arrivals increased to 1.7 million in 1990 and further to 2.64 million in 2000. The growth rate between 1990 and 2000 has been 4.64% annum. A higher growth rate of 6.4% has been achieved in the year 2000 over the previous year. However, India's share in world tourism arrivals has remained virtually stagnant at 0.38% from 1995 onwards. India with about 42% share in the arrivals is the major receiver of international arrivals in the South Asia region in the year 2000 and yet its growth rate lags far behind than that of many countries in the region. The tourism receipts of India went up from US $ 2583 million in 1995 to US $ 3168 million in 2000 showing an annual average growth rate of 4.17% as compared to the world's average growth rate of 3.2% during this period. However, in 2000 India's growth rate of 5.3% compares very poorly with many of the neighbouring countries such as China (15%), Hong Kong China (10.7%), Malaysia (27%), Thailand (12.5%), Macau (25%), Iran (28.4%) and Pakistan (14.5%) (Jha, 2002).

There has been a phenomenal growth in domestic tourism in the country during the last one decade. The domestic tourist visits increased from 63.8 million in 1990 to 210 million in 2000.

On the other hand, tourism development poses special ecological problems, not encountered in other types of economic activity. The environmental resources exploited for tourism attract visitors because of their outstanding beauty, recreational possibilities or educational interest. Often, as in high mountains and islands, the resources of interest for tourism are readily damaged by disturbances. The development of tourism gives some specific ecological problems which concern the utilization of tourist potential. It is not directly related with the community production, it is only in recent years that this has attracted attention it deserves. It is now widely recognized to be a major source of employment and income (Agarwal, 1997).

The aim of conserving environmental amenities of a region and of advancing regional development through tourism are inter-dependent. The more local people benefit from tourism, the more they will benefit from a commitment to preserve the environmental features, which attract tourists. Considerations of the regional ecological characteristics are essential to provide adequate criteria for the design of facilities and viable plans for the use and management of resources for tourism.

Indian Tourism

Tourism is a major social phenomenon of the modern society with enormous economic consequences. Its importance as an instrument for economic development and employment generation has now been well recognized the world over. The existing tourism policy provides a framework for development of tourism with the objective of reaping the socio-economic benefits of the sector. The traditional treatment of a visitor in India is based on the mythological concept of *Atithi Devo Bhavah* (Guest is God). This is the latest mantra of the Indian tourism sector. The ministry of tourism has launched the '*Atithi Devo Bhavah*' campaign under its ambitious programme to attract more number of tourists and the end-results speak volumes about the progress. The concept is aimed at capacity building for service providers and stakeholders in the tourism sector to make the tourists aware of the benefits in India and the need to treat them with traditional care and utmost courtesy. This has been further boosted by the New National Tourism Policy that revolves round a framework Government-led, private sector-driven and community welfare oriented. The 10th plan approach to the sector is also aimed at ensuring that the tourist to India gets "physically invigorated, mentally rejuvenated, culturally enriched, spiritually elevated and feels India within him" (Mohan Rao, 2005).

Kinds of Tourism

Eco-tourism can be defined as travel that conserves the natural environment and sustains the well being of local people. For many countries in the developing world, unspoilt nature is an asset that can be turned into quick profits. But the danger is that tourism could destroy the pristine nature and culture that attract visitors in the first place. Eco-tourism can be a key to saving threatened natural habitats while developing poorer regions (Kumar, 2001).

Environment-friendly travel with a nature dimension is enriching for the tourist. The concept of eco-tourism is also supposed to imply benefits for local people and conservation. But in some cases, it can be more harmful than beneficial. Environmentally-sound tourism may be defined in different ways :

1. **Sustainable tourism** in the spirit of the 1992 Earth Summit in Rio de Janeiro, covers all forms and destinations, mass tourism and small-scale travel and cities and rural areas. A small proportion of the industry as a whole consists of nature-based tourism which also includes eco-tourism.

2. **Nature tourism** simply means that people visit areas of natural interest and beauty; this can be done in the form of pleasure trips, which are not ecologically sustainable. Vehicle safaris in Africa are a case in

point; though inspired by the tourists' interest in nature, they cause erosion, disturb wildlife, and leave behind a trail of rubbish.

3. **Eco-tourism** is a narrower concept, implying more pronounced benefits for nature conservation and local development.

Eco-tourists travel in small groups to areas of natural and cultural interest, preferable taking care to leave no trace of having been there. Visits should be planned in such a way that local people become aware of the economic benefits of protecting natural resources and see this as a long-term goal.

Nature-based tourism as a whole currently accounts for only about 7% of all tourism, and eco-tourism for a much smaller proportion. One basic idea in the eco-tourism concept is less foreign involvement and a greater emphasis on local development and marketing of holidays. One good approach may be locally-owned hotels, built by local labour with local materials, in which tourists are served locally-produced food and drink and provided with well trained local guides.

Tourism can be sustainable if it :

(*i*) operates within natural capacities for the regeneration and future productivity of natural resources,

(*ii*) recognizes the contribution that people and communities, customs and lifestyles make to the tourism experience,

(*iii*) accepts that the people must have an equitable share in its economic benefits, and

(*iv*) is guided by the wishes of local people and communities in the host area.

The seven cardinal principles for sustainable tourism are :

(*i*) use resources sustainably,

(*ii*) reduce over consumption and waste,

(*iii*) maintain diversity,

(*iv*) integrate tourism into planning,

(*v*) support local economies,

(*vi*) involve local communities, and

(*vii*) market tourism responsibly.

Tourism and Wildlife

Tourism can have both positive and negative impacts on the human environment. It has benefited the environment by stimulating measures to protect physical features of the environment and wildlife. Recreation and tourism are normally the primary objectives of establishing and developing national parks and many other types of protected areas. Natural areas are becoming major attractions and constitute the basis of eco-tourism.

Tourism was considered to be life of wildlife by contributing to the national revenue. But with the rise in human population and improvement in transport system the tourist activities have grown to manifold and have practically invaded the peaceful homelands of the wildlife throughout the world. This has adversely affected both the flora and fauna, particularly the large carnivore animals who require peaceful and clean environment for feeding and reproduction. The smoke emitting automobiles and the waste materials particularly the edibles, papers and non-biodegradable plastic bags and cans left behind by the tourists become source of pollution in the unspoiled serene environment of the forest. At times they also caused forest fires (Sinha, 1999).

Recreational, Aesthetic and Scientific Value of Wildlife for Eco-Tourism

The species in natural ecosystems also provide the foundation for numerous recreational and aesthetic interests, ranging from sportfishing and hunting to hiking, camping, bird-watching, photography and so on. Interests may range from casual aesthetic enjoyment to serious scientific study. Virtually all our knowledge and understanding of evolution and ecology have come from studying wild species and the ecosystems in which they live. Pleasure and satisfaction may even be indirect. For instance, one may never see a whale, but knowing that whales and similar exciting animals exist provides a certain aesthetic pleasure. The great popularity of nature films attests to this. Further, knowing that the Earth and its biosphere continue to support and maintain such wildlife provides a sense of well-being.

Recreational and aesthetic values constitute a very important source of support for maintaining wild species. Recreational and aesthetic activities support commercial interests. Eco-tourism - whereby tourists visit a place in order to observe wild species or unique ecological sites - represents the largest foreign-exchange-generating enterprise in many developing countries. As the amount of leisure time available to people increases, more and more money is spent on recreation. Since some, percentage of these recreational dollars will be spent on activities related to the natural environment, any degradation of that environment affects commercial interests. These activities involve a great number of people and represent a huge economic enterprise. To cite one example, 84% of Canadians take part in some form of wildlife-related recreation, spending an estimated $9.4 billion yearly. In the most recent national survey, it was found that some 91 million Americans spent $101 billion on wildlife-related recreation during 1996. Very likely, the broadest public support for preserving wild species and habitats is traceable to the aesthetic and recreational enjoyment people derive from them (Wright and Nebel, 2004).

Potential

Tourism provides enormous opportunity for employment generation. According to an estimate, the travel and tourism industry would have directly generated 9.3 million jobs in India. The travel and tourism industry includes activities such as accommodation, transport, catering, entertainment, recreation and other travel related services. The travel and tourism economy which expresses the impact of travel and tourism and its flow through effect across the wider economy would have generated 17.4 million jobs in India. Travel and tourism jobs are rapidly generated at relatively low cost, are concentrated in small business and local communities, provide significant opportunities for women and young people, offer education, training and skills development and revitalize traditional arts and crafts.

The Tourism ministry, through the **India Tourism** offices abroad, undertakes a series of promotional activities in tourist generating markets for attracting the number of tourists visiting India. These include advertising, participation in fairs and exhibitions, organising seminars, workshops and road shows, publication of brouchers, joint advertising support and inviting media personalities, tour operators and opinion makers to visit the country under the Hospitality programme of the ministry. In India, the focus is to create infrastructure in rural areas having potential for tourism. The objective is to showcase rural life, art, culture and heritage at rural locations and in villages, which have core-competency in terms of craft/handloom/textiles, etc.

For the last four decades, there have been a sweeping revolution in the tourism sector across the world. The number of tourists worldwide has been growing and it is expected to swell to 1.5 billion and the monetary gains from it are estimated to cross 2000 billion US dollars. India has taken note of the boom in the tourism sector and geared itself to meet the challenges. As a result, tourism in the present day world did not confine itself to hotels, restaurants and sea beaches alone, its arena touched rural areas (Rural Tourism), health sector (Health Tourism) and environment (Eco-tourism). That's why it is said that necessity is the mother of invention. The government's policy is to take the benefits of tourism to people in rural areas to ensure socio-economic development of the village, society and the nation as a whole.

Constraints

Despite several constraints facing the tourism sector, India's share in world tourist arrivals was 0.44% in 2004 AD. The constraints include shortage of air seat capacity, high air fares, shortage of hotel accommodation and high hotel tariffs, deficiencies in infrastructure such as airports, roads, railways, facilitation of entry to India by International tourists, multiplicity and high level of taxation, restricted land use policies for tourism protects and absence of single window approach.

The government has prepared 20 year Perspective Plans for tourism development in the country. The tourism policy encourages private sector to act as a main spring of the activities and impart dynamism and speed to the process of development as well as conservation, attaches importance to the improvements and environmental upgradation of the protected monuments and the areas around them.

The Ministry has undertaken studies on taxes levied by the state/central governments in the Indian Tourism sector and the impact of Civil Aviation policies on Tourism in the country. The study on taxes has highlighted the problem of high rate of taxation and multitude of central and state level taxes leading to high cost of packages. The study has recommended rationalization of taxes like expenditure tax, service tax, customs duty and taxation of Aviation Turbine Fuel (ATF), need for introduction of new incentives to increase tourism expenditure and volume and promotion of investment in the industry.

Ecological Considerations

Two most important ecological considerations are peculiar to tourism development and need to be taken into account when integrating it, as it should be integrated, with any over all regional development plan. These are :

1. Despite the demand for various sophisticated facilities, which often accompany it, tourism is basically dependent on unspoiled environment. In most other types of development, some environmental value to be sacrificed in return for the expected benefits, but in the case of tourism, the maintenance of these values at a higher level is essential. Well planned tourism can in fact help both to satisfy and safeguard the quality of environment.

   The environmental amenities which attract tourists have tended to be taken for granted and the preservation of their quality has only recently begun to be of concern to tourists development planners. A certain amount of deterioration in environmental quality may be viewed as a necessary trade-off in some kind of economic activity such as construction and mining etc., but for tourism, the quality of the environment is the basis for attracting visitors and must be conserved.

2. Secondly, however, the infrastructure of tourism hotels and lodgings, roads, vehicles, power lines and the rest including the problem of waste disposal by them, may like that of any other industry bring about deterioration, but it does so to an unusual extent in ways which affect its own survival. There is a definite limit of carrying capacity of the environment for tourism development upon the fragility of the area concerned and the particular nature of tourist activity contemplated. The first important thing in tourist development is therefore, an evaluation of the resources and landscape available, in order that a reliable estimate of this capacity may be made.

   The planning of any region having tourist potential should not be done to profit by maximizing tourism, because it can deteriorate fragile ecosystem and other attractive landscapes through over-building and excessive densities of visitors.

Benefits of Tourism

There are many direct and indirect benefits of tourism development. Some of the major benefits are : (a) Stimulation of economic activities, (2) Employment, (3) Direct revenue, (4) Social and cultural interaction etc.

(a) Stimulation of Economic Activities

The primary objective of tourism is to stimulate economic activity in all spheres of the national economy. Tourism has its impacts on road and air transportation, construction, industry and farming activities.

Economic development inter-governmental and private organisations are deeply involved, whatever kind of development project it may be, whether it is tourism, agricultural development, river valley development and so on must be based on understanding of economic, social and environmental reality. A failure to consider ecological principles which affect all relationship between man and environment has caused unexpected and unwanted consequences from many development projects, and in too many cases has brought environmental damage and human sufferings.

Both conservation and economic development make it essential to consider physical and biological rules within which all the life on earth must operate, proper consideration of the ecological principles will assist those concerned with development or conservation to achieve their goals with a minimum of undesirable side effects, reducing the likelihood of major environmental disturbances which could be harmful to all life within a region or throughout the world. Lack of consideration for the ecological realities of an environment can doom development effects, with consequent waste of money and impairment of the condition of life.

Conflict between conservation and development can be minimized if there is an understanding and partnership among those whose main interest lie on either side. Development planners on the one hand must have due regards for environmental values, the conservation of which is important for scientific, recreational or other reasons; not easily measurable in precise monetary term. On the other, those concerned with conservation must be equally ready to recognize the political, social and economic forces behind the development drive and be prepared to give every assistance in exploring alternatives and reaching reasonable compromises whenever the interests are in conflicts.

In any development activities the ecological principles such as "the need to keep a range of resource use options available to future generations" and "the fact that the conservation of species and natural communities is a logical first step in the development" for the reason that resources of such communities are irreplaceable from the view point of satisfying human needs and aspirations and also because of their long term contributions to the stability and productivity of the planet (Thakur and Bhargava, 1988).

(b) Employment

A good proportion of local people are directly and indirectly employed by tourism. Those directly linked with tourism include tour operators, drivers and hotel employees; in addition the manufacturing and agriculture sectors have their main consumer in the tourism sector.

The travel and tourism industry, international and domestic combined, is the world's greatest generator of employment, today. One guess estimate would have us believe that tourism creates a new job, worldwide, every five minutes round the clock round the year. Yet, in spite of the fact that we hold 16.66% of the world's people, we receive less than 0.5% of the world's tourists (In 1999, according to the Ministry of Tourism, we received 24,81,928 tourists including Pakistan and Bangladesh). And our tourism inflows are not likely to rise significantly unless we overcome the obtuseness of our self-styled leaders who oppose the liberal ideas that tourism brings; reactionaries, the world over, can not hold their followers in a web of fear and hate if they allow them to think for themselves.

(c) Direct Revenue

The revenue collected at the entry point to national parks, national reserves and national monuments goes to the government treasuries. The earnings generated by different forms of tourism activities can be used for conservation of tourist resorts. In the process of conserving the wild life in its natural habitat as a primary objective, another secondary objective has also been achieved, namely the preservation of forests and natural cover which in turn has led to the conservation of soil and water catchments.

(d) Socio-Cultural Interactions

The unavoidable interaction between visitors and the local/resident population brings about better understanding between the interacting communities. Although, in most instances it is the visitors who show greater appreciation for the local culture, local people also become exposed to new ways of life. It is often argued that tourism brings with it social evils but in the final analysis it gives the host country a chance to face new and challenging situations (Sindiyo and Pertet, 1984).

General Impact on Environment

It is not easy to discuss every negative effect caused by a flow of motor and human traffic through a national park or a reserve. Suffice it to say that individual protected areas may experience different or peculiar management problems for a variety of reasons but those that are most common have been summarized in Table 1.

Table 1 : The potential effects of tourism in protected areas

S.N.	Factor involved	Impact on natural quality	Comments	Example
Direct				
1.	Overcrowding	Environmental stress, behavioural changes	Irritation, reduction in quality, need for carrying capacity limits	Amboseli
2.	Overdevelop-ment	Development of rural slums, excessive man-made structures	Unsightly, urban concentrations	Mwea, Keekorok, Ngai Ndathya

Contd.

3.	Recreational use :			
(a)	Power boats	Disturbance of wildlife and peace	Vulnerability during resting seasons	Kuinga marine biosphere reserve
(b)	Fishing	None	Competition with natural predators	Lake Turkana
(c)	Foot safaris	Disturbance of wildlife	Overuse and trail erosion	Mt. Kenya, Kichwa Tempo area in Mara
4.	Pollution			
(a)	Noise (radios, etc.)	Disturbance of natural sounds	Irritation	Many areas
(b)	Litter	Impairment of natural scene	Aesthetic and health hazard	Many areas
5.	Vandalism	Mutilation and facility destruction	Removal of natural features, fossils, facility damage	Sibila
6.	Feeding of animals	Behavioural changes	Removal of habituated animals	Mara, Samburu, Amboseli
7.	Vehicles			
(a)	Speeding	Wildlife mortality	Ecological changes	Amboseli, Nairobi
(b)	Driving off road	Soil and vegetation damage	Ecological changes	Masai Mara
(c)	Night driving			
	Indirect			
1.	Collection of firewood	Small wildlife mortality and habital removal	Interference with energy flow	All areas
2.	Roads and Murram pits	Habitat loss, drainage changes	Aesthetic scars, disruption	All areas

Contd.

3.	Power lines	Destruction of vegetation	Aesthetic impacts	Travo
4.	Artificial water holes and salt provision	Unnatural wildlife concentrations. Vegetation damage	Replacement of soil required	Aberdares, Tsavo
5.	Introduction of exotic plants	Competition with wild plants	Public confusion	Many areas, Mt. Kenya, Elgon.

Source : Thorsell and Pertet (1980)

(a) Habitat destruction

Lack of adequately prepared management plans for parks and reserves development has resulted in an uncontrolled and haphazard development of viewing parks. With increased traffic in the parks, drivers tend to take their vehicles to all parts, thus destroying the habitat (Sindiyo and Pertet, 1984).

(b) Teasing and harassment of animals

It is becoming increasingly obvious that animals are experiencing harassment because of some tourist behaviour. The species mostly affected are carnivores, in particularly lion and tiger, which because of their diurnal habits attract visitors. It is not uncommon to see several mini-buses surrounding a pride of lion or a tiger with the result that often these animals are prevented from making a kill through tourist interference. The attitude of such tourists is extremely selfish (Sindiyo and Pertet, 1984).

(c) Problem of waste disposal

Coupled with unplanned lodge and tented camp development is the problem of discharge of sewage and refuse disposal. Unregulated sewage discharge and often below standard sewage discharge facilities pose some problems in certain parks, for example Amboseli, Masai Mara and Travo in Kenya. Garbage disposal in almost all parks lodges is a particular nuisance to the park management as it attracts carrion-eaters such as hyenas, vultures, marabou storks, baboons and vervets. Elephants have, in some cases, become habituated to garbage and this has led to their being attracted to lodge kitchens, where they pose an obvious threat to the lodge employees. A further problem of garbage lies in the health hazard that could occur through spread of disease (Sindiyo and Pertet, 1984).

(d) Garbage and associated waste management problems

Garbage is made of wastes created by human population, science and technology and industry. There are mainly three types of wastes : solid, liquid and nuclear waste. Bulky solid wastes like plastics, polythenes, rubber and metals are causing a threat for earth's environment to become a garbage store. Solid wastes can be further classified into twin categories of biodegradable and non-degradable wastes. These are non-biodegradable wastes which are causing a serious threat. The chief method followed for disposal of solid garbage are burying (land fill), burning and recycling. The only cost effective environment friendly method is recycling. However, wastes like hospital wastes, due to their specific nature, require special methods of treatment. Dissolved pesticides, fertilizers, treated or untreated sewage, heavy metals, non-degrading chemicals, detergents, DDT and CD-Ni batteries are major constituents of liquid wastes which create difficult problems. Effluents from aquaculture, like prawn farming, are also polluting land and water (Singh and Aggarwal, 1998).

In order to maintain stable economic growth in future and to ensure human health and existence, it is necessary to use our resources carefully and to evolve technologies or recycling or managing otherwise the wastes and residues.

Government Initiatives Towards a New Tourism Policy

The former Prime Minister Sh. A.B.Vajpayee had indicated the need for a new tourism policy in his Independence Day speech on 15th August, 2001. Referring to tourism as a big source of employment generation and foreign exchange earning, he had said the government would unveil a progressive National Tourism Policy.

The 1982 Tourism Policy was drafted in a different socio-economic milieu in an environment of an economy with strict licensing procedures. Foreign investment in the economy was not anticipated, development of new technology was not envisaged and there was no focus on balanced development of various regions. The policy did not differentiate specifically the roles of the government and the private sectors and there was no emphasis on the latter's role in the development and promotion of tourism.

In the post-liberalisation period various developments in the tourism sector have taken place. The sector has been accorded the status of export house and various incentives like income tax exemptions, interest subsidy and reduced import duty are available to the hotel industry, travel agents, tour operators. Several incentives have been made available for attracting private investment in tourism projects including those under the Liberalized Exchange Rate Management System (LERMS).

The economic reforms introduced by the government are integrating India into the global economy and making Indian industry internationally competitive. Foreign direct investment and technical collaborations form a major platform of the economic reforms. With a view to attracting investment in this sector, the hotel and tourism-related industry has been declared as a 'high priority industry' for foreign investment. It is now eligible for automatic approval of direct investment upto 100% of foreign equity.

Non-Resident Indian (NRI) investment is allowed upto 100% automatically. In a fast-changing world, the relationship between suppliers and users of technology, agreements have to be recognized. To promote technology upgradation in the hotel industry, approvals for technology agreements are now available automatically subject to the fulfillment of certain conditions. Applications for automatic approvals for foreign investment or technology agreements and management contracts can be made to the RBI for according such approvals and the entrepreneurs can approach authorized dealers for release of foreign exchange.

New Initiatives in 2004-05

The government has set up a monitoring mechanism for expediting projects sanctioned in the last 10 years. In the 8th and 9th plans, as many as 2,526 projects were sanctioned and these were supposed to be completed within 30 months from the date of sanction. The delay in implementation of the projects by the state governments led to slow progress in these works. As a result some of the projects sanctioned during the 8th plan are still incomplete. In order to ensure timely implementation and also co-ordination between various departments involved in the projects sanctioned under the schemes for Circuit Development, Destination Development and Rural Tourism, the Ministry of Tourism has requested all the state governments and Union Territory administrations to constitute State Level Monitoring Committees under the chairmanship of Secretary (Tourism) including the district authorities concerned, representatives of the implementing agencies such as CPWD, HUDCO, ASI, India tourism and local authorities.

(a) Health Tourism

The Ministry of Health & Family Welfare and the Ministry of Tourism have jointly formed a Task Force with a view to promoting India as a Health Destination for persons across the globe so as to gainfully utilize the health care expertise and infrastructure available in the country. The new domestic and global campaigns for the current year focus on India as a destination for niche segments like Medical Tourism, Cruise Tourism and Spiritual Tourism. The aim is to expand the range of the tourism products in India both for the domestic and international consumers. The Ministry has also promoted Monsoon Tourism in various states. The government has taken up a number of steps to attract foreign tourist arrivals to India. They include : creation of World Class Collaterals, Centralized Electronic Media Campaigns, Direct Co-operative marketing with tour operators and whole-salers overseas. Greater focus is in the emerging markets, particularly in the region of China, north-east Asia and South-east Asia. Participation in Trade Fairs & Exhibitions, Optimising Editorial PR and publicity, use of Internet and Web marketing. Generating tourist publications, reinforcing hospitality programmes including grant of air passages to invite media personnel and tour operators and launching of road shows are the key source of markets in Europe. The government of India has introduced a new category of medical visa (M-visa) that may be given to foreign tourists coming to India for medical treatment for specific period.

(b) Cruise Tourism

The government has constituted a high-power steering group to formulate Cruise shipping policy in the country. The recommendations of this group include formation of working groups to look into issues like-immigration, customs clearances, quarantine restrictions, identification of ports, infrastructural facilities, connectivity, taxation issues, tourism related issue and cabotage to develop cruise shipping policy in India. In the eastern part of the country, Tuticorin port and Chennai port, have been identified.

(c) Eco-Tourism

The National Eco-tourism policy and guidelines aim to preserve, retain and enrich natural resources and to ensure regulated growth of eco-tourism with its positive impacts on environmental protection and community development. Under these guidelines, the government has prioritized several projects in Himachal Pradesh, Uttaranchal and Uttar Pradesh in 2005-06.

(d) Foreign Tourists

As a result of Incredible India campaigns, the foreign tourist arrivals increased from 6% in 2002 to 23.5% in 2004. An estimated 3.54 million foreign tourists arrived in India during 2004. The foreign exchange earnings in 2004 in terms of rupees registered a growth of 32.9%. In absolute terms, the foreign exchange earnings increased from Rs. 16,429 crores to Rs. 21,828 crores. The Bureau of Immigration has estimated that about 6.2 million Indians went abroad during 2004. Foreign exchange earnings through tourism upto June, 2006 has registered an increase of 25.2%. Total earnings during the period were Rs. 12527.04 crore and in Dollar terms is US $ 2821.21 million, up by 26.4%. The number of tourists including these from foreign countries visiting cellular Jail in Port Blair (Andamans) during the last three calendar years has gone up from 48,594 in 2002 to 55,912 in 2003 to 94,311 in 2004.

While the number of foreign tourists visiting the eight North-eastern states has gone up from 22,047 in 2002 to 29,478 in 2003 to 39,437 in 2004.

Conclusions

The development of tourism and industries demand construction of buildings, roads, restaurants and recreation spots which exert unbearable pressure on scarce land resources. Such developmental activities lead to deforestation, defacing and destabilization of land slope in hilly areas.

The tourism industry is a composite of services providers which includes travel agents; tour operators; air, rail and sea transportation operators; guides; hotels, guest houses and inns; restaurants; and shops selling handicrafts, souvenirs, clothing, footwear, leather items and other objects of interest to the tourists. The common factor about these service providers is that all these are involved in meeting the requirements of international and domestic tourists. These service providers are generally in the private sector. Public sector institutions such as the national or state departments of tourism are involved in planning, development and management of tourism-related service providers. In many cases they even provide direct services to the tourists.

If the tourism industry is properly planned, developed and managed at all levels of government in partnership with the private sector, it will strengthen the country's cultural structure and natural heritage and lead to positive economic results including enhanced employment and income opportunities, especially in rural areas. Strict measures to regulate industrial growth and tourist inflow have to be enforced through proper legislation in order to reduce pressure on natural resources.

References

Agarwal, S.K. (1997) Tourism and Environment, Chapter 15, *In : Environmental Issues and Themes.* APH Publishing Corporation, 5 Ansari Road, New Delhi, pp., 343-348.

Hugh and Gantzer, C. (2000) "Indian Tourism : An Overview", Employment News, 25(20) : 1 & 2.

Jha, R.V. (2002) "Towards a New Tourism Policy", Employment News, 9-15 Feb., 2002.

Kumar, H.D. (Ed.) (2001) Transportation and mobility, Chapter 5, *In : Sustainable Human Ecology*, Affiliated East-West Press Pvt. Ltd., New Delhi, pp., 152-153.

Mohan Rao, V. (2005) '*Atithi Devo Bhavah*' is the latest mantra of Indian tourism. Employment News, 30 (30):1-2.

Sindiyo, D.M. and Pertet, F.N. (1984) "Tourism and Its Impact on Wildlife Conservation in Kenya", *UNEP Industry and Environment*, 14-19.

Singh, Y.P. and Aggarwal, A. (1998) Environmental Crisis : A Challenge Ahead. Employment News, 23(9) : 1-2.

Sinhà, Rajiv K. (ed.) (1999) Wildlife Management : Restoring the Ecological Balance. Chapter 15, *In : Environmental Crisis and Humans at Risk : Priorities for Action*, INA Shree Publishers, Jaipur, pp. 198-212.

Thakur, A. and Bhargava, D.S. (1988) Environmental Quality Impacts on Tourism. Ecology, 2 : 10.

Thorsell, J.W. and Pertet, F.N. (1980) "National Parks, Reserves and Protected Areas of Kenya", *In : Proc. 17th meeting of IUCN's Commission on National Parks and Protected Areas, Garoua, Cameroon*, 17-23 Nov., IUCN Gland, Switzerland.

Wright, Richard T. and Nebel, Bernard, J. (eds.) (2004) Wild Species : Biodiversity and Protection, Chapter 11, *In : Environmental Science : Towards A Sustainable Future*, 8th edn. (Eds. Richard T. Wright and Bernard J. Nebel), Prentice Hall of India Pvt. Ltd., New Delhi, pp. 263-285.